LIBERATOR

The Life and Death of Daniel O'Connell,
1830–1847

PATRICK M. GEOGHEGAN

Gill & Macmillan

Gill & Macmillan
Hume Avenue, Park West, Dublin 12
with associated companies throughout the world
www.gillmacmillan.ie

978 07171 5402 9
First published in hard cover 2010
First published in this format 2012

Index compiled by Helen Litton
Typography design by Make Communication
Print origination by Síofra Murphy
Printed by ScandBook AB, Sweden

A CIP catalogue record for this book is available from the
British Library.

5 4 3 2 1

CONTENTS

| INTRODUCTION

This book follows on immediately from the events detailed in *King Dan: the Rise of Daniel O'Connell, 1775-1829*, published in 2008. That book began and ended with O'Connell in 1829, at the height of his powers as a lawyer following the Doneraile conspiracy trials, and having won his greatest victory with the passing of Catholic emancipation. The night emancipation was secured, O'Connell was warned that his career was over, because there was nothing left to achieve. But O'Connell's lifelong ambition was the restoration of the Irish parliament, and he knew that the greatest challenge of his life was yet to come. The 'rise' of Daniel O'Connell had taken fifty-four years, and it represented a number of different ascents. As a lawyer he had triumphed despite the obstacles in his path because he was a Catholic. As a public agitator he had succeeded in energising a moribund Catholic Association and turning it into a dynamic national movement. Through the force of his personality, and his extraordinary oratorical powers, he was able to achieve his objectives through exclusively peaceful means—the use of moral force—and, in doing so, providing an inspiration to democratic movements around the world.

The intention from the beginning had been to subtitle this book 'The Fall of Daniel O'Connell, 1830–1847'. It is a subtitle that reflects the popular perception of O'Connell following emancipation. He entered the British House of Commons, but failed in his attempts to secure Repeal, or even Justice for Ireland, in the 1830s. He attempted to lead a new national movement in the 1840s—which culminated in the massive monster meetings in 1843—but backed down over Clontarf, and shattered the unity of the Repeal movement by his unseemly squabble with the Young Ireland movement. His death in Genoa, during the height of the famine, represented a tragic end for a career that had promised much, but which in the end had seemingly delivered little. The great historian W.E.H. Lecky recognised that there was 'something almost awful in so dark a close to so brilliant a career'.[1] But the more I engaged with the period 1830–1847 I realised this subtitle was misleading and inappropriate. There was a decline and fall, but it took place in the 1830s, when O'Connell's popularity began to fade and, broken-hearted, he considered retiring from politics and entering a monastery. In the early 1840s he faced the same problems as in the early 1820s: an apathetic public and a divided camp. But this time he was an aging man, and was unsure whether he still had the energy and ability, or even whether he was still trusted, to lead the nation once more. The resurrection of O'Connell in 1843 was one of the most remarkable comebacks in world history, as he rolled back the years to travel around the country and speak to his people. It was a campaign that was watched with excitement around the world and which confirmed O'Connell as the prophet of a new age and an entirely new way of conducting popular politics. The transformative campaign ultimately ended in failure, and O'Connell ended his career a broken man. This, then, is the story of the rise, fall, resurrection, and decline of O'Connell, in the dramatic final seventeen years of his life.

'The Life and Death of Daniel O'Connell, 1830–1847' is an attempt to capture this drama in a subtitle. Those who have never heard of O'Connell may mistake this book for the study of a young man who died at the age of seventeen. But the subtitle is also an attempt to show what kind of book this is. Even more than the first book it is a study focused intensely on the character of O'Connell. Therefore it only looks at the events that O'Connell was closely involved with, and does not attempt to provide a wider study of the period. Rather than using O'Connell to try and understand the major events of the time, for example the passing of the Great Reform Act or other important pieces of legislation in the 1830s, it is an attempt to do something very different and provide a first-person camera view of O'Connell—at work and at play, and as he embarked on a number of different campaigns to overturn the Act of Union.

The book begins with O'Connell's attempts to take his seat in May 1829 and his declaration that he would not be easily silenced. Part I then looks at O'Connell's career in Britain in the 1830s, beginning with his determined attempts to make an impression in the House of Commons, and ending with his fear at the close of the decade that his reputation had been compromised. Part II looks at his renewed attempts to win Repeal in the 1840s, and traces his decline all the way to his death in 1847. Chapter 12 is a specialised study of O'Connell's position on slavery, and is similar to the chapter on O'Connell's career as a lawyer in the first book. This may appear incongruous—why provide a study on slavery and not, for example, a chapter on his views on the poor law, or his relationship with his tenants? But the slavery question is fundamental to our understanding of O'Connell's character and, quite apart from the international dimension, it reveals much about his strengths (and weaknesses) as a politician and a national leader. Looking back on the issue now it seems obvious to us that O'Connell was right and his opponents were wrong. But none of this was obvious at the time. Even some leading abolitionists, in Europe and the United States, believed that slavery was wrong because of what it did to the white owner, and were not convinced of the innate equality of the black person. O'Connell was different. He felt the pain of the black slaves, he understood what it was like to be the victim of a real oppression, and he refused to abandon the cause no matter what the cost. It was the same determination—stubbornness—principle—that would prevent him from changing his mind on the use of physical force, and here his reputation paid the price.

Although it may not always be evident in this book, which places O'Connell the man at the centre of things, it is not hard to understand why O'Connell horrified and disgusted so many people in Britain. O'Connell was seen as a coward and a crook, a man who insulted with impunity and then refused to back up his words when challenged, and who appeared to live off the money of the poorest Irish people. Part of this was anti-Irish prejudice, but there was more to it than that. O'Connell confounded people's expectations of what was acceptable public behaviour. By refusing to play by the accepted rules of the game, or even show a passing acquaintance with the accepted political conventions of the day, he was feared and detested. Lecky summarised the views held at the time: 'O'Connell was nothing more than a foul-mouthed, untruthful, vulgar, and venal demagogue.'[2] The stories of O'Connell betraying a private confidence or a public trust were eagerly recited in his lifetime. Some of these criticisms, as this book will show, were well deserved. But the stories which showed O'Connell in a better light were never reported in his lifetime. The Whig peer Lord Ebrington was at one point very close to O'Connell, but they fell out during the Repeal agitation of the 1840s. However, Ebrington was always grateful that 'even in his most angry moments O'Connell never suffered anything he had learnt in the period of their confidence to escape him'.[3]

What made O'Connell such a Promethean figure was his determination to always follow his own path and do whatever he decided was right. At times inconsistent, at times infuriating, he was at all times an inspirational figure who fought an empire on his own terms and almost won.

| ACKNOWLEDGMENTS

At a large evening party in London in 1825 the Irish portrait painter Martin Archer Shee finally met his political hero, Daniel O'Connell. It took Shee some time to find the courage to go up to O'Connell and tell him what an honour it was to meet someone 'whose exertions in the cause of religious freedom in Ireland had deserved the undying gratitude of the country'. Raising himself up, O'Connell replied, 'with oracular sententiousness': 'Sir, *nations are never grateful*.' The style of the response, and the readiness to accept the compliment, offended Shee's idea of what constituted good taste, and had 'a slightly refrigerating effect on the enthusiasm of his hero-worship'.

Authors, on the other hand, should always be grateful. I would like to begin by thanking Fergal Tobin of Gill & Macmillan for guiding this project from the very beginning, when it was a study of the early life of Daniel O'Connell rather than a two-volume account of the entire life. His advice and encouragement have been significant factors in my development as a historian from the very start of my career. I am also grateful to the rest of the staff at Gill & Macmillan, including Deirdre Rennison Kunz, for her meticulous work, and Nicki Howard and Jennifer Patton, for all their help. I would also like to thank Dr Marnie Hay for her assistance in preparing the book for publication.

Anyone who works on the life of Daniel O'Connell owes a massive debt to the exhaustive work of those who have made his extensive correspondence readily available. Maurice R. O'Connell's eight volumes of correspondence, which were published by the Irish Manuscripts Commission and other publishers, are an incredible resource for anyone interested in Irish history in this period, and O'Connell (and Gerald Lyne and everyone else involved in the project) deserve recognition and thanks. At Trinity College Dublin I am very grateful to the Provost, Dr John Hegarty, for all his support, and the Dean of Research, Dr David Lloyd, for the opportunity to contribute in a different way to the work of the College. I would also like to thank my colleagues in the Department of History and on the Trinity Access Programme—in particular, Professor David Dickson, for providing me with a transcript of the James Whiteside correspondence which is in private hands. Dr Daragh O'Connell provided information on (and some photographs of) O'Connell's trip to Genoa, and Dr Trish Ferguson advised on various issues in the text. My sister, Rosena, and her husband, Nick Rowe, made it possible to access key British parliamentary papers, and allowed the project to be completed on time. Cecelia Joyce read the second part of the manuscript and, once again, provided invaluable notes and suggestions. Ted Brady deserves thanks for his enormous efforts in bringing the project to completion, and for his help in so many areas. At Newstalk I am grateful to my producer, Susan Cahill, for making 'Talking History' such a success, and the late Mrs Mary Connellan for everything over the years.

The O'Connell tomb at Glasnevin Cemetery is well worth visiting —'the pre-eminently national symbol of the country', according to W.E. Gladstone—and I am grateful to Shane MacThomais for showing me around and for all his help with this project. The Irish Legal History Society allowed me to present on some of my ideas about O'Connell, and I am particularly grateful to Felix M. Larkin and Mr Justice Hugh Geoghegan for their advice. Professor Michael Laffan provided insights on Bismarck (and the work of T. Desmond Williams), and I would also like to thank Professor James McGuire, Professor Alvin Jackson, and Dr Ian McBride for their support.

Drawing to the end, I would like to thank my mother, Nancy, Thomas, Jennifer, Jack, and Caitlin Geoghegan, as well as the O'Connell family in the United States—Moira, Rory, Adrian, and Benjamin—who have provided so much inspiration. My List 1 class in Trinity College Dublin on 'Ireland in the age of O'Connell' also helped clarify many of the ideas in this book. I should also thank my friends, Alastair McMenamin, Bridget Hourican, Colin Walsh, Declan Lawlor, Paul and Lynne Geaney, Eoin Keehan, John Berry, Rory Whelan, Sean O'Reilly, and Trevor White, as well as Dr J. Vivian Cooke and Dr Robert Armstrong. Final thanks are due to Mr Justice Adrian Hardiman for reading and advising on the entire text, and for his key role in the inception of the entire project. The book is dedicated to Professor Ciaran Brady, who has been a friend and an inspiration for many years and who epitomises the scholar as teacher in academic life.

| PROLOGUE

'O'Connell has come to be nothing but a name . . . But forty and fifty years ago, O'Connell was, and was felt to be, not only a name, but a power.'

(W.E. GLADSTONE ON DANIEL O'CONNELL, 1889)[1]

On Friday 15 May 1829 the House of Commons was 'crowded to excess'.[2] Everyone was curious to see what would happen when Daniel O'Connell finally attempted to take his seat for parliament. Catholic emancipation had been conceded by the government the previous month, following O'Connell's stunning victory in the Clare by-election in 1828, and after British power in Ireland had been 'shivered to atoms', but the terms of the act had been drafted so that O'Connell would not be included within them.[3] In other words, he must take the existing oaths of allegiance, supremacy, and abjuration, and make a declaration against transubstantiation (as well as a declaration that the invocation or adoration of the Virgin Mary, the invocation of the saints, and the sacrifice of the Mass as practised in the Church of Rome were all 'superstitious and idolatrous') or he would not be allowed take his seat. There was no way O'Connell, as a devout Catholic, could denounce the 'impious, heretical, and damnable doctrine' of his faith without humiliating both himself and the Irish nation he represented. The Emancipation Act allowed Catholics to substitute all these things for a new oath when taking their seats, but King George IV had spitefully insisted that O'Connell should not be allowed to fall within this new dispensation.

At five p.m. the Speaker of the House asked if there were any new members who wanted to be sworn, and called on them to come before him. O'Connell rose from his seat under the gallery and made his way to the table of the House of Commons, where he was introduced by Lords Ebrington and Duncannon. 'The sensation Mr O'Connell's appearance caused was intense; the House was crowded, and when he entered all rose, through a feeling of curiosity, to catch a glimpse of the renowned member for Clare.'[4] A journalist from *The Times* wrote that it would be impossible to convey 'the silent and almost breathless attention with which he was received'.[5] O'Connell handed over his return and his qualification papers, as well as a certificate from the commissioners of the lord high steward, confirming that he had taken the preliminary oaths required. The chief clerk of the House, having examined these documents and found that they were correct, immediately opened the large box before him and took out the old oaths (which were affixed to large paste-boards) and a copy of the New Testament on which to swear him. There was 'profound silence' in the House. After some moments, O'Connell announced that as a Catholic he could not take the existing oaths, though he was willing to take whatever new oath was required following emancipation. His refusal was reported formally to the Speaker and he was ordered to withdraw. O'Connell bowed, but made no attempt to move, and remained standing at the table, staring silently at the Speaker.[6] Henry Brougham rose to speak in favour of O'Connell's claims but the Speaker shouted, 'Order! Order!', thereby indicating that he could not proceed until O'Connell had withdrawn. The Speaker turned to O'Connell, and again ordered him to withdraw.

As the *Morning Herald* reported, 'Mr O'Connell once more bowed, and then withdrew, but without uttering, or attempting to utter, one word.'[7] He returned to his seat under the gallery. There, resting against the doorway, was a stack of ten or eleven volumes of the journals of the House, and several volumes of law books, which he had stationed in the doorway ready for use in case he had been called to speak. But the opportunity was denied. A heated debate followed about whether O'Connell could be allowed to present his case before the House, either at the table or before the bar, but it was decided that he could not be heard. Robert Peel, the home secretary and O'Connell's great adversary, denied that O'Connell had any right to speak, and called for the discussion to be adjourned until the Monday. This was agreed and the decision on O'Connell's eligibility was postponed.

On Monday 18 May O'Connell returned to the House of Commons and took his position under the gallery. 'The House was crowded to overflowing' and it was said that 'never before were there in the House so many strangers, peers, or members'.[8] The duke of Orléans, the future king of France, and his son, the duke of Chartres, were among the visitors who came in late and struggled to find a seat. The adjourned debate resumed and it was resolved that O'Connell should be heard at the bar. O'Connell rose to speak. It had been confidently predicted that O'Connell would fail in the House of Commons, with his style of speaking ill-suited for a refined parliamentary setting.[9] But in a thrilling oration O'Connell convinced his critics that a new parliamentary gladiator had arrived. Since 1801 Ireland had sent various MPs to the British House of Commons. But this was the first time that someone had addressed the House with a claim to be able to speak for the entire Irish nation. O'Connell declared that 'the voice of the people had sent him there' and that he spoke as 'the representative of the people'.[10] In a brilliantly structured speech, which traced the history of the various oaths, O'Connell spoke like a lawyer on 'points of legal subtlety' and like a leader on 'the vicious principle' which excluded him. For O'Connell this was nothing less than a question of civil rights. And he asked the House, 'If it be not a civil right, what is it?'[11]

Challenging the arguments that had been made against his eligibility, O'Connell reminded the House that his case could never be made into a precedent, as 'it can never happen again'. Therefore he asked if the House was determined to interpret the Emancipation Act to 'make it an outlawry against a single individual'. This prompted cheers of 'Hear, hear!' In a clever twist, O'Connell shifted his position and denounced the government for deliberately trying to exclude him from the terms of the Emancipation Act. He questioned why his specific case had not been included in the act, and then answered his own question: 'Simply, because it was not intended to be included.' 'What is to become of me?' he asked to loud cheering: 'Am I to remain the representative of Clare? Will the House not let me in, and is it not able to turn me out? What, I ask again, is to become of me? I call the attention of the House to that—what is to become of me?'

In a moving summation, O'Connell presented himself as the representative of 'a divided people', 'a disinterested people', and 'a martyred people'. Finished, he bowed to the House and withdrew 'amidst loud and general cheering'.[12] Attempting to return to his seat under the gallery, he discovered that it had been taken by the visiting members of the French royal family, and he found a new place beside the sergeant-at-arms.[13] In his response, the solicitor general paid a generous tribute to O'Connell's oratory, noting that his temper and ability were exactly what had been expected from 'so distinguished a member of his profession'. But the numbers were against O'Connell. At the end of a long debate it was ordered that he should be asked to present himself before the House the very next day, and if he refused to take the existing oaths it would mean he had disqualified himself and his seat would fall vacant.

On Tuesday 19 May the House of Commons was packed with people anxious to see the conclusion of the drama. O'Connell was brought before the Speaker and reminded of the resolution of the previous night. He was told that he could not take his seat unless he took the original oaths (including the various declarations) prescribed at the time he was elected. 'The excitement was intense; breathless silence prevailed in that crowded assembly' as everyone strained to hear what O'Connell would say.[14] And then O'Connell did something unexpected. He asked to see what he was being asked to swear. 'The clerk was directed to hand him the oath, which was printed on a large card.'[15] Taking his time, O'Connell put on his spectacles and then proceeded to study the card with the deepest attention. A stranger to the chamber might have imagined that O'Connell had never seen the words before, so intently did he study them, and as the minutes passed there was absolute silence. Finally, O'Connell looked up. In a determined voice he said, 'I see in this oath one assertion as to a matter of fact which I *know* to be false. I see in it another assertion as to a matter of opinion which I *believe* to be untrue.' With 'an expression of the most profound contempt', he declared, 'I therefore refuse to take this oath,' and flung the printed card away. It was said that the House was '*struck of a heap*', such was the 'feeling of amazement that pervaded parliament for some minutes after the card was thus contemptuously flung on the table'. The blow struck, O'Connell withdrew from the bar, as a new writ was issued for Co. Clare. After winning one of his greatest victories it hardly seemed to matter that he had lost his parliamentary seat without ever being allowed to take it.

PART I

PART I

Chapter 1 ༺

'THE MAN WHO DISCOVERED IRELAND': O'CONNELL REVISITED

'Yesterday one of my children brought me her book of animals and, pointing to a boa constrictor, asked me its name, and I told her it was an O'Connell.'[1]

(FREDERICK MARRYAT, *DIARY OF A BLASÉ*, 1836)

'Who has not heard of the Liberator?' asked a Scottish clergyman in 1841.[2] Following the winning of Catholic emancipation in 1829 it seemed an unnecessary question to ask. Such was O'Connell's international fame that in 1830, when the Belgian parliamentarians voted on their new king, three of them voted for O'Connell.[3] In later years O'Connell liked to joke that if the election had been held at a later time, and if he had stood against Leopold, then he was convinced he'd have 'run the fellow close enough'. A French captain of artillery once told the bishop of Ardagh that some of his compatriots liked to imagine that O'Connell had been born in France rather than merely having gone there for his education. 'Ah,' the captain sighed, 'if he had been a native of our country, we would have made him king of the French!'[4] Of all the stories of his international reputation told in his lifetime, O'Connell himself particularly enjoyed that of a coachman from Heidelberg in Germany. The coachman was asked by an Irish visitor if he had ever heard of O'Connell. 'I have,' the coachman replied. 'He is the man who discovered Ireland.'[5]

Vanity had always been a key part of O'Connell's character, and the winning of emancipation and the fame and adulation that came with it only encouraged him in his vice. Whenever he met Catholic children he liked to ask them if they knew who he was, before telling them 'that it was I who emancipated you'.[6] O'Connell's popularity throughout the Irish countryside was enormous. One time during the Repeal agitation in the 1840s, O'Connell was travelling by carriage and stopped to have the horses changed. A crowd gathered to watch him, and one old beggar woman with a crutch approached the carriage and pleaded with O'Connell to shake hands with her. He did so and the effect on the woman was immediate. She threw her crutch into the air and exclaimed in delight, 'I've touched his honour's hand—I'm young again!'[7] Similarly, on another occasion, O'Connell spent some days at the house of two English women. Every night they sang a song in his honour, to the tune of 'God save the king', and when one woman had a painful swollen face she applied O'Connell's gold-laced travelling cap to it to see if it would heal her. Visitors to Ireland were often surprised by the extent of O'Connell's popularity. One time an Englishman was travelling with O'Connell to Glencullen when they encountered a funeral. The mourners recognised O'Connell and, despite the solemnity of the occasion, broke into 'a vociferous hurrah'.[8] The Englishman was astonished and made a comment about how odd it was to have a political hurrah at a funeral. But the mourners replied that 'the corpse would have doubtless cheered lustily too, if he could'.

During his lifetime O'Connell's autograph was widely sought. In general he was happy to oblige, although he found the constant writing tedious. The king of Bavaria was anxious to secure his autograph and asked his minister in England to obtain it. O'Connell sent him some lines from one of his favourite poems, John Dryden's defence of the Roman Catholic faith, 'The hind and the panther', and the king was delighted to get something written by the hand 'of that energetical character, inseparable for ever from the history of our age'.[9] However, O'Connell refused a request from the tsar of Russia, and later made this public, declaring that he would not show this courtesy to such a man as Tsar Nicholas because of his tyrannical policies. In later years there was a popular anecdote that O'Connell had once responded to the request for an autograph with the lines 'Sir, I never send autographs. Yours,

Daniel O'Connell.'[10] Old age made the act of writing difficult. When his friend William O'Neill Daunt visited O'Connell in January 1847 he was asked whether he wanted any autographs. Daunt answered in the affirmative. 'Well then', said O'Connell, laughing, 'I'll get my secretary to write as many as you want!'[11]

At the first royal levée after emancipation, O'Connell went up to kiss the hands of King George IV. As he approached, the king muttered, 'There is O'Connell! God damn the scoundrel!'[12] The story made the newspapers and was later confirmed to O'Connell by the duke of Norfolk. O'Connell seemed supremely unconcerned and liked to boast that he was 'the best-abused man in the British dominions'.[13] Thomas Moore, for example, liked to say that O'Connell was a curious mixture of 'high and low, formidable and contemptible, mighty and mean'.[14] When discussing him one evening over dinner, Moore was advised by the noted humorist Sydney Smith that the only way to deal with such a man would be 'to hang him up, and erect a statue to him under his gallows'. Moore approved of this 'balancing of the account'. Once, a friend asked O'Connell if he had ever been upset by the constant attacks. 'Not a bit,' insisted O'Connell. 'I knew the scoundrels were only advertising me by their abuse.'[15]

After his death, O'Connell would be criticised for his apparent dismissal of the Irish language. At a St Patrick's Day dinner in London in 1833 he discussed the decline of the language among the peasantry. O'Connell revealed that he was 'sufficiently utilitarian not to regret its gradual abandonment'.[16] Reflecting on the building of the tower of Babel, O'Connell admitted that although the Irish language was a source of real national pride, the English language was 'the medium of all modern communication' and therefore he could 'witness without a sigh the gradual disuse of the Irish'. These lines should be seen in their correct context: as a commentary on how English was the language needed to succeed, and a prediction that it was also the language of the future. O'Connell's love of the Irish language was clear. He always regretted not changing the spelling of his surname to 'O'Conal' after the winning of emancipation, believing that the other spelling was an English imposition.[17] And he always delighted in speaking Irish. During one Repeal rally at Skibbereen in Co. Cork, when government reporters gathered to record his every word, he enjoyed discomfiting them by delivering the entire speech in Irish.[18]

Returning to Co. Clare for his re-election campaign in 1829, O'Connell was greeted by vast crowds and 'all down the line of road from Dublin to Limerick his progress was a continued triumph'.[19] At every point where there was an opportunity to see him, men, women, and children could be seen 'running at the top of their speed, and waving hats and fragments of garments, or green boughs, shouting all the while at the top of their voices'.[20] It was noted that 'the poor old women' were particularly obsessed with O'Connell. Some of them would throw aside, 'for the moment, their load of years', and 'skip and jump as merrily as the youngest there'. However, the majority would drop on their knees as the carriage approached and, 'raising their aged hands and eyes to heaven, were to be heard praying fervently, and invoking blessings and mercies upon the man who was labouring to upraise a fallen nation, and to vindicate an oppressed creed'. As O'Connell approached Ennis, one elderly woman, working in her cabbage garden, 'threw down her spade and looked around for something green to wave in honour of the Liberator'.[21] There was nothing suitable, so she grabbed a bunch of nettles and held them over her head as she ran towards the carriage, shouting, 'Long life to O'Connell, the man of the people.'

Although O'Connell was not expected to be opposed in 1829, he still insisted on taking every precaution so as not to be taken by surprise. All the canvassing and polling arrangements were made in advance, 'as though a desperate contest was imminent', and it was believed that this level of preparedness frightened off any would-be challengers.[22] Entering the town of Ennis, O'Connell was greeted with white flags at every turn. At first he was confused about what this meant, but was reassured that these were 'the veritable *green* flags of the *great* election of the preceding year, faded and bleached' by the passing of time. Re-elected unopposed, O'Connell was carried by chair throughout the countryside, before retiring to Derrynane to rest and prepare for the new parliamentary session. There was some criticism in Britain of his aggressive language in this period, but shrewder observers recognised what he was doing. As the diarist Charles Greville noted, 'Had he never been violent, he would not be the man he is, and Ireland would not have been emancipated.'[23]

Back in Dublin in January 1830, O'Connell was presented with an address by the Trades' Political Union. Each trade in the city marched with its own leaders and banners to his house at Merrion Square and formed in squares in front of his house. Then their president, and staff of vice-presidents, entered the house and presented O'Connell with the address from the balcony of the house. His response was almost drowned by the 'ringing cheers' of the enormous crowd which had gathered around the square. A few days later, O'Connell set out by carriage by Kingstown, to travel by boat to England and take his seat in parliament. A crowd cheered him at every point of the journey, 'blessing and wishing him success in the new career about to open to him'.[24]

Whenever he wanted to escape from the pressures of work, O'Connell would return home to Derrynane. There he alternated days of relaxation and hunting with days of study and research. If it was raining, or a work day, he usually rose between eight a.m. and nine a.m. Mass was said at nine a.m. in his private chapel, and after attending he would collect the newspapers and post that were delivered by special relays of mounted postboys. O'Connell would begin reading these materials over breakfast, and spend an hour or two afterwards 'wading through his correspondence and the heap of newspapers that he daily received'.[25] Afterwards, he would work in his study for three or four hours, writing letters or dictating them to a secretary. At four p.m., unless the weather prohibited it, he would go outside in his dressing-gown and cap, and walk along the beach between Derrynane Abbey and the sea. At these times he would appear to be in great thought, and suggest 'by the sudden and involuntary motion of the arm, that some vivid thought of Ireland's wrongs had flashed across his mind'. His family were reluctant to join him on these occasions, allowing him time to reflect in private.

The next day, 'the scene was changed'.[26] Shortly after dawn, O'Connell's huntsmen would knock on his door and tell him 'to be stirring and not lose the fine morning'. For O'Connell the great attraction of Derrynane was the opportunity to go 'hare-hunting through the neighbouring mountains on foot'.[27] Within a few minutes he would be dressed and ready to go, carrying a 'tall *wattle*, or long stick, such as is commonly used in mountain-walking there'. There was no question of having breakfast before setting out. Rather, all kinds of breakfast—'Irish, Scotch, and foreign'—were packed up in baskets, and carried with the huntsmen. Nothing would be eaten until at least two hares had been killed, much to the frustration of any less enthusiastic or more hungry hunters. A spot in some mountain ravine would be chosen for the meal, preferably near a mountain stream, and sheltered from the wind. The breakfast would be eaten with enthusiasm, with much banter and joking, 'and the merriest of all was Daniel O'Connell'. Work would then intervene, as his servants would track him down and deliver that day's postbags, and he would quickly read the most important letters. But once the hounds cried out after catching the scent of more hares, all politics would be forgotten, and he would set out once more. He would remain hunting until it became dark, and then return home 'the freshest of the party'.[28] There would be a large late dinner, and O'Connell would be in high spirits from the excitement of the day, 'and he unlocked all his treasures of anecdote and historical and professional reminiscence'.

This would be the routine for the rest of O'Connell's time at Derrynane. By the next morning 'the eager huntsman had relapsed into the studious and absorbed politician'. Twenty-four hours later he would be transformed back into a huntsman, and so it would go on until a Sunday, which would be given over to prayer, exercise, and the settling of quarrels among the tenantry. He had no interest in fishing or shooting and, because he suffered from sea-sickness in his later years, had no wish to go out on a boat.[29] Fox-hunting was not possible because of the mountainous terrain, but in any case he thought it poor sport compared to hunting hares on foot. 'I am the only fellow who understands how to hunt rationally,' he liked to boast, and his beagles were trained to perfection to track the hares. To collect his thoughts, he loved long walks, accompanied by a favourite dog, and he would walk for miles and 'gaze on the seemingly illimitable stretch of ocean below'. Thus 'passed away the few weeks of relaxation enjoyed by the Arch-Agitator'.[30]

Derrynane was open to anyone who accepted its hospitality, whether Catholic or Protestant, Irish or foreign, Repealer or anti-Repealer. One writer left an account of sitting down to dinner at a table set for thirty-three people, Irish, English, Scottish, French, German, and American. One evening a stranger was announced—a young Englishman—who stated that his pony had lost a shoe and he was unable to proceed on his journey. O'Connell rose from the head of the table to welcome him, exclaiming, 'You will oblige us by staying here, sir,' and adding as a joke, 'we are indeed infinitely obliged to your pony'.[31] In a profile of

O'Connell, published anonymously in London in 1839, the writer was generous in his description of O'Connell's hospitality: 'in private life I believe he is a very magnificent fellow'.[32] It had been claimed in *The Times* that O'Connell liked to entice Englishmen into his den and then 'drown them in whiskey toddy'. But this sounded very tempting to the author, who looked forward to visiting some day and toasting O'Connell with a tumbler. As the man noted, 'King Dan is the representative of the country, and he does the honours of hospitality for her.'

In the same anonymous profile it was noted that O'Connell possessed the type of greatness that got things done. Nothing was for show; everything was done to advance the cause.[33] The author had no doubt that when future generations asked the question of how the civil incapabilities of the Catholics had been removed there could only be one answer: 'Daniel O'Connell removed them.' And although there had been many men around him who had helped, 'there is not one who can claim to share with him one leaf of that laurel. Alone he did it.' John Doherty, the solicitor general who had been humiliated by O'Connell in the Doneraile case, had more reason than most to hate O'Connell. But in the 1830s he always spoke of him with a grudging kind of 'awful respect'.[34] One time he told the story of how he had overheard two old women discussing O'Connell in court, following one of his great legal speeches. O'Connell had been defending 'a manifestly guilty man', but had secured his acquittal. 'It is no use talking,' one of the women said proudly. 'He is just a God Almighty upon earth.' As Doherty was forced to concede, this was indeed 'the public feeling'.

Chapter 2 ∾

'KING OF THE BEGGARS', 1830

'It is not vanity, but I shall not be satisfied till in that [Irish] parliament I am hailed by some member as the father of my country.'

(SPEECH OF DANIEL O'CONNELL AT A MEETING OF THE ANTI-TORY ASSOCIATION, 1834)[1]

The House of Commons, inside the royal chapel of St Stephen's at Westminster Palace, so impressive on the outside, was a disappointing sight inside. 'It was dark, gloomy, and badly ventilated, and so small that not more than four hundred of the six hundred and fifty-eight members could be accommodated in it with any measure of comfort.'[2] For an important debate, especially if it was preceded by a call of the house, the MPs were crammed together, and some were forced to take a place in the gallery or the refreshment apartments next door. The members' benches were cushioned and covered with leather, and 'from the floor backwards to the walls, each seat was from twelve to fourteen inches higher than the one fronting it'. The row to the right of the Speaker was for members of the government and its supporters, and the first one on the left was for leading figures of the opposition. The strangers' gallery was immediately above the entrance for MPs and could accommodate one hundred and twenty persons. The back row was used by the reporters and sometimes as many as sixty or seventy would cover an important debate.

Women were forbidden to enter the strangers' gallery, and the only way they could see or hear what was going on was 'by mounting above the ceiling of the house, and looking down through a large hole which was made immediately above the principal chandelier, for the purpose of ventilation'.[3] Not more than fourteen women could follow debates in this way, and the smoke of the candles and the uncomfortable position ensured that few remained there long. Only those 'who were anxious to hear their husbands, or brothers, or lovers, make some expected oration, had the fortitude to endure the semi-martyrdom of remaining many minutes in such a place'. There was a smoking room next door to the chamber, and it was here that members went to write letters. The library was beside it, and some MPs would stop there to research their speeches.

The most important business of the day would commence at five o'clock. But the best orators would usually wait until nine or ten o'clock before rising to speak. This was because the House was comparatively empty before then, with most members preferring 'the more solid qualities of a good dinner to "the feast of reason and the flow of soul"'.[4] If a member wanted to speak, it was necessary to catch the Speaker's eye, and wait to be called. But since the best orators left it until later to speak it was very difficult for a new speaker, or one without a reputation, to catch the Speaker's eye if he waited too long. For the first two years of his parliamentary career, O'Connell complained that the Speaker deliberately neglected him, refusing to make eye contact, but in later years believed that the Speaker went out of his way to compensate for this.[5]

O'Connell was finally able to take his seat on Thursday 4 February 1830 when parliament met for the new session. No controversy was expected this time, and the House was almost empty as he took the required oaths and then shook hands with the Speaker. It was usual to take the oaths on the right side of the table, and there was some consternation that O'Connell chose to take them on the left side, but although this was noted in the records there was no formal complaint.[6] O'Connell took a seat beside Sir Francis Burdett, a longtime supporter of Catholic emancipation, and entered into a long conversation. The speech from the throne had been heard earlier in the House of Lords and in the debate on it that followed O'Connell was determined to announce his arrival as a major parliamentary figure. Most people delivered a set, prepared speech on their debut. But O'Connell had waited long enough for this moment, and had decided in advance to give an unplanned response to the speech from the throne.

Many people entered the House of Commons with great reputations for oratory that were soon destroyed. It was a very different challenge to speaking outdoors, and sometimes speakers who were used to being applauded in other settings were incapable of making the adjustment. A favourite saying among seasoned politicians was that 'a great demagogue out of doors becomes a very minute pygmy in St. Stephen's'.[7] A maiden speech begun badly was said to have 'a paralysing effect', and few recovered from having their efforts greeted with 'marked indifference and inattention'.[8] 'Mortified, disappointed and disheartened', these speakers usually performed no better on their second outing.

Such was the expected fate of O'Connell. John Doherty, the solicitor general, was overheard boasting, 'Mark my words: he will turn out nothing; he will sink down gradually to his proper dimensions.'[9] The pressure was therefore on O'Connell to make an immediate impression. While O'Connell never gave any indication of being nervous before a big speech, either in the courtrooms or at political gatherings, in reality this was just part of his act, the carefully constructed image he wanted to project. In public he was always the showman, laughing and joking, and never appearing anything less than fully confident. But in private he struggled with the usual doubts and insecurities, and often when anticipating a major speech he had trouble sleeping the night before.[10]

Catching the Speaker's eye early on in the debate, O'Connell rose to speak. He began by announcing that 'the people had sent him there to do their business' and that therefore he felt obliged to comment on the state of the country.[11] His review of the speech from the throne was scathing and full of sarcasm. Contrasting it with similar messages from the heads of state in France and the United States, he dismissed it as 'containing such jejune and empty statements' that it would never have been tolerated in either of the other countries. There were cheers of 'Hear!' at this, and O'Connell went on to mock the address for revealing information that was already well known, such as the news that the Russian war was at an end. 'This was an important discovery, indeed,' he joked, adding for emphasis, that 'of course, none of them knew that before'. This earned the first laugh of the speech, and O'Connell grew in confidence as he went on.

Staying with foreign policy, he mocked the ministry for saying that nothing was determined as to Portugal. 'And why?' he asked. 'Ah! We were not told that.' For O'Connell the question was clear-cut. He attacked the regime of Don Miguel for having come to power by treachery and force, and through 'the spilling of innocent blood'.[12] All of this was cheered loudly. O'Connell then moved on to domestic policy, and the state of the United Kingdom. The speech from the throne had mentioned that there was 'distress' in the country, but claimed it was only 'partial'. O'Connell contrasted this with the comments of the three leading supporters of the king's address, who had spoken before him, who had admitted that the distress was 'general', 'extraordinary', and 'overwhelming'. There was more laughter and cheers of 'Hear! Hear!' O'Connell then mocked the chancellor of the exchequer for claiming that there was one 'Oasis in the desert', a country 'where no distress at all existed'. He joked, 'and who would have thought it? That country was Ireland!'

O'Connell claimed that he had never heard anything as astonishing in all his life. He spoke of the seven thousand registered people in Dublin alone who were in poverty, and forced to live off the 'three-halfpence a day' which was distributed by the lord lieutenant. O'Connell then spoke of the three provinces he knew well—Leinster, Connaught, and Munster (and not, revealingly, Ulster)—and declared that 'the agriculturalists in those three provinces were suffering the greatest distress'. O'Connell ended the speech calling for reform of the courts and parliamentary reform, insisting that only 'a radical and complete reform' would satisfy the people. And he demanded that the House of Commons should continue to meet every day until it had discovered the causes of the public distress and how to address them. He sat down to many cheers and much acclaim.

Over the next few months O'Connell spoke regularly, although he did not speak as much as he would have liked and he complained that the Speaker deliberately avoided his eye. But when he did speak, the causes that he championed are revealing. For example, he presented a petition from Co. Cork against slavery in the colonies; he suggested abolishing the practice of arresting people for debt except after judicial procedure; and he spoke in favour of a petition supporting the rights of Jews.[13] In another debate he opposed one member's suggestion that the lord lieutenancy of Ireland should be abolished, arguing that this would increase the suffering of the 'seven thousand persons in Dublin living on the charity of three-halfpence a day'. Instead he suggested that if savings were wanted they should first abolish 'the lords of the bed-chamber, the lords of the admiralty, or the lords of the treasury'.[14]

Jews were prevented from sitting in parliament and O'Connell was one of the strongest supporters of their emancipation. In a letter to Isaac Lyon Goldsmid, the leader of the British Jews, following the passing of Catholic emancipation, he promised to do everything he could to support the Jews' claims. He boasted that Ireland 'had claims on your ancient race as it is the only Christian community that I know of unsullied by any one act of persecution of the Jews', while in contrast, 'The English were always persecutors.'[15] Despite the perception of O'Connell as a Catholic ideologue, he believed firmly in the separation of church and state. He told Goldsmid that it was 'an eternal and universal truth that we are responsible to God alone for our religious belief and that human laws are impious when they attempt to control the exercise of those acts'. This was also his position in parliament. W.E. Gladstone never forgot hearing O'Connell demand a complete separation of church and state during a particularly heated debate. At a banquet in honour of Polish independence in 1831 O'Connell again called for the separation of the two, declaring that it was always 'an adulterous connection'.[16]

Parliamentary reform was another key interest of O'Connell. On 18 February 1830 he rose late in a debate on the subject to respond to comments that had been made. Revealing that he was against paying MPs a salary, he attacked the seventy-eight members who profited from offices of the crown, accusing them of lacking any independence when it came to voting.[17] From this, O'Connell moved to the problem of popular representation. He revealed that 424 MPs were not popularly elected, but were returned for seats controlled by peers or borough proprietors. And he claimed that only twenty-one of the one hundred MPs for Irish constituencies were popularly elected. The national debt of the United Kingdom at that time was eight hundred million pounds, and O'Connell blamed it on the oligarchy which was in control of the political system. Parliamentary reform, he insisted, would solve the problem, as the people themselves were always the best judges of what was best for a country. The speech ended on a dramatic note, with O'Connell calling on the House, 'which had shorn the talons of the monarchy, to use its powers to cut short the fell fangs of the oligarchical faction which lorded it over the land'.[18] In another debate, on 5 March,

O'Connell spoke in favour of the secret ballot, arguing that it was the only way of ensuring that people could vote as they wished without being intimidated.[19] And he ended his speech with another attack on the 'oligarchy that lorded it over them with despotic sway', blaming the aristocracy for burdening the country with eight hundred million pounds' worth of debt.

Despite his great experience as a speaker, O'Connell found it difficult initially to adjust to the demands of the House of Commons. In the early years he spoke often—too often—and became 'a noisy bore' by trying to turn everything into a discussion of the Union.[20] The problem for O'Connell was that he failed to adapt to the style of the House. As a result his parliamentary career, which had begun so well, threatened to slide into mediocrity. O'Connell had not risen to become the leading barrister in Ireland without possessing a quick ability to learn about how systems operated, but it did take him some time to unravel the secrets of the Commons. In his correspondence with the great English utilitarian and social reformer Jeremy Bentham in 1831, O'Connell acknowledged that he had 'shipwrecked his parliamentary fame' by trying to do too much.[21] He blamed this on having too high an opinion 'of the moral worth and intellectual power of the House of Commons', and in thinking he could 'cleanse the Augean stable of the law'. And so he resolved to be less mild and gentle in his fight to secure political reform, justice for Ireland, and Repeal of the Union.

Back in Ireland, in between worrying about growing fat, O'Connell set about organising his Repeal campaign.[22] On 6 April 1830 he founded The Society of the Friends of Ireland of all Religious Persuasions. The aims were economic, political, and moral. It sought to repeal duties on Irish malt, coal, and paper, prevent a duty on Irish tobacco, repeal the Union, reform parliament, campaign against sectarianism, and have slavery abolished in the British colonies.[23] But the society was suppressed by a proclamation of the lord lieutenant on 24 April, after only a few meetings, and O'Connell was forced to find a new way of leading his new campaign.

On 5 March 1830 Lord Francis Leveson-Gower and John Doherty introduced a bill to provide for deserted and illegitimate children in Ireland. This was the first attempt to extend a part of the English poor laws to Ireland, and O'Connell was determined to oppose it. The problem, as he saw it, was that the word of the pregnant woman was taken as fact, and therefore an innocent man was vulnerable to any claims of paternity. The man would then be expected to pay for the costs of the pregnancy and birth (around £40) and be given the choice of marrying the woman or going to jail. For O'Connell this represented nothing less than a threat to Irish morality, with a pregnant woman benefiting from having slept with as many men as possible and then being able to 'pick out the best workman or weaver or shoemaker' to marry.[24] He was quick to enlist the support of the Catholic hierarchy in his campaign against the bill, reminding them that the best protector of female chastity was 'the fear of being so degraded as to lose all chance of matrimony'. In parliament, O'Connell pursued a cautious strategy to prevent the passing of the bill, raising various difficulties with it during the second reading on 26 April, while declaring that he would not oppose it. The bill was reported back from committee on 11 May and O'Connell moved to have the House adjourn without discussing it. Doherty, quite rightly, accused O'Connell of attempting to delay the bill, but was unable to speed up its passing. The bill lapsed at the end of the session. O'Connell was delighted, believing that the bill would have ensured that 'the road to matrimony is prostitution, and pregnancy secures a husband'.[25]

The terminal illness of King George IV meant that a general election was inevitable, and O'Connell began planning his re-election in Co. Clare. The problem was that he had promised Major William Nugent McNamara in 1828, when he had stood as the surprise candidate in the by-election, that he would step aside for him after only one term. McNamara was determined to hold him to that promise. The O'Gorman Mahon, the flamboyant character who had helped O'Connell win election, was also determined to stand, meaning that O'Connell faced a real problem winning one of the two seats on offer. O'Connell attempted to manoeuvre himself out of his commitment to McNamara, claiming to have been released from the promise by a subsequent conversation, but McNamara was not to be placated. Most importantly, he had a letter from O'Connell confirming the promise, and he threatened to make this public unless it was honoured.[26]

The intervention of O'Connell's friend and uncritical disciple Thomas Steele caused further embarrassment. Steele decided that O'Connell's honour had been impugned, and attempted to persuade

O'Connell's son Maurice to accompany him to Ireland and challenge McNamara to a duel. Citing ill-health, Maurice wisely declined to become involved. But Steele went to Ireland anyway, and inveigled Maurice's brother Morgan, a captain in the Austrian hussars who was home on leave, to fight on his father's behalf. Morgan sent an insulting letter to McNamara, challenging him to a duel, but McNamara declined the challenge.[27] The entire thing had been kept secret from O'Connell, who detested duelling, and who was furious when he discovered what had been planned. He was relieved 'the foolish expedition' had ended without any loss of life and without much public attention, and realised he had no choice but to stand down as MP for Co. Clare at the election. As one of McNamara's friends gloated to O'Connell, 'You have been outgeneralled and ill advised.'[28]

Food shortages in Ireland were another distraction. There was much distress in Ireland in the summer of 1830 following prolonged bad weather and O'Connell became concerned with the plight of his tenants in Co. Kerry. He rebuked his agent, John Primrose, for only giving £20 to their relief, and ordered him to kill some sheep or a cow and give the food to anyone who was starving near Derrynane.[29] Any newborn calf was also to be given to the poor, with O'Connell insisting that he could not allow any to be reared while the people needed food. The boats in the area were all to be used for fishing and O'Connell wanted all the salt fish, as well as the fresh fish, to be given away. His beloved hunting dogs were not forgotten about. He left instructions for his dogs to be fed with whatever food was not fit for human consumption.

As there was no salary for being an MP, and as he had virtually abandoned his legal practice, O'Connell was now in need of an income. The rent from his lands was good, but certainly nowhere near what was necessary for organising a national movement, especially given that he was so careless with his own private expenses. But help was at hand. His financial manager, P.V. Fitzpatrick, hit upon the idea of an annual collection for O'Connell, which became 'The O'Connell Tribute', thus allowing him to devote all his energies to politics. O'Connell refused to allow any money to be collected as long as the country was in a state of distress, but by the end of August the harvest had come in and he gave permission for it to go ahead.[30] As with the rent of the Catholic Association, the idea was to collect the money at the chapel doors in each diocese after Mass on a Sunday, having secured permission from the local bishop, and O'Connell calculated that if one shilling was given by one out of every seven Catholics then £50,000 would be raised, 'more, in fact, than would be necessary'.

The first tribute was collected in the early months of 1831 and almost half of what O'Connell had hoped for was raised, which was enough to dedicate his full attention to politics.[31] Close to £14,000 was raised annually until 1834, after which the fund went into decline until the 1840s.[32] For the rest of his life O'Connell would be attacked by his enemies for accepting this income. He was called 'The Great Beggarman', 'The King of the Beggars', and worse. But his critics failed to understand the bond which had been formed between O'Connell and the people, forged in the fires of the campaign for emancipation over close to thirty years. Almost alone amongst his compatriots, Charles Greville recognised what it represented, and described it as 'an income nobly given and nobly earned'.[33]

The king died in June 1830 and a general election was called the next month. Prevented from standing in Co. Clare, O'Connell received invitations from eight constituencies, but in the event decided to run in Co. Waterford. There were two seats on offer but it was expected that one would go to Lord George Thomas Beresford, who was supported by the landowners, leaving only one seat for the popular interest. Both O'Connell and Thomas Wyse, the man who had organised the victory in the by-election in 1826, were standing, which meant the real contest was between them. Wyse was a successful Waterford merchant and, as a popular local man, seemed likely to win the seat. On the second day of polling, 13 August, O'Connell announced that he would step aside rather than risk creating a split between 'several who ought to be friends'.[34] This was a ruse to force Wyse to withdraw, as O'Connell knew that pressure would be exerted on him to make way for 'The Liberator'. Wyse did stand down, and could barely hide his bitterness when asked to explain his decision. O'Connell and Beresford were duly returned as the members for Waterford.

Following a holiday in Derrynane, O'Connell returned to work in the autumn and founded the Association of Irish Volunteers for the Repeal of the Union at a meeting in Dublin on 23 October.[35] It was said at this time that O'Connell 'really appeared as if getting young again', as he attempted to rally opposition to the Union.[36] The new chief secretary, Sir Henry Hardinge, had in the absence of the lord lieutenant issued a proclamation a few days before, suppressing dangerous societies, in another attempt to prevent opposition groups from meeting. At the banquet on 23 October O'Connell denounced the proclamation and dismissed Hardinge as an instrument of despotism, 'that paltry, contemptible little English soldier', and 'a chance child of fortune and war'.[37] Hardinge was furious and wrote to O'Connell demanding that he disavow the comments or fight a duel. In his response, which was written in the third person, O'Connell denied that there were any errors of fact in what he had said. And he revealed that he would refuse to consider any request for a duel: 'He utterly disclaims any reference to such a mode of proceeding.'[38] According to O'Connell he had only been speaking of Hardinge in his '*public* capacity' and had made no reference to him 'in his private capacity'. Therefore he insisted that, 'as a public man, he did speak of Sir Henry as he would of any other man who trampled on the liberties of Irishmen'. And he added, sarcastically, that he thought that 'fighting a duel would be a bad way to prove that Sir Henry was right and Mr O'Connell wrong'.

O'Connell's willingness to abuse, and then when challenged about it to refuse to either withdraw the words or fight a duel, was a serious breach of the 'code of social law' which existed in Ireland and especially in Britain at this time.[39] It horrified all those who considered themselves men of honour, and made O'Connell appear at best an anomaly, at worst a coward and a scoundrel. It was one of the key reasons why O'Connell so offended British sensibilities in the 1830s. As Greville noted with disapproval, O'Connell had declared himself 'self-emancipated' from the code 'by which the intercourse of society is regulated and kept in order'. Thus it allowed him to be irresponsible in words, knowing he would never have to defend them by deeds: 'Out of the reach of danger is he bold, out of the reach of shame he is confident.' Instead of having to be careful with his language, he was free to 'riot in invective, and insult with a scornful and ostentatious exhibition of his invulnerability' and this made him 'an object of execration to all those who cherish the principles and the feelings of honour'. In a heated exchange with John Doherty in the House of Commons on 11 May 1830, O'Connell spoke of the 'vow in heaven' he had made, and accused his opponents of only having the courage to abuse him because they were safe in the knowledge that he would not fight. Wearing a black glove on his right hand—O'Connell explained that there was blood upon it—

he insisted that he would not be deterred from doing his duty by any man.[40]

There was nothing cowardly about O'Connell's renunciation of duelling; it reflected his intense guilt at having killed John Norcot D'Esterre in a duel in 1815, and as he grew older and more devout he became even more concerned about what he had done. He had zero interest in how this looked to a British public. In this, as in everything else, O'Connell was determined to be his own man. In 1832 the *Northampton Mercury* published an article praising O'Connell for his policy on duelling, but advised him to refrain from making any verbal assaults because of his inability to honour the code which existed.[41] O'Connell sent a response in which he defended his conduct, arguing that he would not spare 'the enemy of the people merely because I am not ready to shoot him or be shot for doing my duty'. Instead, he insisted, he would always strive to speak the truth when attacking 'the acts and *selfish motives* of public men . . . Such is my principle, such is my practice.'[42]

The collapse of the Wellington administration on 15 November 1830 led to the formation of a new Whig ministry under Lord Grey. To try and secure the support of O'Connell the British government offered him a high judicial office in November, quite possibly that of the new Master of the Rolls in Ireland. The offer was made through one of O'Connell's oldest and closest friends, Richard Newton Bennett, who urged O'Connell to postpone the question of Repeal. O'Connell was tempted, knowing that office could provide for him and his family. With the change of government there was also a change of viceroy, and it was announced that Lord Anglesey, who had been lord lieutenant during the passing of Catholic emancipation, would begin a second term of office on 23 December. In advance of this, Anglesey arranged a meeting with O'Connell in London, on 15 December, and for two hours the state of Ireland was discussed. Anglesey did everything he could to try and persuade O'Connell to join the government, even going so far as to discuss his precarious financial affairs and how they might be ameliorated if he accepted office.[43] But O'Connell could not do it. He refused the offer in private in London, and then revealed it all in public when addressing the crowd from his home at Merrion Square. A key factor appears to have been the state of Ireland, 'the sober and awful reality', which O'Connell believed could only be improved through having an Irish parliament.[44] He had little faith that Anglesey's return, or the new ministry, would improve things, and was convinced that he, alone, was keeping the Irish people from revolution.

Mary O'Connell was delighted with her husband's decision. She admitted that to have acted differently would have broken her heart, and she claimed that he would only have been betrayed by the government and have died of a broken heart within six months.[45] For her there was no greater honour than to have the love and affection of one's countrymen, and she predicted that he would carry the Repeal of the Union 'without bloodshed as you did the emancipation'. His wife's opinion meant everything to O'Connell, and was a key factor in preventing him from accepting office in the decade ahead. O'Connell himself was content to carry on with his campaign. A few days later, when asked what he wanted, he declared simply, 'For myself *nothing*— for Ireland much.'[46]

The problem was that by making the offer public O'Connell breached the accepted conventions of the day, which held that private communications and offers should remain private. Bennett was understandably furious with O'Connell, and demanded an apology, though none was forthcoming. Tempers became heated and Bennett even appears to have threatened O'Connell with a duel on 4 January 1831. O'Connell scorned the offer, reminding Bennett that he, of all people, should have known 'whether a threat of personal danger was likely to influence me'.[47] And he mocked those who 'deem a duel the proof of valour' for thinking that anyone who 'refuses to fight a duel must be timid'. The men, however, were soon reconciled. Still, in February O'Connell read extracts from Bennett's letters, which detailed the government offer, in parliament, reinforcing the government's belief that O'Connell could never be trusted.

The meeting of Anglesey and O'Connell in London on 15 December rapidly assumed a mythical status. It was widely discussed in the popular press, and stories of what had really happened were eagerly exchanged. Extracts of the conversation had been leaked to the newspapers and the most sensational parts of the dialogue provided much amusement. After O'Connell had rejected the offer before him, it was said that Anglesey had enquired after O'Connell's plans. He was horrified by the response: 'Believe me, my lord, there is nothing personal in my manner of acting, yet I will leave no stone unturned to break the Union of Ireland.'[48] 'Nor have I anything personal towards you, sir,' replied Anglesey with a smile. 'Still, if I can have you hanged, you may depend upon my doing it!' The duke of Cumberland said the exchange was 'enough to kill one with laughing', and reported that his brother, the king, was amused 'amazingly' by the report of the conversation. But O'Connell was not amused, especially when Anglesey declared that if O'Connell persisted in his plans he would be obliged to govern Ireland by force. Furious with these comments, O'Connell decided to return to Ireland and challenge the lord lieutenant. As one commentator observed, 'O'Connell is gone rabid to Ireland . . . resolved to pull down Lord Anglesey's popularity'.[49] It was arranged that Anglesey would be snubbed, and not given any public reception, while O'Connell would be fêted at various events. The clash had become nothing less than a battle to determine who held the real power in Ireland.

Chapter 3 ∾

THE ARREST OF O'CONNELL, 1831

'England's difficulty is Ireland's opportunity.'[1]
(THE MAXIM OF DANIEL O'CONNELL)

On 18 December 1830 O'Connell had a 'triumphant entry into Dublin', his arrival 'greeted by the acclamations of thousands', but Anglesey entered Dublin 'amidst silence and indifference'.[2] O'Connell usually hung the medal of the Order of Liberators around his neck from a green ribbon. But in a show of friendship to Orangemen, O'Connell began wearing it with a ribbon half orange and half green, and he spoke of how he kissed the orange to his lips and pressed it to his heart.[3] He also began holding a series of weekly public breakfasts at Holmes's hotel, on Ussher's Quay, to discuss ways of agitating for Repeal. As a lawyer later joked, 'One of Dan's contrivances was to meet at breakfast around unnumbered tables!'[4] Determined to challenge O'Connell, Anglesey passed a proclamation banning all political meetings arranged 'as a pretext for mischievous purposes'.[5] This marked the beginning of an open war between Anglesey and O'Connell, a conflict that reflected better on O'Connell. It was recognised in England that it was 'glory enough', of a sort, 'to be on a kind of par with the viceroy', to be treated as an equal in this battle for popular opinion, 'and to have a power equal to that of the government'.[6] Sir Edward Stanley (not the Sir Edward Stanley who had been D'Esterre's second in the fatal duel in 1815) was the new chief secretary under Anglesey. Abused by O'Connell as 'Scorpion Stanley', he was to be one of O'Connell's greatest enemies in the years ahead.

To honour O'Connell, the various trades decided to parade through the streets of Dublin on 27 December in solemn procession. This too was prohibited by the lord lieutenant on 25 December on the grounds that it was 'calculated to lead to a disturbance of the public peace'. O'Connell immediately called on the people to obey the latest proclamation, reassuring them that Repeal of the Union could not be stopped. 'At one time', he said, 'Catholic emancipation was far more hopeless, in appearance, than Repeal. However the united force of a class achieved that measure—the united force of a people will achieve the other.' He clarified what he meant by 'force'; it was 'the force of opinion, the force of reason, the force of justice: physical force we abhor and abjure'. Instead of the procession on 27 December it was agreed that two deputies from each trade would march to O'Connell's house and deliver to him their addresses. Greeting them, O'Connell delivered one of his shortest but most effective speeches:

'You are now petty, paltry, provincial slaves. But, with the help of God, and the will of good men, you shall be free, and agitation shall never be put down till the king's speech is pronounced by an Irish lord lieutenant in the parliament house in College Green. I am one of the trades, and my trade is agitation.'

In the speech O'Connell pronounced 'lord lieutenant' as 'lord lewtenant', instead of 'lord leftenant', the Irish and British way of pronouncing it.[7] This was a legacy of his education in France, and there were always certain words which betrayed the slightest trace of a French accent.

Applying his legal mind to the problem of the lord lieutenant's proclamations, O'Connell came up with the idea of forming a new society, The General Association of Ireland for the Prevention of Unlawful Meetings—in other words, a society formed for the very purpose of preventing its own meetings. Upon hearing of this association, the lord lieutenant issued a further proclamation on 7 January 1831 banning it, accusing it of 'intimidating the magistracy of Ireland'. O'Connell was furious and denounced this latest proclamation as an act of despotism and a new crime against his country. Speaking at the Parliamentary Intelligence Office, a newspaper and conversation room on Stephen Street in Dublin, on 10 January, he proposed to form a new association, based around himself as an individual. In other words, *he* would become the association. To great cheers, he declared,

'They may try to put us down by proclamation, but they cannot disperse me. I will be the *Pacificator* of Ireland.'[8]

O'Connell's weekly public breakfasts at Holmes's hotel were already a great success, and these allowed him to continue to organise opposition to the Union. But on 10 January another proclamation was issued which made them illegal. O'Connell responded later the same day with an open letter to the people of Ireland. He declared that he had difficulty restraining his indignation because he was 'living in an enslaved nation, where a proclamation is law'. Poking fun at Anglesey for banning the public breakfasts at Holmes's, O'Connell wondered whether the order should be followed to the letter so that no one should be allowed to have breakfast at the hotel. 'Alas poor Holmes!' he sighed. 'But at breakfast, dinner and supper, let every Irishman recollect that he lives in a country where one Englishman's will is law.' He then proceeded to try and find new ways of evading the proclamation, by forming new associations under a variety of new names. These were also banned by a further proclamation on 13 January. During this period O'Connell did everything he could to effect a union with Protestants, even toasting 'the glorious, pious, and immortal memory' of William III. Later, at a dinner at Drogheda, he drank the same toast from a glass of water taken from the River Boyne.[9] In future years he would be taunted by his enemies for doing this, but his reponse was 'I drank it for Repeal and I am ready to do so again . . . and I hope the day will come when it will be universally drunk in Ireland.'

O'Connell decided to raise the stakes. Believing that Anglesey was being supported by 'base and time-serving Catholics' in the Bank of Ireland and the Irish Provincial Bank, he threatened a run on gold to demonstrate his power. This was carried out by some of his supporters, and the run on the banks caused a panic throughout the country for much of January, with credit drying up for merchants. O'Connell also decided to arrange another public breakfast at Holmes's hotel, to make arrangements for a petition repealing the Union to be sent to parliament. This meeting was raided by two magistrates who demanded that the gathering immediately disperse. O'Connell decided to have some fun with the magistrates. He knew that the statute allowed for people to be given fifteen minutes to disperse, so he took out his watch to count down the time. There then followed a dispute about whether the order to disperse had been given at eight minutes past eleven or ten minutes past eleven, and O'Connell made a big show of waiting until the full fifteen minutes had passed before asking everyone to leave. Humiliated by this further show of defiance, Anglesey decided that O'Connell would have to be prosecuted. It was nothing less, he wrote to his wife, than a question of whether he or O'Connell governed Ireland.[10]

At ten a.m. on Tuesday 18 January 1831 O'Connell was arrested at his home in Merrion Square by Chief Constable Farrell and Peace Officer Irwin. The charge was of conspiracy to evade the Proclamation Act as well as the proclamations recently issued by the lord lieutenant. Upon hearing of his arrest, O'Connell immediately sent word to the *Morning Register* so that two reporters could accompany him to the head police office and take an accurate record of what happened. Word of the arrest quickly spread throughout the city, and when O'Connell set out to walk to the head police office on Dame Street he was soon followed by a large crowd, 'shouting and cheering for him'. Farrell was elderly and suffered from gout, and pleaded with O'Connell to ride with him in a hackney coach, so that he would not have to walk. 'I am very sorry for your gout', replied O'Connell, 'but since the lord lieutenant has chosen to arrest me as if I were a common thief or housebreaker, I think it right the whole city should know it. I must therefore walk.'[11] Poor Farrell was forced to accompany him on foot. The butchers of Castle Market soon joined the crowd, and several carried their cleavers under their coats. Some of the men were spoiling for a fight. 'Ah, Liberator, say the word; only let us at them!' 'No, no!' replied O'Connell. 'That is not my game. I do not want to lose any of your lives. Depend upon it we shall beat them yet, if you do not put them in the right, by your breaking the law!'[12] The butchers were disappointed, but obeyed the instruction, and followed silently behind O'Connell. Within fifteen minutes of O'Connell's arrival at the police station 'the space in front of the office was filled by an immense multitude of persons' and the surrounding streets were 'rendered impassable by the mass of men collected in them'.[13] Iron barriers were erected to keep the crowds away, as the people waited to see what would happen, and the police gathered nervously, fearing a riot.

Upon his arrival, O'Connell demanded to know on whose authority 'common thief-catchers' had been sent to his house so that he could be 'dragged like a felon through the streets'.[14] Alderman Darley admitted that the orders had come from a 'higher authority' and O'Connell seemed satisfied, saying, 'I am glad of it—they may degrade themselves, but they cannot degrade me.' He then asked for any information which had been gathered under oath to be read to him, and when the magistrates hesitated, he put on his hat and said, 'I mean no disrespect to you, but I am a member of the House of Commons—I am the equal of the marquess of Anglesey, and I am determined to maintain inviolable the high privileges of which I am possessed.' The magistrates insisted that they meant no disrespect, and O'Connell said he would remove his hat, but only as a compliment to them. Choosing to remain standing, he listened to the complaint that had been made against him, arising in part out of the speech he had delivered at the Parliamentary Office on 10 January. An argument then developed as to whether a lord lieutenant's proclamations had any legal standing if they were not founded on and authorised by a statute. At this point an officer opened the door of the magistrate's private apartment and a man was spotted inside listening intently. This man then darted behind the door and closed it. O'Connell recognised him instantly: 'There is Baron Tuyll in the other room—I see the lord lieutenant's private secretary looking in at us. You [addressing the magistrates] are, indeed I find, acting under superior authority.' There was much laughter, and when the door reopened a little O'Connell added, 'Baron Tuyll may as well, I think, come into the room at once.' Recognising that the proceedings were turning into a farce, Alderman Darley tried to arrange bail for O'Connell so that he could be released, but O'Connell refused to even consider this, demanding to be discharged without bail: 'Disobedience to the lord lieutenant's proclamation is no crime. What care I for such a proclamation?'

O'Connell proceeded to quote from the statutes regarding proclamations, channelling all his legal training to make a mockery of his arrest, and twisting the warrant so that it appeared he had been arrested 'because he had tried to avoid committing an offence, and was now called upon to give bail precisely because he had taken care not to commit any offence'. The police station was packed with newspaper reporters and O'Connell's friends, and they cheered and laughed at this exposition of the case. The magistrates were beaten. One admitted that he, too, was beginning to wonder if O'Connell had committed any offence. O'Connell just smiled and said, 'I don't doubt it.' Declaring that he was not just the representative of a county, but the 'representative of the feelings and the wishes of the people of Ireland', O'Connell again refused to consider making bail. Hearing this, Baron Tuyll poked his head into the room; O'Connell turned to the gathering and exclaimed, 'Oh, are we to be dictated to by German barons?' Barely concealing the threat, he asked the magistrates if they could guarantee the peace of the city or the country if he was held overnight. They admitted they could not. Then, making reference to the angry crowd which had gathered outside, O'Connell declared that he would 'take care of the peace of the city and country—I will give bail to this foolish charge'.[15] He gave securities for £1,000 and was released.

Once out on the street, O'Connell was greeted with 'long continued and enthusiastic cheers'.[16] First he tried to go into Parliament Street, but the crowd was too large, so instead he turned back to Dame Street. There he addressed the people and called on them to obey the law and disperse, promising them that no exertion of their enemies could prevent a repeal of the Union. 'Yesterday I was only half an agitator,' he declared to much cheering. 'Henceforth I am a whole one.'[17] At an anti-Union meeting a few days later, O'Connell arrived 'clothed from head to foot in deep mourning' and insisted he would continue to wear these clothes until the 'obnoxious' legislation which had seen him arrested was changed.[18] He also revealed that he would refuse to 'taste any excisable article until the Algerine Act [a reference to the detested 1825 act which had outlawed the Catholic Association] is no more', observing that he had refused to drink any tea or coffee that morning.

'We have O'Connell at our mercy,' exulted the chief secretary, Sir Edward Stanley, in a letter to the new attorney general, Francis Blackburne. But the reverse was true, and the prosecution of O'Connell did not get much further. He and five of his associates were indicted on fourteen charges of conspiring to evade the Proclamation Act and with seventeen charges of conspiring to evade the proclamations recently issued by the lord lieutenant. O'Connell's leading counsel was Louis Perrin, with David Pigot assisting. But O'Connell insisted on dealing with the case on behalf of all of the accused and issued a demurrer (where the defendant contests the legal sufficiency of the complaint without admitting or denying the allegations), which was taken by some of his friends as an admission of guilt. Richard Sheil (now Richard Lalor Sheil after assuming his wealthy wife's maiden name in 1830) believed that O'Connell was afraid of going to jail, 'and how can such a man face a battle, who could not encounter Newgate?'[19] Perrin persuaded O'Connell to withdraw the demurrers for the other accused and have them plead not guilty. But O'Connell insisted on continuing with the demurrer for himself, insisting 'he would himself argue the case'.[20] Perrin shook his head and argued that 'O'Connell was self-doomed'. But O'Connell knew what he was doing, and Pigot suspected that he had 'a vague idea that the crown would not argue it'. The Proclamation Act expired in April, and O'Connell used a variety of delaying tactics to postpone his trial until May. As the Whig government now needed O'Connell's support—especially to support the planned Great Reform Act—the charges were allowed to drop.[21] The government's own supporters admitted that this was 'one mouthful of the dirty pudding they have had to swallow'.[22]

Over the next few years O'Connell continued to denounce 'Anglesey the Liar', dismissing him as 'that egregious ninny', 'crazy', 'harsh, virulent, proud', and announcing, 'His name is Scoundrel.'[23] He believed that Anglesey was 'just like a woman, who will hate her most intimate and amiable friend the moment she discovers that men think her prettier than herself'.[24] For his part, Anglesey believed that O'Connell was a 'rogue' and an 'egregious cheat', who willingly sacrificed political principle for personal advantage. When Anglesey was finally recalled in 1833 O'Connell rejoiced in print, mocking him for his 'strange, silly, and wayward career'.[25] There could only be one winner in this contest. Following the clash with Anglesey in 1831, O'Connell's popularity in the country was unchallenged. At the end of the year he attended the opening night of a new play, *The Warden of Galway*. As soon as the crowd saw him they began cheering, and this continued throughout the entire performance. This made things difficult for the theatre critics in the audience. 'It is impossible for us to criticise the performance,' one complained afterwards, revealing that no one could hear a single word that the actors were saying.[26]

Chapter 4 ～

'THE GREAT POLITICAL LEVIATHAN', 1831–1834

'The history of the Irish people can be traced like a wounded man through a crowd—by the blood.'[1]
(SPEECH OF DANIEL O'CONNELL WHICH MADE A LASTING IMPRESSION ON THE ABOLITIONIST FREDERICK DOUGLASS)

Few were as ruthless as O'Connell when it came to dealing with opponents. In 1828 Charles James O'Gorman Mahon (who styled himself 'The O'Gorman Mahon') was an overly dramatic but integral member of O'Connell's election campaign team, and played a key role in helping him win in Co. Clare. But they quickly fell out. On Sunday 18 July 1830, when O'Connell was carried in a triumphal procession from Limerick to Ennis, the procession was attacked by O'Gorman Mahon and his supporters, who attempted to challenge O'Connell's leadership.[2] O'Gorman Mahon quickly became an embarrassment, always following his own line, and refusing to listen to anyone, least of all O'Connell. On 8 February 1831 O'Gorman Mahon delivered a speech in the House of Commons which horrified the government and alienated his few remaining friends. He declared that for eleven and a half years he had been a member of a secret society, consisting of Protestants and Presbyterians, which had attempted to bring about a Repeal of the Union, a measure which he claimed had been 'purchased by treason and blood'.[3] Becoming increasingly heated, he began ranting at the government, much to everyone's embarrassment. The Speaker intervened and threatened to bring him before the bar of the House to answer for his conduct, but to no avail.[4]

The speech marked the beginning of the end of O'Gorman Mahon's political career. He was already under investigation for having used bribery to secure his election for Co. Clare, and was found guilty on 4 March and unseated. O'Connell was delighted with this result, believing that the evidence was overwhelming.[5] Tensions between both men were further exacerbated when O'Connell's son Maurice took the seat in the subsequent by-election. Yet despite their disagreements, O'Connell always believed that the career of O'Gorman Mahon was 'one of the most extraordinary that ever yet was exhibited'.[6]

Another general election was called in March 1831 and O'Gorman Mahon decided to stand in Co. Clare again, despite O'Connell's opposition. It became a three-way contest between Major McNamara, Maurice O'Connell, and O'Gorman Mahon for the two seats. The campaign quickly turned nasty. The *Pilot*, the newspaper which acted as O'Connell's unofficial voice, accused O'Gorman Mahon of being an ally of various illegal agrarian secret societies, and although these charges were denied by the *Freeman's Journal*, they did enormous damage to his reputation, especially following his wild speech in the House of Commons.

What happened next left O'Connell open to charges of being an informer. On 6 and 8 May he sent letters to Dublin Castle warning of O'Gorman Mahon's 'treasonable language' and conduct, and asking, on a separate point, for official support in his own election campaign in Co. Kerry.[7] O'Connell provided the name of a witness who could testify about O'Gorman Mahon's actions, revealing that O'Gorman Mahon had read threatening notices during the campaign and was enlisting the support of Whiteboys (members of an illegal agrarian society) in the county. Insisting that his intervention had nothing to do with his son running for re-election, O'Connell claimed that the defeat of O'Gorman Mahon was necessary to keep Co. Clare peaceful.

While there was a cynical element to the intervention, it was justified by O'Gorman Mahon's erratic and increasingly unstable behaviour. He openly canvassed as a 'Terry-Alt', in other words a Whiteboy, and attempted to terrorise voters into supporting him by threatening all kinds of retaliation if he lost.[8] When that failed to work, he resorted to his old tactic of bribery, and spent close to £1,200 on the campaign. This money had come from the sale of the estate of his younger brother, William Richard Mahon, ruining him in the process. But O'Gorman Mahon was still unable to make an impression and so he decided to reinvent himself as a Protestant loyalist, promising to 'put down the priests'. However, as he had been untrue to every other party, 'and especially to his own', this transformation made little impact, and the voters 'rejected him with scorn'.

During the campaign no scheme was too crazy to be attempted. On 14 May William Richard Mahon assaulted Maurice O'Connell on the street in Ennis, hoping to provoke a duel so that he could kill him and remove the competition. But Maurice coolly replied that he would enquire into the cause of the disagreement after the election.[9] Alarmed by this incident, Daniel O'Connell immediately sent for back-up. Within a short time, two carriages arrived from Kerry and Tipperary, each filled with heavily armed men who acted as bodyguards for Maurice for the remainder of the campaign. Recognising that defeat was inevitable, O'Gorman Mahon attempted to provoke a riot in the town. He gave a violent speech on the evening of 18 May, and ended it by giving thirty shillings to the butchers so that they could purchase whiskey. Within half an hour the butchers were drunk and they took to the streets, waving their long knives and hatchets. The army had to be called out to restore order and O'Gorman Mahon was arrested and charged with causing a disturbance.

At the conclusion of the voting McNamara was clearly ahead in first place, and Maurice O'Connell had a majority of 104 votes over O'Gorman Mahon for the second seat. Upon hearing the result, O'Gorman Mahon raged like a lunatic, shouting at McNamara in the street and calling him 'all manner of abusive names'.[10] But McNamara just glared at him 'with silent contempt', and refused to respond. Afterwards McNamara's friends resolved not to send a challenge, or even have the magistrates prosecute him for the riot, but just to treat him 'with total contempt and disregard'. As O'Connell exclaimed, 'Such then is the result of this mad campaign!'[11]

There was less trouble with O'Connell's own election campaign in Co. Kerry, where he stood for the first time, having decided not to seek re-election in Co. Waterford. In his address to the electors of Kerry he declared that he was 'always proud of being a Kerryman' and that it was the 'height of my worldly ambition to be the representative of Kerrymen'.[12] No claim was too extravagant, no promise too great. In his hustings speech, O'Connell even pledged to never represent another constituency, promising that 'while he lived he would never ask a vote from any man but a Kerryman'. Facing defeat, the knight of Kerry resigned from the contest, and O'Connell was returned on 14 May. Afterwards he decided to visit Co. Clare to make sure that there was no outbreak of violence following the turmoil of the recent campaign. On 5 June he delivered a commanding address to the thousands of people who had gathered at the square in Ennis. Urging them to abandon secret societies as they were incompatible with the Catholic faith, he promised to fight on their behalf in parliament. The speech ended with a ringing appeal to 'let me go to parliament to say: I pacified Clare!'[13]

Former friends might be despatched with ease, but O'Connell could still be remarkably generous to old foes. Sir Abraham Bradley King, former lord mayor of Dublin, had been a leading defender of the Protestant Ascendancy in Dublin corporation in the 1810s and 1820s, and had been one of O'Connell's most troublesome adversaries. But by 1831 he was in serious financial trouble. His family held a royal patent to be the king's stationer in Ireland, an office which it had held since 1760. However, in 1831 the government discovered that the office could be revoked at any time, and did so in a cost-cutting exercise. King was now bereft of his main source of income, and appealed to parliament for compensation. None was forthcoming. O'Connell decided to champion his cause. It was a clever move, as it showed that he was not motivated by sectarian concerns, but was willing to fight for justice for Irish people of all religious and political persuasions. When the matter was raised in the House of Commons on 11 July O'Connell spoke strongly in favour of King, but the House voted against giving any compensation. Shortly afterwards King was declared bankrupt.[14] However, O'Connell would not give up on the issue. He raised it in the House of Commons a year later, on 18 July 1832, demanding that something was done, and succeeded in embarrassing the government into action. O'Connell was delighted, boasting privately that King 'would have been left a beggar' if it had been left to the main parties, and 'if I had not taken him up'.[15] King wrote a generous letter to O'Connell acknowledging that they had once been political enemies, and praising him for 'nobly forgetting this difference of opinion'.[16] He thanked him for his 'continued and unwearied efforts', and promised to spend the remainder of his days offering fervent prayers for 'such reward and happiness, to you and yours'. O'Connell was cynical enough to recognise that the gesture would not be forgotten by leading Irish Protestants, 'when we come to our next effort for conciliation', adding, 'may God forgive me if I be wrong'.[17]

Attempts were made by the government to secure O'Connell's support. In October 1831 he was offered the office of attorney general of Ireland, with Bishop Doyle acting as the conduit.[18] Much as he was tempted to displace the hated Blackburne, he refused the offer. The only thing he accepted was a patent of precedence, which allowed him to be formally admitted to the inner bar on 4 November. This would have made a substantial difference to his income in the 1820s when he had been desperate for one, but by the 1830s, with his legal career all but over, it was more of a symbolic gesture than anything else. Nevertheless, O'Connell was still unhappy that Richard Lalor Sheil accepted one before him, thus giving him precedence over him, and believed he should have waited his turn out of respect.

It was in November 1831 that the name of Ellen Courtenay returned to haunt O'Connell. In that month he was contacted by the radical reformer Henry Hunt, MP for Preston, who had been approached by Courtenay looking for help. Hunt claimed that he would never have believed Courtenay's allegations—namely that she had been raped (or, more likely, seduced) by O'Connell in 1818, had borne him a son, and that both had been left destitute—'had I not personally known your character'.[19] And he revealed that Courtenay had written 'a manuscript of her history' which she hoped to publish to pay for board and lodging for herself and her son. Although he had refused to read the text, Hunt believed that the verbal account of 'her sufferings' was 'enough to soften even the heart of a monster'. Attached to his letter was Ellen Courtenay's covering letter to Hunt, detailing her sufferings. O'Connell had fallen out with Hunt in 1828 during the campaign for Catholic emancipation, when Hunt had published public letters accusing him 'of trafficking in the liberties' of his country, and 'prostituting for gain' his religion.[20] Now describing himself as 'a detester of cant and hypocrisy', Hunt revealed that he was contacting O'Connell so that he could act quickly to prevent publication, though he admitted that he did not expect any gratitude.

Upon receiving this communication O'Connell reacted furiously, accusing Hunt of attempting to blackmail him and of having fabricated the entire thing. He questioned whether the Courtenay letter was genuine, wondering whether it had really been written 'by *another* person'.[21] And he denounced 'the absurd falsehood' contained in both letters, hurling 'contemptuous defiance' 'at the pair of writers, or supposed writers if there really be a second of them'. Over the next few months O'Connell claimed to be investigating the allegations, even going so far as to assert that he had discovered that Courtenay was childless.[22] And he blamed the entire thing on the *Satirist*, a scandal sheet with a history of blackmail, a P.S. Hynes, who he described as 'a half maniac but ingenious', and Courtenay herself, who he insisted was really an elderly strolling actress called 'Mrs. or Madame St. Julien'. O'Connell's refusal to pay meant that the heavily indebted Courtenay ended up in a debtor's prison, from where she published her pamphlet, *A narrative of most extraordinary cruelty, perfidy and depravity perpetrated against her by Daniel O'Connell*, in April 1832. There was a small print run and it made only a slight impression. But for those who hated O'Connell it was a wonderful cocktail of sex and scandal, and provided much entertainment. The scandal returned to trouble O'Connell in 1836, and it served to reinforce British doubts and prejudices about his character and integrity.

The potential marketing opportunities provided by the O'Connell name were tested at this time, as the family became involved in the brewing industry. O'Connell set up his youngest son, Daniel, in a new brewing firm which was called 'Daniel O'Connell Jun., and Co.' in Watling Street, Dublin. P.V. Fitzpatrick was one of the partners and O'Connell was delighted that people could order 'a pint of O'Connell's' instead of supporting the Ascendancy Guinness family. He detested the contemporary Arthur Guinness, who he viewed as a 'miserable old apostate', and he was happy to take whatever profits he could away from the family.[23] O'Connell himself was not a pint-drinker. When some of O'Connell's barrels arrived at Derrynane he tried only one pint, judging it 'strong and palatable' but complaining of 'a sourishness of taste'.[24] Despite some initial success, the brand never became anything more than a novelty, and the partnership was dissolved on 21 June 1841, though the brewery continued under a different name.[25]

A cholera epidemic hit Britain in early 1832, and it was rumoured that O'Connell was 'horridly afraid' of it.[26] It was said that he 'shirks the House of Commons from fear of the heat and the atmosphere'. Certainly he decided to rest at Bath, and partake of the recuperative waters, during this period. But his real anxiety seems to have been about conditions in Ireland, where the cholera arrived in March. O'Connell monitored events in Ireland carefully and worried about the people of Cahirciveen in Co. Kerry, because 'the back yards of several of the houses were exceedingly filthy', and he knew that this would assist the spread of the contagion if it reached the area.[27] Therefore he sent instructions to his agent in the county that all of the houses were to be 'cleansed, whitewashed, and as far as possible purified'. He also insisted that the old prison was to be converted into a hospital if necessary, and that money should be given to provide food for the poorest in the area. O'Connell was optimistic that the contagion could be contained to the large towns, and was confident that 'nourishment and cleanliness' would protect the countryside from 'this malady'. Cholera reached Kerry in the first months of 1834. O'Connell immediately sent instructions for some cattle to be killed and distributed in beef and broth for the people, and also ordered a ban on the sale of whiskey so as to avoid public drunkenness.[28] Money was no object to O'Connell and he ordered for meat to be provided to people twice a day, for coal to be ordered from the largest nearby towns, and for doctors to be paid to look after the sick. He declared that he would happily sacrifice an entire year's income if it would save even a single life.[29]

In this period O'Connell was friendly with Edward Lytton Bulwer, MP for Lincoln, editor, and novelist. Bulwer was hailed at the time as 'the most popular writer now living', and O'Connell admired the way he supported the 'cause of genuine reform'.[30] Bulwer would later memorialise O'Connell in verse in his epic, *St. Stephen's*, published in 1860:

> Peace to his memory! Grant him rash and vain,
> 'Twas the heart's blood that rose to clog the brain;
> No trading demagogue, in him we can scan
> That pith of nations, the bold natural man,
> Whose will may vibrate as the pulses throb,
> Now scare a monarch, now despise a mob.[31]

Bulwer attempted to describe in poetry what it was like to witness O'Connell delivering one of his great outdoor addresses:

Once to my sight the giant thus was given,
Wall'd by wide air, and roof'd by boundless heaven;
Beneath his feet the human ocean lay,
And wave on wave flowed into space away.
[. . .]
Then did I know what spells of infinite choice,
To rouse or lull, has the sweet human voice;
Then did I seem to seize the sudden clue
To the grand troublous Life Antique—to view
Under the rock-stand of Demosthenes,
Mutable Athens heave her noisy seas.[32]

At one of the parties which Bulwer threw in the summer of 1832, O'Connell met the notorious Comte d'Orsay, a man who revelled in his reputation as 'the most unprincipled man in Europe'.[33] D'Orsay had been having an affair with Lady Blessington in the 1820s, and it was rumoured that together they arranged for him to marry her daughter, Lady Harriet Gardiner, so that they might gain access to her fortune. The reality was a little more complex, with Lord Blessington having made the marriage a condition of his daughter's inheritance.[34] The marriage took place in 1827 but was never consummated, despite D'Orsay's best efforts, and they later separated. D'Orsay liked to say that she was 'a virgin wife, through no fault of his, for he spared no pains to promote her seduction'. Perhaps it was no wonder that Sir Denis Le Marchant, a clerk of the chancery who was also present at the party, believed that O'Connell was one of 'the only decent men' at it.

The 'foul, unnatural murder' of four people on 5 September 1832 upset O'Connell deeply. The incident took place outside the village of Wallstown, Co. Cork, after the local rector had gathered a group of magistrates, police, and soldiers, and brought them to the field of a local farmer, James Blake, so that the standing crop could be valued. But this was seen as an unacceptable infringement upon the rights of the farmer, and a crowd of a couple of hundred locals, armed with stones and scythes, gathered to block the way. The crowd refused to allow the rector to pass, and began shouting, 'Hurrah for O'Connell!'[35] The soldiers opened fire, killing four and injuring a dozen more, and afterwards a verdict of 'justifiable homicide' was returned at the inquest. O'Connell was furious and attacked the 'Wallstown massacre' in print.

He blamed the Irish administration for what had happened, accusing it of a cover-up, and he demanded that changes be made to the system of government in Ireland.

There was another general election at the end of 1832 and O'Connell had his greatest electoral success yet, with 39 MPs returned who promised to follow the Repeal pledge.[36] O'Connell himself was returned for Dublin city on 17 December, alongside another Repeal candidate, Edward Ruthven. On 5 February 1833 the new parliament was opened by the king, and the address in the House of Commons was moved by Lord Ormelie. In it he accused O'Connell of being 'a harpy' and 'a bird of prey', and O'Connell replied in such furious terms that Lord John Russell moved to have his words taken down. He was particularly upset that O'Connell had denounced the king's address as 'bloody, brutal and unconstitutional' and called it 'a declaration of civil war'.[37] However, although Ormelie's attack was 'warmly cheered', it was 'not approved of' and was considered far too intemperate.[38] O'Connell's response, in contrast, was 'artful and persuasive and made a deep impression'. He continued in the same tone, 'not of an apologist, but an accuser'.[39] O'Connell was equally unforgiving towards the prime minister, Lord Grey. He believed Grey had a 'foolish and envenomed prejudice against everything Irish' and, as a result, refused to recognise the support of the Irish MPs in passing the Great Reform Act.[40] When Grey was praised during the debate he shouted out, 'No, no! Blood, blood!' The exchange soon passed into parliamentary folklore. It added considerably to O'Connell's standing in the parliament, as 'the new members thought he had much right on his side'.[41] Afterwards it was said that on that day O'Connell 'was the great agitator, not the member of the imperial parliament'.

In the new parliament O'Connell faced one of his greatest challenges, the coercion bill which the Whig government introduced on 27 February 1833 'for the more effective suppression of local disturbances and dangerous associations in Ireland'. This was one of the most repressive pieces of legislation ever imposed on Ireland. The bill allowed the lord lieutenant to declare that certain areas were disturbed and that therefore no meetings of any kind could be held there. The lord lieutenant was also given the power to replace the ordinary courts with courts martial, suspend *habeas corpus* (thus allowing internment without trial), and ban all meetings called to discuss the petitioning of parliament unless permission was given in advance.[42] If the bill passed then O'Connell believed that despotism would become law and he was determined to block it.[43]

Almost single-handedly leading the opposition, O'Connell performed some of the greatest oratory of his life. At the first reading of the bill on 5 March O'Connell denounced it as a 'cruel, ensnaring act' which was 'so utterly untechnical and indefinite in its phraseology'. And he claimed that if the bill passed then 'personal freedom in Ireland is at an end'.[44] During the introduction of the bill a few days earlier, Sir Edward Stanley had gone out of his way to insult O'Connell. He quoted at length a ballad, 'The downfall of the tithes', forty-eight lines in total, which he claimed had been sung in Kilkenny after a murder. The intention was to link O'Connell to the violence of the peasants, with lines such as 'Poor Irish captives are liberated/All by the means of our noble Pan'. In his response, O'Connell destroyed Stanley with his sarcasm. 'I really pity you,' he said. 'You do this because my name [Dan] is made to rhyme with a line of a miserable ballad. Oh, it was excellent wit—it was superabundant cause of merriment. You may delude yourselves with this, but you will not delude the sensible people of Ireland or of England.'[45] And he abused Stanley for bringing in a piece of legislation purely to stop O'Connell's agitation: 'you are legislating against a single individual'.

Perhaps the most dramatic section was the damning review of how the legal system in Ireland had been corrupted and abused by similar pieces of legislation. He told the story of a magistrate in 1798 who owed money to a woman with three sons. Instead of paying it, he arranged for the three sons to be arrested and imprisoned, and threatened the woman that all three would be hanged unless she immediately released the debt.[46] O'Connell dared his opponents to check the veracity of the story, by speaking to the Cursitor of the court of chancery, because he would inform them 'that the lady was his [the Cursitor's] own mother, that she was thrown into prison, that he also suffered a long imprisonment, during which he was treated with much cruelty, and manacled with irons sixty-eight pounds in weight'. O'Connell praised the mother for not backing down, and he used the story to show how people could be arrested on spurious grounds under the kind of system which the bill would make law. And he promised that with the legislation the government would sow dragon's teeth which would result in the rise of armed men. Francis Jeffrey, the Lord Advocate of Scotland, and no real admirer of O'Connell, believed that O'Connell's clause-by-clause resistance to the bill made him 'indisputably the greatest orator in the House—nervous, passionate, without art or ornament; concise, intrepid, terrible, far more in the style of old Demosthenic directness and vehemence than anything I have heard in this modern world'.[47]

The leader of the government in the House of Commons was Lord Althorp. Unfortunately Althorp was one of the worst speakers in the House and he was incapable of withstanding the attacks of O'Connell. 'He could not put three or four sentences together without stammering, and recalling his words over and over again' and it was said that he became 'a mere plaything' in O'Connell's hands.[48] However, despite his campaign the bill passed by large majorities. 'The die is cast,' lamented O'Connell. 'We are slaves'.[49]

There was a run on gold in some places in Ireland at the start of March, and O'Connell considered making a public call for gold in Ireland and Britain as a way of disrupting the economy and forcing the coercion bill to be dropped. But he hesitated, recognising that it would hurt his friends as much as his enemies.[50] This was a time when he was much criticised by his opponents. On 1 March when Henry Grattan Jnr showed the chief secretary, Henry Hobhouse, a petition to the king to dismiss his ministers, he told him, 'I wish to heaven you would hang or shoot O'Connell, and pass some Algerine Act if you like, but not this bill.' Despite bitter opposition the Coercion Act became law on 2 April. O'Connell declared war on the 'Algerine administration' and did everything he could to bring about its defeat. He had little interest in office, believing that he could become Master of the Rolls in England, never mind in Ireland, if he wished. However, he insisted that his ambition and pride 'as well as my first and most sacred duty bind me to struggle for Ireland'.[51]

In early June it appeared that Lord Grey's government would fall. O'Connell was delighted at first, but changed his mind when he realised that the alternative was the return of the Tories. He was also tempted by the possibility of the Whigs coming to some arrangement with him. On 6 June he spoke in the Commons in defence of the ministry and played his part in keeping it alive.[52] At this time Feargus O'Connor, the MP for Cork, was anxious to bring forward a motion in parliament in favour of

Repeal, but O'Connell opposed it. First, he knew it would be rejected and did not want to suffer a humiliating defeat that would make public their weakness. Second, he considered it a ruse by those who were normally supporters of the government to cloak themselves in 'a fictitious patriotism'.[53] Third, he viewed it as weak politics, aiming for the impossible instead of doing the groundwork to try and make it possible.

Feargus O'Connor was an extraordinary character, a brilliant speaker and a committed radical, who came from a Protestant family in Co. Cork; both his father and uncle were United Irishmen. He had been arrested for robbing the mail coach a few years previously and, although acquitted, had not convinced many of his innocence. When running for election in Co. Cork in December 1832 he told the crowd, 'My lads, you all know me.' 'Yes,' one man replied, 'you robbed the mail!'[54] O'Connor was a perfect example of the kind of brilliant young men who were first attracted to, and then repulsed by, O'Connell. For his part, O'Connell admired O'Connor initially, saying emphatically, 'He is a man!'[55] But enthusiasm soon gave way to suspicion, and finally dislike. He found O'Connor's oratory exciting, but believed there was 'too much bragging about conquering and trampling under foot', and too many attempts to assert his own leadership rather than allowing it to develop naturally.

Elected a Repeal MP, O'Connor immediately began demanding that a motion on the subject be brought forward. In later years O'Connor would accuse O'Connell of having backed away because he did not really want to see Repeal passed, believing he would lose his power in Ireland. He quoted O'Connell as having told him in 1833, 'Well Feargus, you are a bad general. You cannot take a hint.' When O'Connor asked him what he meant, O'Connell allegedly replied, 'Ah! Feargus, you want to destroy both our trades in Ireland!'[56] In a series of public letters published in October 1836, O'Connor accused O'Connell of being a complete cynic when it came to politics, sacrificing the interests of Ireland for his own relentless self-promotion. For example, he believed that O'Connell could have secured a reform of the Irish jury system but instead chose to withdraw the bill, citing it as 'another melancholy instance of the mode of treating my unhappy country'.[57] Afterwards, when he sought an explanation, O'Connor claimed he was slapped on the thigh by O'Connell, who told him, 'Never mind, I am better pleased that they opposed me, it will give me more power in Ireland.' O'Connor said he left the Commons in disgust, and from that point on considered O'Connell 'a most artful man'. But O'Connor was a most unreliable witness, and his reading of O'Connell's political strategy was misguided. O'Connell was playing a more sophisticated political game, waiting for the right moment to press for Repeal, and taking little interest in the schoolboy posturing of naïve enthusiasts.

Working in the shadow of O'Connell ate away at O'Connor, and bitterness soon turned to hatred. Denouncing O'Connell in print in 1836, he called him 'this Dictator', and a 'licensed defamer' who only succeeded because 'timid individuals submit to his slander'.[58] 'You are the great political Leviathan of the day', he said, 'and many an unsuspecting man has been wrecked against your wiles and sophistry.' But he insisted he would rather 'dash myself at once to pieces, than be constantly covered with your foam'. And so he set out to list 'the catalogue' of O'Connell's 'treasons against Ireland'. Having worked alongside O'Connell, even briefly, gave him some insights into his character. He recognised that whenever O'Connell addressed an assembly he always took the pulse of the audience, 'and then with amazing tact and the rapidity of lightning' suited the speech to his hearers. O'Connell's 'domineering manner' was also discussed. O'Connor was not the first person to fall victim to it, and he described it as 'the wicked resolve to accomplish by extravagant bullying that which was refused'.[59] In short, the determination to be '*aut Caesar aut nullus*'—either a Caesar or nobody.

The meeting of the Repeal MPs on 10 June was pivotal. Thirty-four members attended and O'Connell outmanoeuvred O'Connor from the start. First, he placed one of the members supporting O'Connor in the chair, thus preventing him for voting. He then despatched a second O'Connor supporter to the House of Commons, telling him that he would be back in plenty of time for the crucial vote. The member returned too late. That left thirty MPs, excluding O'Connell and O'Connor themselves, to convince. O'Connell quickly made the debate personal, claiming that O'Connor's family had ruined Ireland before (a reference to the United Irishmen), and accusing him of wishing to ruin it again.[60] This infuriated O'Connor, and he responded in such angry terms that someone had to take him by the arm to calm him down. When the vote was taken, O'Connell defeated the move to bring forward the motion by twelve votes to ten, with ten abstentions.[61]

Afterwards, O'Connell was heavily criticised in some quarters for postponing the debate, but he knew what he was doing. A few days later, O'Connell attempted a reconciliation: 'Feargus, if in the heat of argument on Monday last I said anything to annoy you or to hurt your feelings, I beg your pardon. Will you forgive me?' But O'Connor was not to be placated. A few days later, when O'Connell gave him a lift in his carriage to the House of Commons, he exploded in venom. He told O'Connell that he would not be stopped: 'I know your talons are over me, and that you are watching the first opportunity to crush me, but you never will.' It was the ranting of the delusional. From that point on the men were bitter enemies.

Some Irish newspapers, such as the *Freeman's Journal*, sided with O'Connor, and the praise went to his head. Without checking with O'Connell he decided to go ahead with his Repeal motion on 16 July. O'Connell was contemptuous and believed that O'Connor had 'had his brains blown out by the trash in the *Freeman's Journal*'.[62] However, on the appointed day O'Connor was completely unprepared and, recognising that there would be little support for the motion, he announced that he would not proceed. But although O'Connell had seen off the challenger, his position remained vulnerable, and there was growing pressure on him to take the lead and bring forward a debate on Repeal.

O'Connell returned to the chamber on 12 June to speak in favour of abolishing tithes, and faced aggressive opposition. There were attempts to shout him down, but O'Connell boldly confronted his challengers. 'Extending his arm and erecting himself with a lofty boldness of mien and gesture', he exclaimed with indignant vehemence, 'What talk to me after this of your Union! I am an Irishman; it is my crime in this House that I am an Irishman, but what has my country done, what have I done that you should dare assail me thus?'[63] The Irish MPs shouted, 'Hear! Hear!', but they were drowned out in the shouts of 'Order! Order!', occasional cries of 'Oh! Oh!' and general confusion. 'Why', demanded O'Connell, 'should that House dare to assail me with those ruffian shouts?' There were objections to O'Connell's use of the word 'ruffian', which was considered unparliamentary, but the Speaker intervened and declared that although O'Connell had been 'undeniably disorderly' he had been provoked into it. O'Connell was allowed to proceed without interruption.

The issue of tithes, the means by which Catholics were forced to pay for the upkeep of the Protestant church in Ireland, was a central one for O'Connell. Indeed, he himself refused to pay any tithes and insisted that the bailiffs could 'sell the very bed from under him, but he would never consent to pay a single farthing'.[64] He stated it as a principle of his political life that 'no one Christian should be compelled to contribute to the support of a church to which he does not belong, or a religion from which he dissents'.[65] But he was furious when he discovered that his contribution to the tithes debate had been misreported in the newspapers. Indeed, some reporters quoted him as saying that he would vote a certain way on the subject even though, as he later joked, this was 'directly in the teeth of all his former opinions on the subject!'[66]

Increasingly O'Connell was finding that his best speeches were being ignored in the newspapers or, worse, deliberately misrepresented. For example, a speech on electoral malpractice in Liverpool on 4 July was only given 'a few insignificant lines'—much to his annoyance, as it was more cheered than any of his previous speeches in the chamber.[67] In addition, his speeches on the anti-slavery bill were barely reported at all.[68] Defending their actions, the reporters claimed that O'Connell had become spoilt by the Irish press during the emancipation campaign.[69] In particular O'Connell blamed *The Times* for censoring him, and he was determined to get his revenge. At a public meeting in the Globe Hotel he attacked press standards in Britain, and accused *The Times* of 'designedly false' reporting.[70] In response, the parliamentary reporters issued a statement on 25 July insisting that until O'Connell apologised they would not report any of his speeches. If O'Connell's speech was a declaration of war then this was an acceptance of that declaration. Few politicians who had challenged the press had survived the battle, but O'Connell was determined to emerge victorious.

O'Connell brought the matter before the House, claiming a breach of privilege, and the matter was investigated. The journalist who had reported on the tithes debate claimed that while walking from the House to the offices of *The Times* he had been caught in a heavy shower of rain. The water, he insisted, went into his pocket and washed out the notes he had made of O'Connell's speech. Upon hearing this, O'Connell exclaimed that it was the most extraordinary shower of rain he had ever heard of, because not only had it washed *out* the speech he had made, it had also washed *in* an entirely different one!

The reporters joined together to defend the attack on one of their number. In addition, they resented the list of grievances which O'Connell had compiled against them, and decided to punish him by not reporting another word he said in the chamber until he backed down. After three nights of this, O'Connell retaliated. By claiming that he 'saw strangers in the gallery', he was able to ensure that the Speaker ordered the reporters' removal. The benches for the reporters were emptied. 'Like a set of children suddenly let out from confinement', the MPs moved around the chamber, taking positions under and even in the gallery, as they took full advantage of the extra space on the warm summer's night.[71] The removal of the reporters prevented them from doing their job and also had a serious effect on the eloquence on display. MPs knew that their speeches would not be reported in the newspapers the next day, and this 'had a most paralysing effect'.[72] 'There was no animation in their manner, scarcely any attempt at that wit and sarcasm at each other's expense' usual on other occasions. This state of affairs continued for almost ten days until a compromise was reached, and the reporters were allowed back in. O'Connell was delighted and claimed to have defeated 'the tyranny of the press'.[73] Indeed, he believed he was the only man in either house of parliament who would have dared to challenge so powerful a press. But it was at a price, and *The Times*, in particular, was to wage a vicious campaign against O'Connell for the rest of his life.

On 26 September 1833 Lord Wellesley succeeded Lord Anglesey as lord lieutenant, and O'Connell celebrated the replacement of the 'Saxon oppressor'.[74] Edward Littleton, Wellesley's son-in-law, was appointed chief secretary and, from the outset, made attempts to win favour with O'Connell.[75] O'Connell immediately requested a pardon for Daniel Leary, wrongly convicted and sentenced to transportation in the first Doneraile trial, but despite his best efforts he was unable to secure it until 1837 and the accession of Queen Victoria.[76] He was, however, able to secure the release of ten Catholic prisoners in Enniskillen jail, whose release had been requested by the local bishop.[77]

The question of 'Who is the traitor?' became a popular game at this time. In a speech in Hull on 22 October 1833, the local MP, Matthew Davenport Hill, claimed that during the debate over the Irish coercion bill an Irish MP, who had spoken with great violence against the measure, told ministers in private not to change 'one single atom, or it will be impossible for any man to live in Ireland'.[78] O'Connell insisted that the story was a lie, but the search was soon on to identify the traitor. Although he refused to name the MP, Hill promised to exonerate in public any member who wrote to him. The finger of suspicion soon turned to Richard Lalor Sheil, because although he denied the allegation many times he showed great reluctance about contacting Hill. In the House of Commons on 5 February O'Connell questioned Lord Althorp about the allegations. Althorp denied the exact wording used by Hill, but he did admit that someone who had voted and spoken against the bill had used very different language in private. O'Connell asked if he was the man, and was told 'No', but, when Sheil asked if it was him, Althorp responded, 'Yes.' There was uproar in the House and the sergeant-at-arms was obliged to take both Althorp and Sheil into custody to prevent a duel. Afterwards, O'Connell refused to abandon Sheil and insisted loudly that he had done nothing wrong. In part, it was because the evidence was so slight, but he also refused to give his enemies the head of one of his oldest allies.

The judicial career of Baron Smith was another matter. O'Connell had long been an enemy and had long been looking for a way to bring about his downfall. He had plenty of material to work with. For example, there were stories of Smith beginning trials after midnight and continuing them until six a.m. It had also become clear that he had lost his impartiality and showed marked favour to Orangemen over Catholics. On 13 February 1834 O'Connell seized his chance. He moved for a committee of enquiry into Smith's conduct, accusing him of neglecting his duty as a judge and of compensating for that neglect by becoming 'a violent politician'.[79] Edward Littleton and the government ministers attending the debate determined to defend Smith, but when they heard the list of allegations they voted for O'Connell's motion and it passed by 167 votes to 74. However, Smith had many allies and the vote was overturned a week later. O'Connell was not too disappointed, having made his point at Smith's expense.

By the start of 1834 O'Connell's standing in the House of Commons was at its lowest. No matter what he tried, he seemed unable to catch the spirit of the House. It was thought that his opinions were too imprudent, the way he expressed them too extreme. His influence decreased the more he spoke in the House, and experts predicted that he had 'sunk to rise no more'.[80] To a certain extent his failure to be accepted as a first-rank orator reveals the prejudice of his listeners. Some of O'Connell's speeches between 1830 and 1834—for example on the coercion bill— were the greatest of his life. For example, Lord Ellenborough enjoyed watching O'Connell's speeches from the gallery, and recognised that he did not receive the respect he deserved. After one debate he noted that O'Connell 'was not supported by the House, nor was he cheered when he ought to have been'.[81] Even when he delivered 'a great speech' it was still 'the general opinion that it was a failure'. Ellenborough believed that O'Connell was 'so very unpopular that the world does not do him common justice'. The turning point was the debate on the Repeal of the Union on 22 April 1834. This was the moment when O'Connell conquered the prejudices of the MPs and was widely accepted to have 'established his reputation'.[82] By demonstrating his complete mastery of a subject in a blaze of rhetorical glory, he was finally able to convince his critics that he had the ability to dominate parliament in the way he had dominated the courtroom and the platform.

The irony is that once again O'Connell had wished to postpone the debate. The man who forced him into the motion was Feargus O'Connor, increasingly unhappy with his subordinate position to O'Connell. He announced publicly at the start of the 1834 session that he would no longer delay the testing of the Repeal question in parliament, and 'that if no one else would "bell-the-cat", he would make a motion on the subject' himself.[83] In vain O'Connell pleaded with him to postpone the discussion, claiming that the subject was still too new to be brought before the Commons, and that they lacked sufficient strength. But a clamour was raised in Ireland and O'Connell was forced to relent. He gave notice of a motion in April. O'Connell admitted that he never 'felt half *so nervous*' as he did when he thought about the debate, and he spent weeks in preparation reading books on Irish history from medieval times to the present day, parliamentary papers, and detailed accounts of how the Union had affected Ireland.[84] Beforehand he joked about whether he should make 'a quiet or a wicked speech', before deciding, 'Wicked for ever.'[85]

In the lead-up to the debate O'Connell visited Canterbury Cathedral and was eager to see the exact spot where the twelfth-century saint and martyr Thomas Becket had been killed. The verger showed him the place, and O'Connell knelt down and kissed 'the stone which had received his life-blood'.[86] The verger was horrified and complained that he would be sacked if the dean saw him allowing any 'Popish work'. To assuage his concern, O'Connell asked him the fee for visiting and, when told it was a shilling, paid him a half-crown, 'saying that the additional one and sixpence was for his fright'. The verger accepted the money gratefully and did a quick search of the grounds to make sure the dean was not around. He then invited O'Connell to kiss the stone a second time for free, telling him, 'When a real gentleman comes, I let him do as he likes for I am very liberal.' O'Connell was shrewd enough to realise that the man was just hoping for another half-crown and afterwards he joked that although he was never in office, he 'remained on that occasion under the crown'.

The night before the great Repeal debate O'Connell was unable to sleep, consumed by anxiety, as sometimes happened before a big event.[87] That, however, was the private O'Connell, and on the day he presented an image of supreme self-confidence and appeared to be in 'his usual buoyant and light-hearted mood'. Walking from his residence at Langham Place to the House of Commons, O'Connell was followed by a large crowd of cheering Irish supporters. Ever the showman, when he passed Westminster Abbey he took off his hat, made the sign of the cross, and made a speech praising Henry VII for leaving 'so magnificent a monument to your piety', and attacking 'that ever execrable brute', Henry VIII. Along the way he was joined by one of the celebrities of the time, John Gully, who slapped him on the back. Gully had for many years been a champion prize-fighter in England, and was now the MP for Pontefract. He was also a successful racehorse owner, having won the Derby with 'St. Giles' in 1832. 'There you are, Dan O'Connell,' he joked, 'going down cool and quiet to your work.' 'Yes,' replied O'Connell, assuming a boxing stance, much to the enjoyment of the spectators. 'Tell me, Gully,' he asked, 'is not that the way to do it?'[88]

The debate began at five p.m. on Tuesday 22 April 1834 and O'Connell opened with a speech that lasted five and a quarter hours. Recognising the challenge before him, he began by announcing that 'no man ever yet rose to address a more unwilling audience'.[89] He then recounted a conversation which had taken place in the lobby of the Commons a few days previously. When the Repeal debate was mentioned a passing MP told him, 'The Canadas are endeavouring to escape from us; America has escaped us; but Ireland shall not escape us.'[90] O'Connell blamed this 'claimed superiority', this assumed 'right of dominion', for 'all the evils which you have for centuries inflicted upon Ireland'. At this there were shouts and cries from opponents of Repeal, but he was prepared for this, and was not distracted. By the end, his opponents had settled into a state 'of scornful indifference'. The speech contained a lengthy analysis of the constitutional history of Ireland, 'the reckless and shameless policy by which she was robbed of her rights', a listing of specific grievances, and a suggestion for how the two countries could work together.

O'Connell questioned the claim that Britain had over Ireland, and said that it was 'an assertion of rights founded on atrocities', a subjugation which had been achieved by 'shameful deceit and devastation' and not through conquest. He praised the great revolution of 1782, when Ireland had won her legislative independence, and attacked the Union which had been passed through corrupt and unconstitutional means. The text-book of O'Connell's political career was also discussed, his first political speech on 13 January 1800 against the Union. He spoke of how the glass door and some of the windows at the Royal Exchange had been broken by 'the clashing of arms and the rush of soldiers' attempting to stop the meeting, and how he had stood forward to denounce the measure. Here he quoted some of the key passages taken from Francis Plowden's *History of Ireland*, in particular the lines about preferring a return of the penal laws to 'the political murder of our country', and how the Catholics of Ireland would never accept 'any advantages as a sect, which would debase and destroy them as a people'. These lines, he said, were quoted to show that from his early life he had been opposed, 'as he ever would be opposed, to a measure so pregnant with shame and disaster to his country'. There followed perhaps O'Connell's greatest oratorical assault of the Act of Union, a measure which he said was 'marked by malice' and whose enforcement had been 'stained with blood and tears'. But it was also an assault on British rule in Ireland, denounced for being corrupt in its origin and malicious in its execution.

Perhaps the most devastating section was the review of British rule in Ireland in the thirty-four years since the Union had come into operation. O'Connell listed the periods when the constitution had been suspended in Ireland, because of martial law, the various Insurrection

Acts, Algerine Acts, and even the recent Coercion Act, and revealed that for twenty of the thirty-four years the country had been 'gagged and fettered' and 'shut out from the light of liberty'. 'There are the results of your Union!' he exclaimed. It was, he declared, a Union between 'the master and the slave—between the oppressor and the oppressed—it cannot, and it ought not to continue'. It later became part of parliamentary folklore that during one of the finest parts of the speech O'Connell began untying his cravat, seemingly unconsciously, and took it off completely. Indeed, it was considered one of the 'most singular things' that had ever been seen in the chamber.[91]

The speech ended with a prophecy and a threat. O'Connell warned that if the Union was not repealed then it was only a matter of time before the two countries would separate and that the future of the connection depended on Repeal. And so O'Connell urged the parliament to do his country justice 'and restore her national independence'.[92] The speech was considered the best single statement on Repeal, and unusually for O'Connell he showed a complete mastery over all the details of the case, with a wealth of facts and figures about Irish poverty and the ill effects of the Union. But ultimately it came down to two points. The first was that Ireland had prospered between 1782 and 1800; the second was that this prosperity had died with the Union. In public afterwards O'Connell was buoyant, though in private he was dissatisfied, believing that the bringing forward of the motion had been premature.[93]

That night O'Connell left the Commons without wearing a cloak and the next day was ill, suffering from a sore throat and headache, although he refused to let this prevent him from hearing any of the speeches on the motion.[94] There followed an exhausting five-day debate on the subject. It was during this time that Emerson Tennant, the MP for Belfast, gave a brilliant three-hour speech against Repeal. The speech was filled with 'minute calculations and figures', and Tennant delivered it without any notes, having memorised it all in advance.[95] Indeed, he was so confident that his memory would not fail him that he sent the full text of his speech to the newspapers before he delivered it. O'Connell dismissed it as a 'long abusive speech' and claimed Tennant had only delivered the bits he could remember.[96] Two of the best speeches in favour of Repeal were by Feargus O'Connor, who gave 'a "rollicking" rattling off-hand sort of speech, in his ordinary fashion', and Richard Lalor Sheil, who delivered a 'clever' speech on the subject.[97] But the numbers were so overwhelmingly and so obviously against Repeal that it was barely a real debate, and the final vote was never in doubt.

The House of Commons was packed for the fifth and final night of the debate on 29 April. Everyone had come to see the defeat of the Repeal motion and watch how O'Connell would respond. Here O'Connell had an opportunity to speak for a second time. He had three objectives: to defend the Repeal motion, to answer the attacks which had been made on it, and to cover his retreat. Always a good judge of how long a speech should be, O'Connell met his three objectives in a speech three-quarters of an hour in length. He noted that no matter how great the majority by which the motion was defeated, it did not remove the legitimacy of his claims. The speech was so effective that it even drew a few cheers from his opponents and word was given from the treasury benches to restrain the vehemence of the cheers when the result of the division was announced. Only one MP for a British constituency voted for the motion. That was James Kennedy, MP for Tiverton, who said later that he opposed Repeal but believed it was a subject worthy of closer examination. When the vote was announced there were only 38 in favour of Repeal, and 523 against it, and 'a very general cry of "Hush" enforced the obedience' of some of the members who wanted to be 'particularly noisy'.[98] It would be the first and final time that O'Connell would ever bring a Repeal motion before the House of Commons.

O'Connell followed the defeat of the Repeal motion by unintentionally bringing down the Whig government. The problem was that his view of how politics operated—what was honourable conduct and what was dishonourable—sometimes differed markedly from that of those around him. He made decisions on his terms, based on what suited his interests at the time, and this enabled him to sacrifice discretion and friendship for political advantage. In the summer of 1834 his lack of discretion caused a major political crisis. Wellesley, the lord lieutenant for Ireland, had been anxious to placate O'Connell, and so persuaded the prime minister, Lord Grey, to drop the courts martial clauses from the Coercion Act. However, Grey was determined to keep the ban on public meetings, but he faced a divided cabinet, with many willing to do whatever was necessary to placate O'Connell.[99] In an attempt to get O'Connell on side, the chief secretary, Edward Littleton, arranged a meeting. Littleton was unsuited for politics, 'his talents were slender, his manners unpopular, and his vanity considerable'.[100] When colleagues warned him to be careful in his dealings with O'Connell he brushed them off, saying, 'Oh, leave me to manage Dan.' But as the diarist Charles Greville noted afterwards, O'Connell ended up managing Littleton, 'and manage him he did with a vengeance'.

The meeting was confidential and off the record, and Littleton convinced O'Connell that the liberals in the cabinet had won the argument, and that the ban on public meetings would be dropped. Indeed O'Connell left the meeting under the impression that both Wellesley and Littleton opposed the Coercion Act and that 'the game was in my hands if I did not throw it away'.[101] Foolishly, Littleton did not report back to the cabinet on what had been discussed, or what he had encouraged O'Connell to believe. Thus when O'Connell read in the newspapers that no changes would be made, and that the Irish government was willing to go along with this, he was furious. In the House of Commons on 3 July he demanded to know whether this was the case, and, when Littleton confirmed it, he revealed that in that case he had 'been exceedingly deceived by the right honourable gentleman'.[102] By making a confidential conversation public O'Connell breached an accepted political convention of the day. Indeed Littleton considered it nothing less than 'a black act of perfidy'.[103] But O'Connell was unrepentant and claimed that Littleton had promised him a few days previously that he would resign if the changes were not made.[104] The damage was done and Littleton's reputation was in tatters.

Littleton tendered his resignation on 6 July, though Lord Althorp refused to accept it. The next day, however, both Althorp and Grey submitted their own resignations, bringing the government to an end.[105] O'Connell boasted that his 'triumph over Littleton is admitted to be complete' and celebrated the news of the fall of 'that unworthy gentleman'.[106] For his part, Littleton never forgave O'Connell for the breach of confidence. He admitted ruefully that his 'entire confidence in O'Connell's assurance that he would consider my communication confidential was not warranted by his character, or even by my own experience of it'.[107] As O'Connell's nineteenth-century biographer, Michael MacDonagh, has put it, 'Thus fell—destroyed by O'Connell— the great Reform administration.'[108]

On 16 July Lord Melbourne was invited to form a ministry. He was an unexpected choice as prime minister, given that he was 'lax in morals, indifferent in religion, and very loose and pliant in politics'.[109] Duncannon became home secretary and immediately attempted to effect a reconciliation with O'Connell. Together with the Whigs, O'Connell worked on a tithes bill that would abolish arrears and reduce the amount payable, but although the bill passed the Commons it was thrown out by the Lords. Duncannon was wary, however, of working too closely with O'Connell in the future. He believed the problem with O'Connell was that he was 'so vain and excitable and ambitious' that no matter what deal was done, as soon as he returned to Ireland he forgot everything he had promised, 'the demon of agitation regains the ascendant, and he bursts into all those excesses which have made him so odious and formidable'.[110]

Around this time O'Connell came to know the young Tory MP William Ewart Gladstone. They served together on a parliamentary committee which had been established, on O'Connell's request, on 13 May 1834, to investigate the four inns of court in London and the King's Inns in Dublin.[111] This was because of the treatment of Daniel Harvey, MP for Colchester, a solicitor who had been refused admission to the bar because of mistakes he had made in his youth. Listing his problems with the inns of court, O'Connell gave other examples of prejudice. There was the case of a working printer who had been denied admission to train as a barrister because of his profession, and another man who had been denied admission because a friend had quarrelled with a bencher. O'Connell thought back to his own time as a student, when the inns had been neither 'seminaries of learning' nor 'seminaries of accomplishments'. Rather, they were places for the eating of a required number of dinners, where the students 'drank bad port' while the benchers and barristers were 'provided with excellent claret'. And so O'Connell demanded a complete reform of the system of admitting and training barristers.

Gladstone was no admirer of O'Connell in this period, and voted consistently against him on Irish questions. He later acknowledged that the prejudices he held against him were established, 'not by conviction, but by tradition and education'.[112] O'Connell was 'the symbol of his country' and the hatred that was felt towards him was the hatred the ruling elite feels 'towards those whom they have injured'. But although he detested his politics, Gladstone from the beginning of his parliamentary career in 1833 recognised O'Connell as 'the greatest popular leader whom the world had ever seen'. He was also astonished by his energy and attention to detail. Although O'Connell did not know Harvey, he was determined to get justice for him, and Gladstone was amazed by the 'amount of personal sacrifice for one with whom he had no connection'. In the committee O'Connell 'took the chair, conducted the examinations, carried the report, and presented the result to parliament in five hundred folio pages of hard work'. Gladstone, however, dissented in the final judgement of the committee, and so three of the members were required to go to Coggeshall in Essex to interview one of the witnesses (an elderly and infirm man called Skingley).

And so O'Connell, Gladstone, and a third committee member set out in a carriage on a Sunday morning at five a.m. to interview Skingley. O'Connell had already been to Mass, and he carried with him a book of theology which he used to show Gladstone that the Roman Catholic church did not hate Protestants; rather, it considered them all to be Christians by virtue of their baptism. Gladstone was not so easily impressed, and recognised that the Roman Catholic church claimed jurisdiction over Protestants by the same token. But he was much taken by O'Connell's character, and he enjoyed 'the frank and kindly conversation of this most remarkable man'. O'Connell recounted how he had fled the French Revolution in 1793, and indeed how his ship had been the one that carried news of the execution of Louis XVI to England. He also told stories about his legal career, and how he had been able to earn huge amounts as a barrister in the 1820s despite the restrictions on his practice because of his religion.

In the years ahead O'Connell kept a close eye on Gladstone. In late 1838 he read his book *The state in its relations with the church*, and noted that Gladstone seemed to be flirting with the Oxford Movement (a religious movement in England). The next time the two men met in the House of Commons chamber, behind the Speaker's chair, O'Connell put his hand on Gladstone's arm and joked, 'I claim the half of you.' Not a warm man himself, Gladstone was moved that O'Connell was 'most kindly and genial to one who had no claim to his notice, and whose prejudices were all against him'. Gladstone was not blind to O'Connell's faults. He believed he was too quick to resort to violent language, and too ready to abuse people who did not deserve it. They had only one serious fight, when during a debate on Ireland Gladstone remarked that there was nothing to be gained from dwelling on either English atrocities or 'the bloody and terrible retributions which they had provoked'. O'Connell interrupted him 'so loudly and vehemently' that the Speaker was forced to rise from his chair and call him to order. It was only in later years that Gladstone accepted he had been insensitive in his language when discussing 'the hideous massacres perpetrated on the Irish under supreme direction'.

When it came to parliamentary oratory, Gladstone recognised that O'Connell was of the first class, though he wasn't sure where exactly to place him in the rankings. He believed that O'Connell was at his best 'in extemporary bursts, and least great when charging himself with extended and complex exposition'. He also recognised that few other men had achieved similar greatness as lawyers and public orators. Indeed, he wondered whether the nineteenth century had produced 'anyone more eminent' in the law. However he was certain that as an 'orator of the platform, O'Connell may challenge all the world. For who ever in the same degree as O'Connell trained and disciplined, stirred and soothed, a people?' Towards the end of his life, Gladstone considered O'Connell one of the greatest Irishmen in history: 'His was the genius and the tact, the energy and the fire, that won the bloodless battle of emancipation.'

In the summer of 1834 O'Connell worked on his plan for setting up a new bank in Ireland, The Irish National Bank, which would challenge the monopoly of the Bank of Ireland and the Irish Provincial Bank. He disapproved of both banks because of their 'rascality', their narrow 'anti-Irish' principles, and their unwillingness to provide credit for Catholics.[113] In particular he detested the Bank of Ireland, 'an Orange confederacy', whose directors interfered in political cases in Dublin and intimidated juries by abusing their power:[114] 'Dishonest and bigoted they are and have been.' The National Bank—with a picture of a bust of O'Connell on each note—proved a success in the short term, and provided another example of O'Connell establishing institutions in Ireland to represent the interests of Catholics as well as Protestants. Thomas Mooney, a baker who was working on the foundation of another bank, the National Agricultural and Commercial Bank of Ireland, sought O'Connell's advice at this time, but O'Connell wisely chose to keep him distant.[115]

In later years Mooney emigrated to San Francisco and set up a bank there, but absconded with all of the funds.

In October 1834 O'Connell's intervention in the Co. Clare election three years earlier returned to haunt him. Sir William Gossett, the former Castle undersecretary, leaked a story to the *Observer* newspaper that O'Connell had provided information against O'Gorman Mahon. The story was reprinted in the Irish newspapers and was potentially very damaging, as O'Connell stood directly accused of having acted out of 'selfish interests' and 'personal malignity'.[116] The way O'Connell handled the story reveals much about his understanding of the media. First, O'Connell denounced the story as 'a perfect lie' and dismissed Gossett's allegations with contempt.[117] This was relatively easy to do, because Gossett had claimed that O'Connell had provided the information to him in a personal interview. As that was not the case, O'Connell had no hesitation in denying the specific charge (which was false), while avoiding the more general allegation (which was true). A master of misdirection, O'Connell then launched into a 'violent attack' on the *Courier* newspaper for something it had published on a completely different issue, recognising that this 'artifice' would throw 'the public attention to the other *scent*.'[118]

The first ministry of Lord Melbourne only lasted from 16 July to 14 November 1834. O'Connell considered him 'a sham reformer', in part because of his refusal to dismiss the law officers in Ireland, and he complained publicly of the tragedy that the 'destinies of the Irish people should depend in any degree on so inefficient a person'.[119] The death of Lord Spencer on 10 November 1834 provided an excuse for the king to dismiss Melbourne's ministry four days later. O'Connell was glad to be 'rid of the humbuggers', but had no reason to look forward to a new Tory ministry.[120] The duke of Wellington was invited to form a government, but he declined in favour of Robert Peel. As Peel was holidaying in Italy, Wellington agreed to conduct the government until his return. O'Connell loved abusing Wellington, and at a reform meeting in Dublin on 21 November mocked him for merely being 'the chance victor of a battle'.[121] He also promised to abandon Repeal temporarily until the Tory government was driven from power.

O'Connell had to deal with some family affairs at this time. Maurice had embarked on a relationship with Mary Scott, the only daughter of Bindon Scott, a Protestant landlord in Co. Clare who had supported

Vesey Fitzgerald in 1828. Bindon Scott's hatred of the O'Connell family propelled the romance, and on 29 September 1832 Maurice decided to elope with Mary, sailing away in his yacht, without telling anyone. They married, and when Mary gave birth to a daughter in August 1833 O'Connell made every effort to reconcile the families, even going so far as to concede that Scott's objections to the match were 'quite natural' and 'perfectly reasonable'.[122] He promised to call on Scott when next in Clare, to talk 'on business, or not, precisely as you choose'. But the divisions were not so easily healed, especially as Maurice was not quite so willing to be conciliatory. When Scott's daughter-in-law was put on trial for bigamy in Cork in October 1833, Maurice was examined and he made a number of jokes about the fact that he had married without Scott's consent.[123] He referred to his father-in-law as 'Old Scott' throughout, much to the amusement of the crowd. O'Connell disapproved of the match, recognising from the start that it was unlikely to last, but he accepted that his son had no one to blame but himself. As he later confided to his wife, 'What a prize my unfortunate Maurice drew for himself in the lottery of life.'[124]

In late 1834 Maurice's wife was expecting their second child, though O'Connell became convinced that it was a phantom pregnancy, and that she had just grown very fat. This was because she had miscalculated the date of conception by some distance, making it 'an eternal pregnancy', though she was proven correct in the end.[125] As the estimated due date passed, and there was still no sign of a baby, he began to mock 'the silly woman' for confusing 'her excessive corpulence and great appetite' with a pregnancy.[126] The baby was born just before Christmas, a girl named Mary. O'Connell was unapologetic about having got things so wrong, and instead sent instructions for the child to be baptised as soon as possible.[127] His thoughts turned to the approaching general election. From the reports he was receiving he was convinced Maurice would lose his seat and he ordered him to go to Tralee immediately and begin campaigning. He had little faith that things would work out for his son, concluding sadly that Maurice was '*not a lucky young man*'.[128]

In December 1834 O'Connell returned to the Four Courts in Dublin. Since entering parliament he had allowed his legal practice to dwindle considerably, but every now and then a case (or the money that went with a case) attracted his interest. On this occasion he was in the court of exchequer representing Thomas Hodgens, who was bringing a case against a Dr Mahon, a surgeon in the artillery, for seducing and running off with his wife. The case was heard on 22, 23, and 24 December, with O'Connell successfully preventing a postponement of the case until after Christmas. In his closing address on 24 December O'Connell 'drew beautiful and affecting pictures of wedded happiness—of the sacredness and sanctity of the domestic hearth', and ended with a moving description 'of the wife and husband clinging to each other with a passionate and devoted fondness, until the adulterer came to dissolve the dream'.[129] It was an emotionally charged appeal, and the judge was clearly affected by it. According to one newspaper reporter, the tears could be seen rolling down his cheeks during the most affecting passages of the speech. Based on the evidence, O'Connell had only been expecting to win damages of between three and five hundred pounds. But the speech changed everything and he got a verdict for £3,000. O'Connell was cheered loudly when the verdict was announced and, as he later boasted to his wife, 'even the judge did not interfere to prevent it, that is, the continued cheering'.[130] Delighted with his victory, O'Connell hailed the speech as one of the most successful of his career. Little did he realise that he was about to enter the darkest period of his life.

Chapter 5 ∾

PUBLIC ANGER, PRIVATE
AGONY, 1835–1836

'Scum condensed of Irish bog!
Ruffian—coward—demagogue!
Boundless liar—base detractor!
Nurse of murders—treason's factor!'

('THE WHIG MISSIONARY OF 1835', *THE TIMES*,
26 NOVEMBER 1835)

'This is King Dan, that "mighty great" man, who sold the
county of Carlow.'

('THE COUNTY OF CARLOW', *THE TIMES*, 1 DECEMBER 1835)

O'Connell's troubles began with the general election which was held in January 1835. Once again he stood in Dublin city, but all his political instincts warned him that victory was not a formality. No matter how many times his friends assured him that success was certain, his own feelings were 'naturally desponding' and he refused to get carried away.[1] As he admitted to his wife, 'I am prepared for the worst.' He did not believe his campaign team was 'sufficiently prepared for the contest', and he had little faith in the canvassing that was being done. There were four candidates for the two seats, O'Connell and Edward Ruthven standing as Repeal candidates against George Alexander Hamilton and John Beatty West. At the hustings on Monday 12 January O'Connell was jeered by some Orangemen when he rose to speak, but he soon won them over by promising to go to parliament as the representative of all—'Orangemen, Protestants, and

Dissenters'.[2] By the end of the speech the applause was universal. Polling began the next day and continued until 17 January.

The campaign was a dirty one, with Arthur Perrin, the lord mayor of Dublin, signing a placard to be posted around the city which insulted Ruthven directly, and which claimed that he did not possess the property qualifications needed to be a member of parliament.[3] County members in England, Wales and Ireland were required to have an income from property of £300 a year, although these qualifications were not always rigidly checked. Ruthven was enraged and challenged Perrin to a duel. The two men met on the morning of 13 January and fired two shots each, but no one was hurt.

This was one of the most difficult periods of O'Connell's life. He suffered intense 'mental agony' as the tension of the campaign got to him, and he waited to see if he would be returned.[4] By Wednesday 14 January he was convinced he was going to lose the election. The polling for the day had not gone well—he estimated he had lost by about 120 votes—and he believed that 'we have now no prospect of success'.[5] At evening time he was given the bad news that he was behind by 48 votes, with three days of polling left. Part of the problem was that every obstacle was being put in the path of his voters, in an attempt to delay and demoralise them. They were asked to take every single oath that was required, while those voting for the other candidates were not impeded in any way.[6] As a result, his voters were left waiting for hours until they were called to vote. O'Connell became withdrawn and brooding. As he admitted, 'I am naturally of a desponding disposition when anything goes against me.'

Things, however, improved dramatically on Thursday 15 January. By the close of polling O'Connell was topping the count, on 2,234 votes, just ahead of Hamilton on 2,162, West on 2,157, and Ruthven on 2,000. His confidence returned and at the close of the election two days later both he and Ruthven were returned. The final count was O'Connell 2,678, Ruthven 2,630, Hamilton 2,461, and West 2,455. The turnaround in fortunes after the first day was impressive, though it seemed a little too good to be true. Certainly allegations of bribery were prevalent at the time, with stories of voters being paid ten pounds to vote for O'Connell and Ruthven.[7] There were genuine grounds to challenge the result, but O'Connell's enemies decided to go one step further, forming a plot to destroy him and his family politically and remove them from public life for ever.

The plan was to challenge the validity of the returns of everyone connected personally to O'Connell. This included his three sons: Maurice, who had been returned for Tralee; John, who had been returned for Youghal; and Morgan, who had been returned for Co. Meath. It was an ingenious plan. Even if it failed O'Connell would be put to considerable expense, and if it succeeded it would remove each family member from parliament. Thus a petition challenging the return of O'Connell was presented in the House of Commons on 25 February, with a second, challenging Ruthven's return, presented on 5 March. In each case it was claimed that their return had been secured through fraudulent votes. Following this, a petition challenging Morgan's return was presented in the House of Commons on 9 March, and the next day petitions were presented against Maurice and John. There were also petitions against O'Connell's son-in-law and his nephew, making it six election results in total that O'Connell had to defend personally.

O'Connell recognised the challenge: 'The Orange enemy is resolved to run me down if he possibly can.'[8] The potential expense of the Dublin challenge was immense. If the hearings were held in London then O'Connell would have to pay for all his witnesses (in other words, his voters) to travel over and testify, something that was likely to cost £40 per person. This would destroy him financially, and he admitted that he saw 'nothing but ruin staring me in the face'.[9] Normally so confident about any approaching conflict, for once O'Connell began to despair. His health and strength began to fail him, and he could not raise his spirits for the fight. But he still would not back down, and was determined to go bankrupt rather than let his enemies win unopposed. One idea for fundraising was to write his autobiography, and he even contacted a publisher through an intermediary, but he failed to secure the lucrative terms he desired and the proposal went no further.[10] A subscription was raised in Ireland to help with his expenses, but it was barely enough to pay for the costs of the clerks, attorneys, porters, printing, and stationery in Dublin. In a moment of profound melancholy O'Connell admitted that it was the first time in his life that he was 'disposed to feel heartbroken', and he prayed that 'God's holy will be done'.[11]

In the short term there was some success. Following an appeal by the *Pilot* newspaper it was agreed that a commission would be established in Dublin to examine witnesses, thus saving O'Connell the expense of bringing them to London. Following this, the attempt to unseat Morgan fell apart on 24 March when the petitioners failed to enter into a recognisance. Then on 2 June the election committee declared that John had been duly elected, and on 17 June the petition against Maurice was abandoned. But the attempts to unseat O'Connell and Ruthven continued into the next year and provided a deep source of anxiety. The burden of the costs of the Dublin and Youghal petitions fell almost completely on him, and came to almost £8,000.[12] Gradually, O'Connell's health and spirits began to recover, and he claimed that he would await the result 'in perfect tranquillity'.[13] But it was hard to maintain his good cheer as the challenge dragged on. The financial implications frequently left him despairing, and he feared that he would have to mortgage his entire property to meet the costs.[14]

With the return of O'Connell's strength came a desire for vengeance. He blamed 'the Dublin corporation and Orange factions' for the plot to unseat him, and vowed that, after five years of attempting to conciliate, he would never again 'enter into any compromise with *the scoundrels*'.[15] The attacks on himself and his family had left him embittered, and he noted his 'political education has been *perfected* by the conduct of this faction' towards him. 'The unrelenting hatred' shown by the attacks convinced him that it was 'a faction that may be beaten, but cannot possibly be otherwise conciliated or even mitigated'.

O'Connell was also determined to tackle the ingratitude of some of the Irish MPs he had helped get elected. Richard Sullivan had stood for election in Kilkenny city and had been opposed by William Fletcher, who had claimed at the hustings that O'Connell was no friend of Sullivan's. But Sullivan had anticipated this move, and had contacted O'Connell in advance pleading for his support. Agreeing to help, O'Connell had sent a letter to Sullivan assuring him of his support and when this was read out at the hustings it helped settle the contest in Sullivan's favour. But after the election Sullivan ignored O'Connell, and did not respond to his requests for help with the committee investigating the Dublin election. O'Connell was furious with this 'treachery' and was determined to get his revenge.[16] In 1836 he found a solution to a number of problems. He bullied Sullivan into sending him a letter resigning as MP for Kilkenny city, promising to only activate it if he was unseated for Dublin. Sullivan had little choice but to agree, rather than have O'Connell as an implacable enemy. O'Connell now had a backdoor into parliament if things went against him.

It was only on 16 May 1836 that the commission delivered its verdict on the disputed Dublin election and O'Connell and Ruthven were both unseated.[17] Sullivan's resignation letter was immediately processed and O'Connell was returned, unopposed, the very next day as the new MP for Kilkenny city. Ruthven had been in poor health for some time, a situation almost certainly exacerbated by the stress of the long controversy, and he died on 31 March 1836, before the result of the commission was announced. The long contest had also taken its toll on O'Connell. He admitted that for the fifteen months the controversy had dragged on he had possessed no peace of mind, though he was now able to relax.[18] On 20 May O'Connell presented one of two petitions to unseat the men who took the seats, West and Hamilton, claiming that bribery had been used in their election. But the attorney general ruled ten days later that the petitions could not be received. With this defeat, the long controversy finally came to an end.

O'Connell's mission in this period was to secure good government for Ireland. The ambition—he called it his 'dream'—was to become a government minister, and sit in cabinet with responsibility for Ireland. This would keep the 'Orange faction' down, and ensure that the days of misgovernment 'for our country and our creed' would be brought to an end.[19] He hoped that this would happen soon, believing that 'it is time they [the British government] should act honestly by Ireland'. Following the general election of 1835 the balance of power was held by O'Connell and his party, and he was determined to do something with it. Therefore he embarked on a series of meetings with the Whig leadership in 'the dusty, unfurnished drawing rooms' of Lichfield House, the 'dingy-fronted mansion' of the radical Whig Lord Lichfield.[20] The loose agreement which emerged from these meetings was described in parliament by Richard Lalor Sheil as a 'compact', and the name stuck, although in reality it was more of a loose alliance.

Resolving his differences with the Whigs led to a swift change of fortunes. Suddenly his 'great talents' became visible again. On 19 February 1835 the House of Commons met to elect a new speaker. The result of this contest was to reveal the respective strengths of the Whigs and the Tories and provide a good indication of which party would form the new government. Sir Charles Manners-Sutton had been Speaker since 1817, but he was a Tory, and had been so partisan when the Melbourne ministry was dissolving that the Whigs were determined to punish him. The Whigs and the Tories were almost equally divided, with Stanley having formed his own party around him, so the support of the Irish MPs was pivotal. O'Connell issued an instruction that any man who absented himself from parliament for the vote (or presumably voted the wrong way) would 'forfeit all claim upon his constituents' and should be considered a traitor.[21] Betting on the election was intense, with as much wagered as would normally be put on the Derby or the Gold Cup. On the steamer over to Liverpool O'Connell was offered a sizable wager on the result of the election of the Speaker, but he did not consider 'the occasion quite weighty enough to depart from his established rule of never betting'.[22]

At one of the earliest Lichfield House meetings O'Connell had agreed to support the Whig candidate, James Abercromby, and had given his word that the Irish Repeal MPs would not be too triumphalist if Manners-Sutton was defeated. This was a real concern of the Whigs, so it was agreed that there would be no loud cheering no matter what the result. The vote for Manners-Sutton was taken first and he received 306 votes. Rarely would attendance at the Commons go above 600, so it appeared certain he would be re-elected. The counting of the votes against Manners-Sutton was therefore conducted in a tense atmosphere. As John O'Connell reported, 'at last—at last—came the welcome sounds, 304—305—306—307!' which was followed by an incredibly loud cheer from O'Connell's party.[23] The final total was 316, and Abercromby was elected afterwards without a division. As John noted without much sincerity afterwards, 'It was *very* wrong of us to cheer in that way!'

'Victory, victory!'[24] O'Connell celebrated the result afterwards, a victory which not only indicated the defeat of the Tories, but which also suggested a new, closer relationship between O'Connell and the Whigs. In the packed library of the Commons afterwards O'Connell was forced to go down on one knee so that he could write to his friends in Ireland, and send the news that 'The Tories are down, and for ever.'[25] Over the next few weeks O'Connell continued his meetings with the Whigs at Lichfield House, and agreed the terms of the alliance. In return for 'Justice for Ireland', a series of reforms to help the country, O'Connell would suspend his campaign for Repeal. O'Connell announced this change of direction during the debate on the king's address on 26 February. At the start of his speech he was jeered when he spoke of his 'unfortunate and neglected country', but he turned the jeering to his advantage by wishing that 'the slight incivility of such interruptions' was all the people of Ireland had to bear.[26] In a dramatic section he promised to give the Whigs a 'fair trial to show whether *they* could produce good government in Ireland'.[27] And if they succeeded he promised 'to give it [Repeal] up for ever'.[28] But he also threatened that if they failed then 'he would come back with tenfold force to "the Repeal"'.

To some observers (and historians) the Lichfield House alliance was evidence that O'Connell never really cared about Repeal, that it was merely the means to an end, a negotiating tactic to secure better terms for Ireland. The truth was very different. Even during this period he admitted that there 'is nothing else for it' except Repeal; 'everything else is trifling and childish'.[29] But following the humiliating defeat of the Repeal motion in April 1834 O'Connell realised that he needed a change of direction, or he would risk becoming irrelevant. Continuous pressing of the Repeal issue had eroded his standing in parliament between 1830 and 1834; to persist with it threatened political oblivion. The Lichfield House alliance was both a masterstroke and a piece of misdirection. It was a masterstroke because it made it appear that O'Connell was suspending the campaign for Repeal from a position of strength, which was certainly not the case. It was a piece of misdirection because it also allowed O'Connell to switch attention away from the issue that meant the most to him, secure good terms for Ireland, and then return to the issue at some later date. As W.E. Gladstone shrewdly observed, 'He never for a moment changed his end; he never hesitated to change his means.'[30] Rather than representing the end of the Repeal campaign, the Lichfield House alliance was the moment when O'Connell finally came to terms with the challenge of British parliamentary politics, and showed his mastery of the political game.

The debates over the speakership and the formation of the new government provided plenty of opportunities to score points off the despised Stanley. O'Connell blamed Stanley for the coercion bill which had ruined the Whigs, and accused him of being 'the "calamity" of every party to which he belongs or belonged'.[31] Even though Stanley had voted against Manners-Sutton, O'Connell went out of his way to mock him, '*and all his influence*', convinced that he was now 'politically defunct'.[32] O'Connell detested his 'thimblerig style of bitter but

pointless sarcasm', and believed that he was 'as vindictive and spiteful as
possible'. During the debate on 26 February O'Connell dismissed
Stanley's party as being unworthy of the name, nor was it 'a faction—
that would be a harsher title . . . we ought to call it the tail'.[33] And he
enlisted a famous quote from John Philpot Curran to make fun of
Stanley's appearance, comparing his smile to the 'silver plate on a coffin'.
The 'tail' was dismissed in a couplet adapted from George Canning,
which played on Stanley being the heir to the thirteenth earl of Derby:
'Down thy hill, romantic Ashbourne, glides "The Derby dilly", with his
six insides.' There was much laughter at this, but O'Connell reminded
the chamber that it was 'quite consistent with the genius and disposition
of my country to mix merriment with woe' and he noted that 'the
sound of laughter is often heard while the heart is wrung with bitter
anguish'.

There was a distinct possibility of O'Connell taking office. The two
posts that he aspired to were those of attorney general and chief secretary
for Ireland. But his main priority was to replace the existing office
holders in Ireland, and especially secure the removal of Blackburne, the
attorney general. This, combined with '*liberal* measures being adopted
towards Ireland', would strike 'a brain blow to the Orange faction'.[34] His
motto was '*Delenda est Carthago*'—'Carthage must be destroyed'—
meaning that all that mattered was the destruction of his enemies in
Ireland.[35] After the anguish of the past number of months, when he and
his family had been attacked and assailed, this was the time for revenge.
He made it clear that he would refuse to support the ministry if it left
even one of his enemies in power: 'They *must* ALL go.' The time for
conciliation was over, after 'the unrelenting hatred with which they
came out against me and my family', and he vowed that he would 'never
again enter into any compromise with *the scoundrels*'.

As Lord Melbourne moved to prepare a ministry the prospect of
O'Connell taking office receded. First, Melbourne did not really want to
give him anything, and the king was also an obstacle. It seems
O'Connell was offered the position of Master of the Rolls for Ireland,
but he refused it, especially when he discovered that the king had made
'a personal objection'.[36] Many of the Whigs continued to distrust
O'Connell, despite the alliance. O'Connell was one of the founders of
the Reform Club in 1835, and was a member of its first committee of
management.[37] But his involvement was 'a bitter pill' for many Whigs,

and only accepted with great reluctance. During the formation of the government, it was rumoured that O'Connell had been given a veto over the appointment of the lord lieutenant and had been allowed to nominate the Irish attorney general and solicitor general. This was not the case, but it served to increase O'Connell's stature in Britain. It was said that 'O'Connell holds the destiny of the government in his hands, and is acknowledged to be the greatest man going.'[38]

In a debate in the House of Lords on the formation of the ministry on 18 April, Lord Alvanley accused the Whigs of having made dishonourable terms with O'Connell. His entire speech was a bitter denunciation of O'Connell, a man whom he accused of attempting to subvert the constitution by his support for Repeal. It was inevitable that O'Connell would respond, and his speech two days later contained some of his best insults yet. In an excoriating attack, he dismissed Alvanley as a 'creature, half idiot, half maniac' and a 'bloated buffoon'.[39] And in a passage that left no room for misinterpretation, he warned Alvanley that he had used language in parliament 'which he knew he would not be allowed to use in other places'. This was unambiguous, and Alvanley immediately wrote to O'Connell demanding satisfaction. Particularly wounding was his observation that O'Connell had assumed the right 'to insult with impunity,' and he hoped that O'Connell would 'make an exception in my favour' and do 'what any other gentleman would do'.[40]

But O'Connell refused to fight. He mocked Alvanley for the 'absurdity' of sending a challenge when his 'sentiments on that subject have been so publicly and so frequently proclaimed'.[41] And he joked of the 'absurdity' of Alvanley sending the challenge from Clifden in Co. Galway, to his second, George Dawson Damer, in London, to be transmitted to O'Connell in Dublin, an unnecessary complication which he said added an 'air of more comicality' to proceedings, and which 'bangs Banagher'. Scorning the challenge, O'Connell threatened to bring the entire affair before parliament, claiming a breach of privilege.

The challenge was soon leaked to the newspapers, and O'Connell once again was criticised for his eagerness to abuse and his unwillingness to fight. Twenty-two members of Brook's Club signed a requisition to have him expelled as a member, though O'Connell was protected by his new Whig allies, who decided the club was not

competent to deal with the private affairs of members.[42] It was said that
when O'Connell next attended the club many members turned their
backs on him. O'Connell's son Morgan was embarrassed by the affair,
and felt the family honour had been stained. He sent his own challenge
to Alvanley and the men met near Regent's Park on 4 May. A Methodist
minister intervened and attempted to persuade the men to stop the
duel. 'Pray, sir, go and mind your own affairs', replied Alvanley, a noted
wit, 'for I have enough to do now to think of mine.' 'Think of your soul,'
pleaded the minister. 'Yes,' said Alvanley, 'but my body is now in the
greatest danger.'[43] The men were placed twelve paces apart, but Morgan
fired first, before the signal was given. Alvanley agreed to consider this
a mistake, and begin again as if nothing had happened, and they each
fired two shots. It was said that Morgan jumped back, 'very much
startled', when Alvanley fired at him, and after the second exchange of
fire he withdrew, saying he was satisfied.[44] When Alvanley returned
home he paid the coachman a sovereign, telling him, 'I give you that,
not for taking me here, but for having brought me back.'

The Alvanley affair was soon overshadowed by a much bigger clash.
The opponent here was the foppish novelist Benjamin Disraeli, a man
whom O'Connell had assisted in 1832 when he had attempted to enter
parliament as a reformer. When that was unsuccessful he reversed his
positions, and became a committed Tory. In the general election in 1835
he stood at Taunton, and abused the Whigs for having done a deal with
O'Connell and for having grasped the 'bloody hand' of a man they had
previously denounced as a traitor. Responding to the attack at a
meeting in Dublin, O'Connell delivered perhaps his most vicious (and
shocking) speech ever. He began by mocking Disraeli for having
enlisted his support when running for election in 1832, reminding him
that he was a 'greater incendiary' at that time than 'at present'.[45] As to
the reference to being a traitor, O'Connell responded by calling Disraeli
a liar: 'He is a liar in action and in words. His life is a living lie. He is a
disgrace to his species.' The speech left O'Connell open to allegations of
anti-Semitism, unfair given his consistent support for Jewish rights in
parliament. But when the rage was upon him O'Connell used whatever
weapons were at hand, and chose words to hurt and words to wound.
He demanded to know what kind of society 'could tolerate such a
creature'. Conceding that his language was harsh, O'Connell admitted
that he owed an apology, but an apology for there not being 'harsher

terms in the British language' to describe 'a wretch of his species'. The conclusion was the most offensive part of the speech. O'Connell insisted that Disraeli possessed 'just the qualities of the impenitent thief who died upon the cross, whose name, I verily believe, must have been Disraeli'. And he suggested that, for all he knew, 'the present Disraeli is descended from him, and with the impression that he is, I now forgive the heir-at-law of the blasphemous thief who died upon the cross'.

Infuriated, Disraeli immediately sought revenge. Knowing that O'Connell refused to fight, he sent a challenge to his son Morgan, claiming he had established himself 'as the champion' of his father. But Morgan declined the challenge, insisting that the Alvanley affair had been a different matter. Disraeli then issued a public letter on 5 May 1835, denouncing O'Connell as a public beggar deriving a 'princely revenue' from 'a starving band of fanatical slaves'. The Catholic church was also attacked. Disraeli claimed it was a church which 'clamours for toleration, and labours for supremacy'. He promised that he would be a member of parliament before too long, and assured O'Connell, 'We shall meet at Philippi.'

Frustrated with the House of Lords for consistently blocking his reform agenda, in September 1835 O'Connell began a campaign to abolish (or at least radically reform) the chamber, hoping to intimidate it into backing down on various Irish concessions. Over a ten-day period he addressed enormous crowds at Manchester, Newcastle, Edinburgh, and Glasgow (with stops along the way at Falkirk, Greenock, Paisley, and Kilmarnock), and unleashed some of his greatest invective. Wellington was dismissed as 'a stunted corporal' and 'the chance victor of Waterloo'.[46] Hardinge was 'a one-armed ruffian'. Peel was 'the greatest humbugger of the age, and as full of cant as any canter who ever canted in this canting world'. The lords themselves were mocked for being '[t]he soaped pigs of society'.

On a wet day in Manchester on 11 September O'Connell was greeted by over thirty thousand tradesmen, and he delivered an address that he estimated a third of them were able to hear. Afterwards there was a dinner for three hundred people and O'Connell boasted that he was 'never so well received in Ireland'.[47] The tour of Scotland was an even greater success. An estimated 200,000 waited to hear him in Glasgow, and O'Connell delivered a stirring oration which discussed the legacy of William Wallace, 'a legacy of freedom won from tyranny', a 'nation determined never to submit to slavery'.[48] Attacking the House of Lords for being an outdated and narrow-minded institution, he mocked the idea that 'wisdom was hereditary', noting that there were no hereditary doctors or hereditary tailors. Repeal was also discussed, to much cheering. He quoted the old Irish phrase 'Ireland her own, or all the world in a blaze', and said that while he did not want to see the world in a blaze, he did wish that Ireland would have her own parliament. At the dinners afterwards, guests were astonished to find that O'Connell was nothing like they expected. He had none of the airs of a great orator or statesman, and was not anxious to show off or display his powers. Instead he became simply 'one of the party. He laughs at all their jokes and merry sayings, and gives his own in return. There is a continual play of laughing good humour on his countenance.' Guests were surprised to see no evidence of 'the profound lawyer, the bold orator', or the 'wary pacificator of his turbulent country'.

In a review of O'Connell's oratory published in Scotland, England, and Ireland after this tour, it was suggested that 'any man of common sense and tolerable talent may, by perseverance, become an eloquent speaker'.[49] But it was argued that no man would ever 'acquire the art of affecting an audience, as Mr O'Connell does, through sheer study'. What was impressive about him was the way 'he throws so much of his internal soul into every word he utters, that the words are the expression of his feelings at the time'.[50] It was said that his oratory had no literary merit—it was to be experienced rather than read—but it did inspire action. In this way he was compared to the ancient orator who inspired his audience to cry, 'Let us march against Philip,' rather than the one who drew the response, 'How well the orator has spoken.' 'By a glance, a curl of the lip, or a change of the voice', O'Connell was able to produce 'an electric effect on the listener'. For example, when discussing the Tories he had said, 'But they never shall succeed.' Coming from a man 'of slight physical powers, or of little influence in the political world', the words would have produced laughter and would have made the speaker appear ludicrous. But with O'Connell, 'the triumphant glance of the eye, and the bold menacing attitude of defiance suddenly assumed by so powerful a looking man', ensured that the words had 'a startling and rousing effect'.

The tour of Scotland took place during another period of profound crisis in O'Connell's life. Separate to the controversy over his return for

Co. Dublin, he had become embroiled in a second electoral controversy which ultimately proved much more costly and damaging. Financial worries played their part in entangling him in the mess, but it is harder to be sympathetic to him this time. The problem began on 27 May 1835 when the two recently elected MPs for Co. Carlow, Henry Bruen and Thomas Kavanagh, were unseated following a petition and a new writ was issued for the county. In an incredibly cynical manoeuvre, O'Connell decided to use the opportunity to make some money. The very next day he called at the home of a wealthy Catholic banker, Alexander Raphael, in London and invited him to run as a Repeal candidate. Raphael was a British-Armenian, of Jewish descent, and had been sheriff of London in 1829. More importantly, he had money. He 'was known to be a man of almost unbounded wealth' and had been looking for a seat in parliament for some time.[51] Arising out of this, he had contacted O'Connell and had discussed ways of entering parliament 'some two or three years' previously.[52] O'Connell later claimed to have heard stories of Raphael's dishonesty at this time, and said that 'more than once' he was told that 'there was no relying upon him—that he was a faithless person'.[53] But O'Connell insisted that he had ignored these charges, because he himself was used to being regularly abused and calumniated against. As a result, O'Connell recommended Raphael for the seat in November 1834, in advance of the general election (at a cost of £3,000), though Raphael declined to stand.[54] He invited him to stand again in advance of the election in January 1835, but once more Raphael refused. But following the unseating of the sitting MPs in May 1835 Raphael was willing to be persuaded.

O'Connell promised to take care of all of the details of the election, assuring Raphael that he would only have to contribute £2,000 towards the costs of the contest. 'You will never again meet so safe a speculation,' promised O'Connell.[55] Half the money would be paid in advance, the other half in the event that Raphael was elected, with O'Connell promising that he would not have to spend any 'other expense whatsoever, whether of agents, carriages, counsel, petition against the return, or of any other description'.[56] In fact, O'Connell went so far as to guarantee that Raphael would not have to pay 'one shilling more in any event or upon any contingency'. Raphael accepted these terms and arranged payment of the first £1,000. It is hard to see the transaction in a good light. If the actual cost of the election was £2,000, as O'Connell later insisted, then he would have asked for that amount up front. Otherwise O'Connell was promising to make himself responsible for half the costs of the campaign in the event that Raphael was defeated. In reality O'Connell was using his own name and reputation to get a man with no Irish connections elected for an Irish constituency, with the intention of using any profits to defray the costs he was facing elsewhere.

In the beginning the plan worked perfectly. On 19 June Raphael was elected MP for Co. Carlow, with another pro-Repeal candidate, Nicholas Aylward Vigors, taking the second seat. O'Connell immediately went looking for the payment of the first £1,000 insisting, 'It is time this were done.'[57] But a petition was soon presented against Raphael and Vigors challenging the validity of their election. Fearing the result, O'Connell asked Raphael if he would like to be made a baronet, though he was unable to deliver on this offer. He also pressed Raphael for the payment of the second £1,000. Raphael refused initially, claiming that under the terms of their agreement this was only to be paid in the event of victory, and that he had been promised that any petition expenses would be covered. But O'Connell reacted angrily, demanding the money, and accusing Raphael of shrinking 'from performing your engagement with me'.[58] Embarrassed, Raphael paid the second £1,000 over to O'Connell, as a sign of good faith on his part. But he was understandably hurt that the terms of the original agreement were being broken, and he reproached O'Connell for the unwarranted tone of his accusations.[59] Things quickly became worse for Raphael. On 4 August he discovered that he had to pay entirely for the defence of the Carlow seat, and was placed 'in the painful dilemma of either running away from the fight' or spending even more money.[60] By this time O'Connell was ignoring all pleas for help, and Raphael continued on, feeling insecure and abandoned. The verdict went against him and on 19 August and both he and Vigors were unseated, with their opponents, Bruen and Kavanagh, returned in their place.

It is not clear where the £2,000 went. It seems that part of the first £1,000 went to pay for some of the legal expenses which had accrued following the initial petition which unseated Bruen and Kavanagh. According to O'Connell the rest of the money went to the Carlow Liberal Club to secure the election of Raphael. O'Connell was left vulnerable despite his claims. Even if none of the money ended up in his account, it was still wrong to be trading in parliamentary seats. It was also clear from the correspondence that he had broken his word to Raphael, and should have paid for the costs of the disputed election. And if financial gain was at the heart of it then he risked charges of pecuniary corruption, and the destruction of his reputation.

Unable to get compensation from O'Connell, Raphael reluctantly decided to make the whole thing public. He published the entire correspondence of the transactions—copies of his letters as well as O'Connell's—as a pamphlet in the autumn.[61] By posing the question 'Can O'Connell be made to blush?', the pamphlet exposed his obdurate refusal to ever accept he was wrong.[62] The controversy was widely discussed in Ireland after the *Freeman's Journal* reprinted the most damaging letters on 3 November 1835. People were able to read everything in black and white, and make up their own minds, and the whole affair reflected terribly on O'Connell. Not only had he tried to sell a seat in parliament to someone with no connection to the county (or even the country), he had then reneged on his promises when things went wrong. It was shabby treatment at best, outright corruption at worst, and the affair exposed the very worst aspects of O'Connell's character. The weakness with money, a problem since the age of fourteen, now appeared to have developed into venality. Worse, his callous disregard for those who differed from him was also revealed, and his brutish determination to get his own way. According to Charles Gavan Duffy it was not unusual to hear 'influential adherents whisper' that the farmers of Carlow should have been fighting for something more worthy than trying to secure a baronetcy for 'a successful Cockney confectioner'.[63]

The Times, which was continuing its long-running feud with O'Connell, could not believe its good luck. Over a number of months it mocked 'King Dan' in verse for 'selling the county of Carlow'. One poem, 'The Three Thieves', was representative:

> Let Englishmen talk of their brave Robin Hood,
> Let the Scotch to Rob Roy fill a can;
> But "ould Ireland" can show them a thief quite as good
> She can show them her beautiful Dan!

Though Robin made booty, as sure 'twas his duty,
Of many a lawyer 'tis true;
Yet O'Connell (great thief!) has surpass'd all belief,
For, by Jove, he has cheated a Jew![64]

This affair was an excuse to attack him on all fronts, and the poem 'The Whig missionary of 1835' did so viciously on 26 November 1835. Catching the Irish nation in the crossfire of its racist rant, it abused O'Connell for his refusal to duel, and expressed a hope that he would end up being hanged for his treason:

Safe from challenge—safe from law
What can curb thy callous jaw?
Who would sue a convict liar?
On a poltroon who would fire?
Then grant the monster leave to roam,
Let him slaver out his foam,
Only give him length of string,
He'll contrive himself to swing.

It was as nasty an assault as O'Connell had ever withstood. But he had known for a long time that those working for the paper hated him, and he welcomed their hatred.

With so much heat being generated, it was only a matter of time before the Raphael affair reached the House of Commons. On 11 February 1836, when parliament resumed, John Hardy, the MP for Bradford, moved for a parliamentary enquiry into the allegations, accusing O'Connell of trafficking in seats. Hardy liked to call O'Connell the 'Agitator', and on the day of the debate he 'abused O'Connell right and left', and with such boldness and bitterness that he made a considerable impression on the House. The speech was credited with, in the short term at least, raising Hardy from 'the size of an oratorical dwarf to the dimensions of a giant'.[65]

In the course of the discussion John O'Connell's role as intermediary was mentioned. This guaranteed a response, and when Hardy rose to present his petition he was interrupted by O'Connell, who rose at the same time. When it was suggested that O'Connell should give way he replied, dismissively, 'No, I will not,' and he proceeded to address the

House.[66] He began by welcoming the inquiry, claiming that it was necessary to clear him completely. But he then denounced Hardy for dragging his son John into the matter without giving any advance notice. O'Connell became increasingly emotional as he attacked the conspiracy of what he called 'the Orange den' to destroy him and his family. And he declared that he did not envy 'the Orange triumph, which amounts to aiming a dagger at my heart, that falls blunted from the shield of the honour and integrity of my upright, loved, pure, and (except through falsehood) my unimpeachable son'. Mocking the men arrayed against him for having discovered a 'new-born love of purity', while themselves paying twenty pounds for a vote, he reaffirmed his principles as a radical reformer.[67] In a subsequent debate he mocked his opponents for thinking that elections were only about patriotism and had nothing to do with 'pounds, shillings, and pence'. He reminded them, 'Alas, Sir, pounds, shillings, and pence are absolutely necessary!'[68]

The committee examined Raphael on 29 February but it was unable to produce enough evidence to support his allegations. And so in April the committee issued a report exonerating O'Connell of all charges of corruption, although it did criticise him for having acted intemperately. Hardy attempted to return to the affair in parliament, but he was voted down and the discussion was brought to an end on 22 April. The entire controversy was deeply wounding for O'Connell, with his conduct and his finances discussed daily in the English newspapers for six months, and the affair raised at every Tory meeting and dinner. During the general election in 1837 it was claimed in Carlow that Ireland had become 'the arena of strife, of violence and corruption, where every adventurer, provided he had a sufficient sum in his hand—be he Christian, Heathen, Turk or Jew, is welcome'.[69]

There was also anxiety closer to home. In March 1836 John O'Connell was arrested for assaulting Ellen Courtenay's son, and the case went to court.[70] The return of the Courtenay scandal caused further distress to O'Connell and his family. O'Connell had planned another crusade against the House of Lords, this time across the manufacturing centres of England, but the tour collapsed in the wake of the Courtenay story and the accompanying attacks in *The Times*. At the start of the tour Mary O'Connell, although seriously unwell, accompanied her husband to show she did not believe any of the stories about his immorality. At Nottingham the women of the area presented her with a lace veil in 'admiration of the domestic support and zealous encouragement which she has always given her husband in his political career, especially in periods of the greatest trial, difficulty, and discouragement'. Whether or not the stories of O'Connell's infidelities were true, they were certainly very distressing for Mary O'Connell, and the public scandal and the public attention were likely to have exacerbated her final illness.

Disraeli continued his attacks on O'Connell throughout 1836. In a series of articles, published under the name of 'Runnymede' in *The Times* but soon attributed to him, Disraeli asked, 'Who is this O'Connell?' before denouncing him as 'the hired instrument of the papacy'.[71] O'Connell's 'moral character' was also dissected: 'he has committed every crime that does not require courage; the man who plunders the peasant can also starve his child'.[72] And it was claimed that his sole objective was 'the destruction of every thing which is English'. Disraeli was attempting to make his name in politics (and secure a seat in parliament in the process) by attacking the character of O'Connell, and the alliance with the Whigs. Proclaiming himself to be defending the British empire, he accused O'Connell of being 'a rebel without dignity, and a demagogue without courage', who represented a people who could never be conciliated. With startling aggression he insisted the Irish hated 'our order, our civilisation, our decorous liberty, our pure religion . . . our free and fertile isle'.[73] If ever people might question O'Connell's use of violent language or his relentless determination to vindicate the rights of his countrymen, they would understand him better if they studied a selection of these letters: '[The Irish] are a wild, reckless, indolent, uncertain, and superstitious race . . . A savage population'.[74]

Disraeli's mentor was Lord Lyndhurst, a man who had cynically switched sides on the question of Catholic emancipation for political advancement in the 1820s. Even Lyndhurst's sympathetic biographer considered it 'the least brilliant part of his history'.[75] Twice lord chancellor of England, he was so close to Disraeli it was rumoured (probably correctly) that they shared a mistress, Henrietta Sykes.[76] Always an enemy, O'Connell dismissed Lyndhurst as a 'lying miscreant' and 'a contumelious cur' during his mission to Scotland in September 1835. In the summer of 1836 Lyndhurst became a national hate-figure in Ireland, quoted as having dismissed the Irish as 'aliens in blood, language, and religion'. The reality is that he never said those exact words, but however much he tried to deny the attribution he was never believed.[77] The phrase became indelibly linked to him, and the Irish MPs went to great lengths to attack and abuse him for it. Nevertheless, what he actually said was close enough in content, and almost identical in intent, and it is clear that he was being disingenuous in his denials. What had happened was that during the debate on the Irish municipal corporations bills on 9 May 1836 Lyndhurst spoke about the problems of the Protestants of Ireland, and described them as being surrounded by 'a population alien to Englishmen, speaking, many of them, a different language, professing a different religion, regarding the English as invaders, and ready to expel them at the first opportunity'.[78]

It was only a matter of time before O'Connell responded. In the autumn he launched a withering attack on Lyndhurst, lashing out not just on the specific attack on Irish Catholics, but also attempting to get revenge for all the attacks on his character. Calling Lyndhurst 'the accursed', and the bitterest enemy of Ireland, he threatened to bring forward all 'the hideous details of his life' unless 'the miscreant' stopped his attacks on Ireland.[79] Not surprisingly, *The Times* rushed to the defence of Lyndhurst. It laughed at what 'an unredeemed and unredeemable scoundrel is this O'Connell', who threatened other politicians with disclosures 'with his own wife dying under his eyes'. And the editors threatened that if he dared invade the privacy of Lyndhurst, 'or of any other man, woman, or child', they would 'carry the war into his own domiciles at Derrynane and Dublin, and show up the whole brood of O'Connells, young and old'. In a furious response, O'Connell told the editors that he hurled at them, 'foul miscreants as you are, the most contemptuous and emphatic defiance!' And he promised them that while they were free to write whatever stories they wanted, he would not 'condescend to contradict a single falsehood you publish', but would ignore their assaults. 'Defiance, loud and indignant, is hurled at you, vile instruments,' he raged, 'and at your more vile employers!'

Grief and anxiety consumed O'Connell in this period. His eldest son, Maurice, became seriously ill, and O'Connell feared he would die. He consulted with some of the leading medical men in Ireland to see what should be done, and made plans to send him abroad to a warmer climate.[80] It is hard to diagnose Maurice's ailment. In part it was physical, caused by a problem with his lungs, but it also seems to have been to some extent psychological, related to problems connected to his marriage. The marriage seems to have become unhappy very quickly, and broke down completely in 1841. It has been claimed that his wife, Mary, had mental problems, and that Maurice fathered several children with local women in Co. Kerry, which 'contributed to the folk image of his father as a promiscuous seducer'.[81]

The worst blow of all was the death of O'Connell's beloved wife. She had been ill for much of 1835 and declined rapidly in 1836. On 4 September 1836 O'Connell realised that his wife had not much longer to live. He despaired that 'She may linger weeks. One week may—Oh God help me!'[82] Becoming increasingly gloomy, he said that 'Hope, which comes to all, comes not to me.'[83] For the rest of his life O'Connell would be unable to discuss his wife in public without breaking down in tears, and his grief seems to have been tinged with guilt at having not been able to protect her from the attacks of his enemies. Mary O'Connell died at Derrynane on 31 October. O'Connell mourned the loss of a woman who he described as '[t]he purest spirit that ever dwelt in a human breast'.[84] He claimed that she 'did not believe in the existence of evil', and insisted that she would demand that he devote his energies, 'even in misery, to Ireland'.

O'Connell's first public event after the funeral was a meeting of the General Association of Ireland, a new short-lived organisation which sought municipal and tithe reform, on 10 November. Appearing to be suffering 'great mental affliction', he began by announcing that he was determined to 'devote every moment of the rest of my existence to the cause of my country'.[85] Death, he claimed, no longer had any fear for him, and he promised to keep working until he saw his country happy, 'and her injuries avenged by liberty'. And so he resolved that his 'great consolation will be a dogged and determined activity in the cause of Ireland'.

O'CONNELL IN PARLIAMENT, 1835–1840

'There he is! That's O'Connell!'[1] There was always great excitement whenever Daniel O'Connell made his way into the chamber of the House of Commons. Wearing a cloak and a wide-brimmed hat, he would elbow his way along, with 'a grin, a jest, and an Irish greeting for every one he meets', and always seem to be in the best of spirits. This was all part of the performance, for at times he would have trouble sleeping 'when any matter of importance impended'.[2] Indeed, his son John later claimed that he was 'one of the most sensitive and nervous men that ever lived'.[3] But O'Connell was the consummate actor, the master performer, and could mask his inner feelings while exuding an outward image of confidence and determination. An expert observer of public speakers noted that whenever O'Connell spoke of the degradation of his country, 'not a man among them but felt his own degradation and hers, and bemoaned it in his heart'.[4] And whenever he spoke of the people responsible for this degradation 'there was not a man among them but who felt his soul stirred to action, and upon whose ear every word fell like the blast of the trumpet upon the war horse'. No wonder it was said, 'He is a dangerous man, is that O'Connell.'[5]

Tall and athletic, O'Connell was one of the most muscular figures in the House. Those who did not know of him might have thought he was a man in his thirties, so healthy did he appear, and indeed he liked to boast that he would follow his uncle, Hunting Cap, and live until he was nearly one hundred.[6] His face was large, but not fat, and had a freshness and ruddiness about it which seemed to reflect his 'good health and excellent spirits'. Close up, it was noticable that he wore a dark brown wig, which had a 'rough and uproarious appearance', and which seemed rarely to have been combed. Most days he wore a dark green coat, and a wide-brimmed hat which was cocked to the right side of his head in the style of a ship's captain. Indeed, he was often mistaken for a ship's captain by strangers. He would usually take a seat, 'upon the second row of the benches', and cross his right leg over his left, while following the speeches that were being made.

James Grant, a gallery reporter and one of the shrewdest judges of the quality of speakers in the House of Commons, considered O'Connell an orator 'of the highest order of genius'.[7] Although Sir Robert Peel had greater tact and dexterity in debate, he believed that there was no one who compared to O'Connell 'in point of genius'. 'You can see the greatness of his genius in almost every sentence he utters,' Grant insisted, adding that 'it ever and anon bursts forth with a brilliancy and effect which are quite overwhelming'. According to Grant, it was impossible to weigh up the quality of his arguments when he was speaking, for you were 'taken captive wherever he chose to lead you, from beginning to end'.[8] Any 'untenable positions' or 'inconclusive reasonings' were only detected once he had sat down, 'and his voice no longer greets his ear'. To appreciate his oratory, then, you had to hear it rather than read it, as the energy and enthusiasm cast a spell on its listeners, even on those who 'despised the cause and hated the advocate'.[9] Contributing to the success of O'Connell was his ability to incorporate into his speech things which had just been said in the debate, something that few of his contemporaries were able to do.

'Ten to one but the first sentence he utters is a joke.'[10] Some speakers were good at delivering humorous speeches, others were better at serious topics, but O'Connell excelled at doing both within the same speech, making the transition from one to the other without any difficulty. Indeed, he often seemed to be 'himself insensible of the transition'.[11] When O'Connell discussed some topic of an affecting nature, Grant observed on many occasions 'the tear literally glistening in the eyes of men altogether unused to the melting mood', and, 'in a moment afterwards, by a transition from the grave to the humorous, the whole audience convulsed with laughter'. O'Connell's 'careless comicality of manner' was quite irresistible, and usually brought forward 'an unanswerable peal of laughter'. Making a hostile crowd laugh (or cry) is no easy task, but the genius of O'Connell as a speaker was his ability to dominate his listeners and control their emotional response. Indeed, Grant often heard O'Connell begin many speeches 'in a strain of the most exquisite humour and, by a sudden transition to deep pathos, produce the stillness of death in a place which, but one moment before, the air was rent with shouts of laughter'.

In this way he was able to manipulate the emotions of his listeners: 'The passions of his audience are mere playthings in his hand.'[12] Charles Dickens's first job was as a parliamentary reporter and in later years he spoke of the impression which O'Connell's oratory had on him. He long remembered the description of a widow seeking her only son among the peasants killed by soldiers, and of a young girl shot while leading her blind grandfather down a country lane, images that were so powerful emotionally that for some minutes he was unable to continue and had to put down his pencil.[13] In the same period James Grant attended a dinner at Hackney, in London, where O'Connell addressed an audience of two hundred and fifty people, most of whom were strangers. O'Connell spoke of a young Irish girl, who had been murdered by soldiers who were enforcing the collection of tithes, in such moving terms that there was 'hardly a dry eye in the meeting'.[14] At the end of the speech there was a standing ovation and 'almost every person present' rushed to shake his hand. 'Modern times cannot furnish a parallel to this splendid proof of the effect produced by oratory,' wrote Grant in amazement.[15]

In 1835 there were many examples of O'Connell's use of humour to neutralise an opponent. For example, on 22 June 1835 O'Connell was attacked by Sir Robert Inglis, who accused him and the other Roman Catholic MPs of violating their oaths and acting against the interests of the British constitution.[16] Inglis always spoke in a 'drawling, whining sort of way', in a style that was more suited to the pulpit than the senate. O'Connell chose to use humour to destroy him. He dismissed Inglis as 'fat, sleek, and contented', and exclaimed, 'amidst bursts of laughter', 'Oh! The misery of being taunted with perjury in such a drawling, hum-drum speech! Why, the whining manner in which the charge is made is worse than the charge itself!'[17]

A month later, during the second reading of the Irish church bill, on 23 July 1835, O'Connell noticed that John Walter, the MP for Berkshire and proprietor of *The Times*, had gone over from the government side and was now sitting with some friends who had recently joined the opposition. Seeing an opportunity to have some fun, O'Connell exclaimed, 'Oh, the honourable member has gone over!' And he joked that Walter had grown bored sitting by himself, quoting some lines from a popular song of the day, 'Like the last rose of summer left blooming alone/All its lovely companions being faded and gone.' According to one MP who was present, it was 'impossible to convey any idea of the effect which this produced'.[18] There were shouts of laughter, and even Walter's close friends 'could not refrain from joining in the loud peals of laughter which burst from all parts of the house'. Immediately afterwards, Walter resumed his seat on the government benches, and it was speculated that his humiliation at the hands of O'Connell was the cause of his return.

The rapidity with which O'Connell could construct a devastating attack on his opponents was one of his greatest strengths. He was the master of the spontaneous response, and had a talent for producing at will something that was both humorous and cutting. During the debate on the grant to Maynooth College on 30 July 1838 three MPs, William Verner, MP for Armagh; Charles Sibthorp, MP for Lincoln; and Alexander Perceval, MP for Sligo, made violent attacks on the Catholic clergy in Ireland. All three men held the rank of colonel, and so O'Connell decided to mock 'these gallant colonels' by parodying the famous lines of John Dryden, 'Three poets, in three distant ages born', from the poem *Lines printed under the engraved portrait of Milton*. He began:

> Three colonels, in three distant counties born,
> Did Lincoln, Sligo, and Armagh adorn;
> The first in gravity of face surpassed—
> In grace the second—
> Sobriety the last.
> The force of nature could no further go;
> To beard the first she shaved the other two.[19]

'There was much laughter at this sally', and the verse left the three colonels red-faced and humiliated.

Many noted that O'Connell did not excel as a logical debater. Rather, his strength was in creating an impression, or a feeling, and then using humour to discomfit an opponent. He spoke in short, pithy sentences. His 'broad Irish accent', though 'somewhat strange' to an English ear, was not a problem, and his voice was considered 'rich, clear, strong, and often musical'. Some believed that O'Connell's intonations were regulated, unconsciously, by 'his feelings alone'. If the subject was not one 'involving important principles, or one which appeals to his feelings' there was a certain coldness about his manner, 'and a monotony about the tones of his voice, which is sure to make a person who has never heard him before, go away with an unfavourable impression of his talents, and wondering how he could ever have attained to so much popularity'. Occasionally he would stammer slightly, 'simply from two or more ideas struggling at the same moment in his mind for priority of birth'. Grant sometimes observed O'Connell, 'in the conflict of ideas', breaking off abruptly mid-sentence because of some 'brilliant thought suggesting itself at the moment'. A more artificial speaker, Grant believed, would finish the old sentence first before discussing the new idea.

'The great characteristics of Mr O'Connell's manner are its boldness, its fervour, and its utter disregard for all artificial forms.'[20] When speaking, O'Connell's gestures were awkward and ungraceful. Sometimes mid-speech he would raise his arms above his head, his fists clenched as if he was about to start a fight, but at the next moment his head would be thrown back with 'his arms placed akimbo on his breast'. At times he would grab at his wig violently as if he was about to tear it into pieces, but then calm down and adjust it carefully.

Few, if any, could match O'Connell when it came to vituperation. It was said that he did not strike at an enemy, rather he seized him 'with Herculean force, squeezes the breath out of him, and then bandies him to and fro as though he were tossing him in a blanket'. His enemy would then be dismissed 'with a contemptuous kick—and a nickname that sticks to him for the rest of his life'.[21] O'Connell gave every indication that he loved being in the 'midst of the political storm and tempest and whirlwind'. Indeed, he once admitted that independent of the merits of the struggle, he exulted in the struggle itself. In the House of Commons he always appeared in great spirits, radiating confidence that he would succeed in his mission: 'You see a perpetual smile on his countenance, whether he be addressing the house or reclining in his seat.' As a result, he never held a grudge over something that was said in the chamber. In

1835 he was attacked by Hughes Hughes, the MP for Oxford, who accused him of ordering skulls and cross-bones to be painted on the doors of those electors in Cork who would not vote for his candidate. In a violent response, O'Connell denounced Hughes as a calf's head. A few nights later both men were observed walking arm in arm up Parliament Street, on their way home from the House.

O'Connell took the job of being an MP very seriously. 'From twelve to four o'clock every day I was in regular attendance at the committees,' he once told a friend.[22] 'Going home, I took a hearty dinner, and proceeded to the House, and continued in it until twelve or one. I was never absent. By the time I got to bed it was generally two.' O'Connell recognised that age was creeping up on him, and 'a man at my time of life generally requires some sleep'. But, as he 'was never fond of it', he would get up and have breakfast at nine a.m. From ten o'clock until twelve o'clock he would attempt to read his large daily correspondence. 'Heaven help me! I don't exaggerate when I say I generally got two hundred letters a day.' This was also a considerable expense, as postage for most letters at this time was not prepaid, and so he would have to have paid approximately ten pounds a day for his mail. All anonymous letters were burnt unread, but he made sure the others were all gone through. Most were requests for jobs. O'Connell later admitted that there was not an office 'from lord high admiral down to scavenger that I have not been asked for'. Following the Lichfield House alliance the Whig government was regularly abused for being under the control of O'Connell, and O'Connell believed that this made securing patronage even more difficult. He admitted that 'it has caused a reaction against me, and I believe there is not a man who votes with them who gets less from them than I'. Many of the requests from Ireland began with the salutation 'Great Liberator and Father of your Country'. But O'Connell was particularly amused by one letter which began 'Awful Sir!'

On 29 July 1835 there was a debate in committee on a proposed grant to Maynooth College. This was opposed by Frederick Shaw, the MP for the University of Dublin, who argued that only the established church should be supported by the state. O'Connell attacked Shaw for his 'spiritual ferocity' and for seemingly thinking that the Protestant religion consisted of nothing more than 'pounds, shillings, and pence'.[23] In response, Shaw accused O'Connell of attempting to subvert the established church which he had sworn to uphold. O'Connell was furious, accusing Shaw of uttering 'falsehoods', and there was uproar in the chamber which did not subside for several minutes. Shaw became deeply upset, and abused O'Connell for adopting as his symbol 'a death's head and cross-bones'. But O'Connell dismissed him for being 'a calf's head and jaw-bones'. There were cries of 'Order, order!' and 'Chair, chair!' from the floor, before the committee continued.

Sometimes O'Connell would go out of his way to be rude in the chamber. To disconcert an opponent he would occasionally yawn as loudly as he could, 'as if he was infinitely weary of the commonplaces and inanities of a member attacking him'.[24] For example, during a debate on the municipal corporations (Ireland) bill on 7 March 1836 he yawned loudly twice during the speech of Sir James Graham, who was so distracted he pleaded with O'Connell not to again subject him 'to so unseemly an interruption'. A few nights later O'Connell again emitted a loud yawn during a particularly boring speech by Sir Henry Inglis.

14 June 1836 was a date that was long remembered in the history of the House of Commons. An ordinary debate on the municipal corporations bill for Ireland was turned into one of the most entertaining exchanges in memory. Afterwards it was said that if a foreigner had entered the gallery on that day he would have thought he had entered into 'some theatre for the performance of farces of the broadest kind', rather than the imperial parliament.[25] The 'farce' began when O'Connell began abusing John Walter, the MP for Berkshire and proprietor of *The Times*, because of his running war with the paper. O'Connell joked that Walter was confused and believed he was 'writing a paragraph instead of making a speech'.[26] John Hodson Kearsley, the MP for Wigan, interrupted O'Connell, insisting that MPs would not submit to his bullying. But O'Connell responding by joking that he hoped Walter enjoyed his new ally: 'They are two kindred spirits—they are admirably suited to each other.'[27] There were shouts of laughter, much to the annoyance of Kearsley. O'Connell continued his attack on Walter, when John Richards, the MP for Knaresborough, rose to intervene. Although a feeble and monotonous speaker, Richards was never afraid of challenging O'Connell, and he announced that he would not allow him to 'browbeat and ruffianise' the MP for Berkshire. O'Connell was delighted with this intervention and he congratulated Walter on his second defender, joking that 'nothing could be more flattering to him than the first—except the second'. This was delivered

in such a 'sly humorous way' that there was 'a deafening peal of laughter from all parts of the House'. O'Connell followed it up by saying that Richards was so 'remarkable for his own exceeding delicacy and extreme polish' that it was no surprise that he 'must necessarily shrink from anything which savours of the kennel'. There followed much laughter and confusion, but Richards was not to be humiliated so easily. He rose to accuse O'Connell of bringing into the House 'the manners of a blackguard', to almost equal amounts of cheering and condemnation. All the time O'Connell sat with his arms akimbo and his hat cocked on one side. It was said that 'his countenance told with what zest he enjoyed the scene'.[28]

The Speaker intervened and said that improper terms had been used on both sides, and called on members not to make personal allusions to one another. One MP demanded that Richards withdraw the word 'ruffianise', which he insisted he would only do if O'Connell withdrew the word 'kennel'. But O'Connell assured the members that he considered the application of the epithet in question by Richards 'as the greatest compliment which could be bestowed on him'. His 'laughing countenance', and the tone in which these words were delivered, threw everybody, except Walter, Kearsley, and Richards, into another 'fit of laughter'. Again Richards was called upon to withdraw the word 'ruffianise', but by now he was so angry that he merely suggested that if O'Connell had not applied the word 'kennel' to him then he had not applied the word 'ruffianise' either.

This should have settled things, but O'Connell reignited the controversy by observing that Richards was such an unfortunate speaker he did not even seem to be aware of what he was saying. There was further uproar and Robert Scarlett, the MP for Norwich, rose to his feet to lecture O'Connell on his unparliamentary language. O'Connell listened patiently and then rose to reply. Crossing his arms on his breast, he looked at Scarlett with 'a most contemptuous smile', and exclaimed, 'Behold a third advocate!'[29] He joked that this should be a source of congratulation for the honourable MP for Berkshire, adding that he did not think 'a *fourth* could be found in the House!' It was said afterwards that 'never did the performance of any farce at a theatre' produce as much laughter as these exchanges on the floor of the House of Commons. Eventually order was restored and Edward Goulburn, MP for Leicester, rose to ask the Speaker whether O'Connell's behaviour should be permitted in the House. Before the Speaker was able to reply, O'Connell again rose to his feet and said, 'I thought that a fourth advocate of the honourable member for Berkshire could not be found; but I forgot at the time that the right honourable gentleman [Goulburn] was in the House.' This provoked further laughter, and loud calls for order, and Joseph Jackson, the MP for Bandon, rose and shouted at the Speaker for something to be done about O'Connell. 'What!' exclaimed O'Connell, pointing at Jackson with his finger, 'a *fifth* advocate! Are they . . .' But he was never able to complete his sentence because the laughter from one side and the shouting from the other produced such a cacophony that nothing more could be heard. Later it was speculated that he had intended to ask, 'Are they to stretch to the crack of doom?'

Few enjoyed the cut-and-thrust of parliamentary politics as much as O'Connell. On 23 February 1838 he was called to order in the House by a new MP, the twenty-three-year-old Lord Maidstone, over comments he had made at a dinner in the Crown and Anchor two days earlier. At this dinner O'Connell had accused the Tories of committing gross perjury when sitting on election committees and the comments had been reported widely. Maidstone's request was greeted with 'deafening noise', and the government (Whig) benches looked 'as grave as if their own doom' was at stake as they waited to see how O'Connell would respond. There was a sudden transition 'to the most death-like stillness' as O'Connell rose to speak. Everyone expected O'Connell to challenge the accuracy of the published report or to explain away the offensive matter as having been misinterpreted. But, 'in a firm and steady voice', O'Connell thanked Maidstone for having brought the matter before the House, and declared, 'Sir, I did say every word of that.'[30] 'It is impossible to convey an idea of the emphasis and energy of the manner with which the honourable gentleman delivered this last sentence.' The Whigs cheered, the Tories shouted and jeered, and the entire scene, according to one observer, baffled description. With even greater emphasis and energy, O'Connell added, 'Yes, sir, every word of that; and I do repeat that I believe it to be perfectly true.' 'The violent contention of sounds again burst' forth, this time 'with redoubled fury', and many MPs kept shouting until they were out of breath. Supporters clapped or struck their hands on their knees, while opponents also displayed their disapproval with 'violent bodily gestures'.

When the noise died down, O'Connell provoked further scenes by asking, 'is there a man who will put his hand on his heart, and say upon his honour that he does not believe this to be true?' To loud shouts of 'No! No!' and 'Yes! Yes!', O'Connell added, 'If there be such a man he would be laughed to scorn.' There were cries of 'Oh! Oh!' and 'vehement cheers'. Describing it as 'a hideous abuse', O'Connell attempted to remind the House of a previous time when he had spoken on the subject but he was interrupted by cries of 'Order! Order!' The Speaker called on Maidstone to reveal what motion he meant to submit on the subject, and the Tories were filled with confusion, having not expected O'Connell to admit and repeat the charges. About ten men surrounded Maidstone, each suggesting a different course, and 'Poor Lord Maidstone was most of all to be pitied.' He looked imploringly to Peel for advice, but none was forthcoming. Deciding to go on the attack, Maidstone gave notice of a motion the following week which would bring O'Connell's conduct before the House. The Tories exulted, the Whigs appeared defeated and downcast, but the positions were reversed within a few minutes when Lord John Russell rose and gave notice that on the same day he would put forward the allegations of the bishop of Exeter respecting a charge of perjury against certain members of the House. This was only a delaying tactic, though, for the bishop's charge related to an MP who had lost his seat in the last election, and thus was not relevant.

On Monday 26 February, the motion of Lord Maidstone respecting O'Connell's comments was introduced and it passed by nine votes after a tense two-hour debate. What followed afterwards was even more extraordinary than the events of the previous week. Joseph Hume, the MP for Kilkenny, denied the right of the House to censor what members said outside of parliament, and he was joined in this by Daniel Callaghan, the MP for Cork, who delivered a stirring defence of O'Connell. Henry Grattan Jnr dared the House to send O'Connell to Newgate, which was greeted with ironical cheers by the Tories, and Lord John Russell called the reprimand 'the most faint-hearted, the most pusillanimous course that ever could be adopted'.[31] Morgan O'Connell attempted to defend his father, but there were too many interruptions, and he could only make himself 'occasionally understood'. Two hundred and fifty Tory MPs rose as one to call for order as the debate went on, and finally the proceedings were adjourned for the day. It was considered one of the most violent exhibitions in the House of

Commons for over fifty years.[32] The debate resumed the next day and concluded the following night when the Speaker called O'Connell to his place to reprimand him. 'Mr O'Connell!' shouted the Speaker. 'Here, sir!' replied O'Connell, rising to his feet. In the name of the House, the Speaker delivered a severe reprimand to O'Connell for the intemperate and improper language he had used at the Crown and Anchor. O'Connell seemed to enjoy the rebuke, and he 'never seemed more in his element in his life'. A few minutes later he quitted the House. As he was leaving he was joined by an MP who said, 'So, they have been reprimanding you!' 'Yes,' replied O'Connell with a smile, 'and *I* have been reprimanding *them*.'[33]

The debate on 11 June 1840, on a bill for the registration of voters in Ireland, was also long remembered. Once again Lord Maidstone was O'Connell's key adversary, but this time he was quite drunk on his feet. Affecting a superior tone, Thomas Macaulay wrote in his diary that Maidstone was 'so ill-mannered that I hope he was drunk'.[34] Attacking the legislation, which had been presented by Maidstone, O'Connell highlighted the hypocrisy of those who championed the Union but who still insisted on an entirely different system for Irish voters. There was uproar when he dismissed the bill as 'a bill to trample on the rights of the people of Ireland', a phrase which he repeated three times in the face of persistent whistling and shouting. Scorning this abuse, O'Connell observed that even if his opponents were 'ten times as beastly in your uproar and bellowing, I should still feel it to be my duty to interpose to prevent this injustice'.[35] There arose such a storm of protest that Macaulay believed that no outdoor mob could have equalled the noise: 'Men on both sides stood up, shook their fists, and bawled at the top of their voices.'[36]

O'Connell was in his element. Macaulay said he 'raged like a mad bull', but that many people 'thought it much extenuated by the provocation'. Asked to explain his language, O'Connell was unrepentant. He admitted that he used the words 'beastly' and 'bellowing', but he demanded to know if anyone had ever heard of any bellowing that was not beastly, asking, 'What sounds were they? Were they human sounds?' When challenged a second time on whether he had used 'certain expressions' which were unparliamentary, O'Connell was equally defiant: 'Yes, sir, I have.' He then abused the architect of the bill, Lord Maidstone, for long being an enemy of Ireland, and assured him that although the legislation was 'tyrannical and despotic' it would not pass. Sir Benjamin Hall rushed to Maidstone's defence and attempted to insult O'Connell by telling him that he could not understand what he was saying, though 'if he will speak in plainer terms, perhaps I may'. But O'Connell retorted that he had not that misfortune: sadly, he understood Hall well enough.

The clash had begun at six p.m. and had continued until after one a.m., and only ended 'from absolute physical weariness'. Amidst all the tumult, Maidstone addressed O'Connell directly and told him, 'If the word beastly is retracted, I shall be satisfied. If not, I shall not be satisfied.' O'Connell was unmoved. 'I do not care whether the noble lord be satisfied or not,' he replied. Maidstone was infuriated and tried to challenge O'Connell to a duel: 'I wish you would give me satisfaction.' But O'Connell had the ultimate put-down: 'I advise the noble lord to carry his liquor meekly.'[37] It was a one-line answer that captured the supreme self-confidence of O'Connell in parliament and the absolute dominance which he had at long last attained.

Chapter 7 ∾

DESPAIR AND DECLINE, 1837–1839

O'Connell 'was exceedingly fond of good novels', and he particularly enjoyed the works of Charles Dickens.[1] In 1837 he was impatient to follow the story of *Oliver Twist* (Dickens's second novel), which was serialised in *Bentley's Miscellany*.[2] He was equally impressed with Dickens's follow-up novel, *Nicholas Nickleby*, and was 'charmed' by the story of the idealistic young hero. But he was less happy with the ending of *The Old Curiosity Shop*, which was serialised weekly in Dickens's own publication, *Master Humphrey's Clock*, between 1840 and 1841. The story of what would happen to the young heroine, Nell Trent, captured not only O'Connell's imagination, but the imagination of the English-reading world. It was even said that some people stormed the piers of New York City to discover the fate of 'Little Nell' from visitors arriving from England. Lord Jeffrey famously declared that there had been 'nothing so good as Nell since Cordelia'.[3] As Michael Slater has noted, 'the story of Little Nell's wanderings around England with her helpless old grandfather, fleeing from Quilp, a grotesquely hideous, anarchic, and sexually predatory dwarf, is the most Romantic and fairy tale-like of Dickens's novels'.[4]

Dickens's decision to kill off Nell proved controversial. When O'Connell (who had been reading the story as a collected hardback) arrived at the death of Nell he threw away the book 'with a gesture of angry impatience' and exclaimed that he would never read another line that Dickens wrote: 'The fellow hadn't enough talent to keep up Nell's adventures with interest and bring them to a happy issue, so he kills her to get rid of the difficulty.' Of course, this was just the frustration of the moment, and O'Connell's love of Dickens survived the death of Little Nell. As he admitted some years later, 'Few people admire more the writings of Dickens, or read them with greater interest.'[5] O'Connell might have enjoyed the story more if he had realised his own contribution to its genesis. Given that Dickens often spoke in later years of how moved he was by a speech of O'Connell's about a young girl who died while helping her grandfather, it seems likely that the speech influenced one of the most famous sections of the book. O'Connell would later appear (although his name was never mentioned) in *Martin Chuzzlewit* (serialised monthly between 31 December 1842 and 30 June 1844), and his agitation for Repeal and the abolition of slavery was discussed over a number of pages.

O'Connell was also becoming a subject for biographers. In 1837 a lawyer, A.V. Kirwan, was asked to write a short biographical sketch of O'Connell for a French publication. And so he wrote to O'Connell requesting information on his birth and education, pressing for an immediate reply as the deadline was approaching.[6] O'Connell never responded, although he did acknowledge receiving the letter when he encountered Kirwan on the streets a few days later. Kirwan proceeded with his short biography and, when it was published, sent O'Connell a copy. It was, as he later admitted, 'a "biography" which even your most fulsome adulators call "flattering"'. But O'Connell was not flattered. Indeed, he was furious with what he perceived were serious inaccuracies and wrote an abusive letter to Kirwan demanding that the work be suppressed or corrected. There were three specific claims which made him consider it 'one of the most detailed libels that ever was penned against anybody'.[7] The first was the suggestion that O'Connell's family background was humble; the second was that he had not excelled as a student at St Omer; the third was that his rise at the bar had not been meteoric. O'Connell sent back the publication with thirty passages marked out, claiming he could have marked out as many more. And he threatened to bring legal action through the French courts if something was not done. He was not impressed by Kirwan's mention of 'fulsome flattery', insisting that his real problem was with the 'flagrant untruth'.[8] It was, even by O'Connell's standards, a massive over-reaction, especially as Kirwan had not been too far wrong. O'Connell's pedigree was not as great as he sometimes asserted; he was not 'first in the first class' at St Omer; and while he may have risen rapidly at the bar, it was certainly no reason for abusing someone who had interpreted his rise differently. Closing the correspondence with some dignity, Kirwan wrote to O'Connell that he was 'your candid and just "Biographer", but not your "fulsome flatterer" and *certainly* not *your abject slave*'.[9]

At the start of 1837 O'Connell felt obliged to issue a public statement clarifying his involvement with the Freemasons. This followed an article in *The Freemasons Quarterly Review* which claimed that he had once been 'a most prominent' member, and had only withdrawn because of the pressures of public business.[10] O'Connell admitted that he had once been a member, but that he had 'unequivocally renounced Freemasonry' after learning of the censure of the Catholic church. And while he accepted that there was 'no evil tendency' to Freemasonry in Ireland, he criticised the 'wanton and multiplied taking of oaths'. Archbishop Murray of Dublin was also contacted to make sure that there was nothing further that O'Connell needed to do to satisfy the Catholic church on the subject.

There was a by-election in Co. Longford in December 1836 and afterwards stories emerged of voter intimidation and corruption. In particular it was revealed that Peter Prunty, an illiterate Catholic farmer and registered voter, had been taken against his will and held prisoner at the home of Thomas Lefroy, and ordered to vote for Charles Fox, the Conservative candidate.[11] Prunty was led under guard to the place of voting, but when he passed his wife, Bridget, she shouted, 'Oh! Prunty, remember your soul and liberty!' Emboldened by this, Prunty voted for Luke White, the Repeal candidate, who was elected. O'Connell was impressed with the story of Bridget Prunty's courage, and ordered that 'some small token' should be presented to her, 'a shawl, a cloak, or other suitable article'.

The alliance with the Whigs brought some advantages. A measure of municipal reform for Ireland finally became law in 1840 and, although not as ambitious as O'Connell had hoped, it had important consequences for O'Connell's own career in the decade ahead. The Orange order was also forced to dissolve itself or risk being suppressed. A reform of the tithes system was passed in 1838 which went some way towards easing the burden on the peasants. More Catholics were appointed to office, and there was less overt prejudice against them. But in so many other ways it failed to bring the advantages O'Connell had hoped for. As time passed, and 'Justice for Ireland' remained as far away as ever, his popularity began to fall, as was clear from the declining annual returns to 'The O'Connell Tribute'. However, as O'Connell liked to joke, 'A Whig government is like Paddy's old hat thrust into a broken pane; it is true it doesn't let in much light, but at any rate it keeps out the *cold*.'[12]

O'Connell found it increasingly difficult to control his party in parliament. On 17 April Sir Henry Hardinge proposed a motion in parliament calling for the withdrawal of the British Legion, which was fighting in the Spanish civil war in favour of Queen Isabella's government and against the forces of Don Carlos.[13] The British Legion was a voluntary force which had government approval and many of the officers were Irish, including O'Connell's cousin, Colonel Maurice Charles O'Connell. O'Connell rushed to defend the involvement of the legion, claiming that if Don Carlos took power the inquisition would return and plunge the country into 'the deepest moral degradation'. After a three-day debate the motion was defeated but many of the Irish MPs absented themselves from the vote. O'Connell was furious, believing that their countrymen had been 'violently calumniated' by Hardinge.[14] He arranged for an article to be published in the *Pilot* under the heading 'Are they faithful or traitors?' Two MPs in particular were singled out for criticism, Frederick William Mullins, MP for Kerry, and William Smith O'Brien, MP for Limerick, who were called 'deserters and betrayers', with O'Brien accused of playing 'the fast and loose game'. The article contributed to Mullins's defeat in the general election in the summer.

In that general election O'Connell was determined to make absolutely certain of the result. He decided to be returned for Co. Kilkenny, where there wouldn't be a contest, and also stand in Co. Dublin, where there would be one. While he claimed that his plan was to remain as MP for Kilkenny, and let in another liberal to sit for Dublin if elected, it was clear that he had set his mind to representing the capital one more time.[15] His mission was to 'liberate Dublin', and after the trauma of the previous disputed election he was determined to succeed. Men were required to take an oath before voting, swearing that they had not received a bribe, and O'Connell made sure that there was no misconduct in any of the elections of his party. '*We must not be bribers*' became his constant refrain.[16] During the campaign King

William IV died and his niece, the eighteen-year-old Victoria, succeeded as queen. On 5 August O'Connell was elected for Dublin, and he celebrated his return as MP for the constituency. Almost as a matter of course the result was challenged by his opponents, and it was only on 26 March 1838 that the Dublin election committee confirmed the result. The challenge cost him close to £1,300, but he considered it 'a most glorious *escape* from the villains'.[17]

The first parliament of Queen Victoria's reign met on 15 November 1837. It was noticeable that when the MPs came forward to take the required oaths those on the Tory side delivered the lines attacking the Roman Catholic religion with great emphasis, while the Whigs ran through that section carelessly. There was a separate oath for Roman Catholic members, which was administered at the same time as they were being 'denounced by the Protestant members as idolaters'.[18] O'Connell entered the chamber by himself, and his appearance made an impression on his friends and supporters; 'his athletic person was recognised passing the bar, and swaggering up towards the table'. Indicating that he was ready to take the oaths, O'Connell was handed the oath of allegiance on a card, which he placed on the table. The clerk then began reading his copy, with O'Connell expected to follow. However, O'Connell was unable to read the card without his spectacles and began searching for them, 'first in one pocket, then in another', all the time attempting to repeat what the clerk was saying as best he could. By the time he found his spectacles, the clerk was already considerably further ahead, and O'Connell began reading the oath rapidly, and to observers it appeared to be a race between him and the clerk to see who would finish first. O'Connell seemed to place particular emphasis on certain expressions, for example the reference to being one of the most loyal subjects in her majesty's dominions. He then read the oath required by Roman Catholic members and, after finishing it, 'contemptuously tossed it down again on the table, as if he had either some private quarrel with it, or deemed it an altogether unnecessary affair'.[19]

The debate on the 'Spottiswoode conspiracy' was one of the most heated of that parliament. It was named after Andrew Spottiswoode, the queen's printer, who had organised a meeting at the London Coffee-House at Ludgate Hill on 30 August 1837. At this meeting resolutions had been passed accusing some of the Repeal MPs of being elected through intimidation and corruption, and called for a national subscription in Britain to protect the Protestant establishment by contesting these results. On 7 December William Smith O'Brien moved a motion in the Commons to have the whole thing declared a breach of privilege and a furious debate ensued. Earlier in the debate, there had been a controversy over a point of order, on which O'Connell intervened to resolve. Later, when he rose to speak on the 'Spottiswoode conspiracy', he was assailed by the opposition benches, who cried, 'Spoke! Spoke!', meaning that he had no right to rise a second time. O'Connell appeared supremely indifferent to their shouting, and he stood with his arms folded across his breast, 'in an attitude of perfect calmness'.[20] The uproar continued for several minutes, until finally O'Connell threatened to move an adjournment of the House. Things quietened down and O'Connell began speaking but after a few second he was 'again assailed by cries of "Spoke! Spoke!" and "Order! Order!"'. But again he stood defiant, and finally was allowed to speak.

Addressing the House, O'Connell denounced the meeting as 'an English Protestant conspiracy' put together to block Irish Catholics from being returned to the imperial parliament.[21] And he demanded to know if there was 'sufficient love and sympathy for Ireland in the legislature of Great Britain to justify those who wished to preserve the connexion between the two countries'.[22] He was jeered by the Tories, but he warned them that there was 'no instance in the history of the world in which seven millions of people once roused to the truth by a sense of injustice have ever failed to right themselves'. Ireland, he said, had a population of eight million. 'A million of them are opposed to us. I make you a present of that million; but I tell you that the remaining seven millions will not lack the power sooner or later of righting themselves'.

The much anticipated maiden speech of Benjamin Disraeli, the MP for Maidstone, took place on this occasion. He rose to speak immediately after O'Connell, hoping to make his reputation by an attack on the celebrated orator. For the first few minutes he was cheered loudly by his Tory friends and jeered by everyone else. Even Sir Robert Peel, who rarely offered any encouragement to speakers, turned his head to cheer Disraeli 'in most stentorian tones'.[23] Disraeli accused O'Connell of delivering 'a long, rambling, wandering, jumbling speech' and defended the Spottiswoode subscription as 'a defensive fund'. But his attack on O'Connell and his 'well-disciplined band of patriots' was barely heard. The numbers supporting O'Connell were too great: Disraeli's speech was submerged in the shouting and eventually his voice was drowned. Even *Hansard* reported that 'during the greater part of the time the hon. member was on his legs, he was so much interrupted that it was impossible to hear what he said'.[24] Losing his temper, Disraeli paused mid-sentence and said 'in remarkable loud and almost terrific tones—"Though I sit down now, the time will come when you will hear me"'. Then he sat down to the loudest uproar, which lasted for several minutes. In later years his closing words would be read as a prophecy of future greatness, but at the time it was seen as the pathetic wailing of a man who had been comprehensively humiliated on his debut.

At a dinner given in his honour by the radicals of Norwich on 28 November 1837, O'Connell delivered a speech about electoral corruption, and his words caused offence when they were reported back in Ireland.[25] O'Connell had recounted the story of Blake Foster, 'a gentleman in Ireland, at least so he called himself', who had sold the votes of his tenants to one candidate on the first day, then to a different candidate on the second day, and on the third day allowed the tenants to go out and 'sell themselves'. Foster's logic was that, 'now he was bribed on both sides, he felt bound in honour to vote for neither, and being thus disengaged, why should he not let the poor men make the most of themselves'. Foster was dead, but his son, Robert Blake Foster, was furious and demanded a retraction as well as a promise that O'Connell would never speak on the subject again. O'Connell was apologetic and admitted that had he known, 'or recollected', the death of Foster he would not have mentioned his name. But although he said that he would like to make '*any atonement in my power*' to Foster and his family, he insisted that 'it is not in my power to retract a statement which is strictly true in its essential particulars'.[26] Promising never to speak on the subject again, O'Connell did reveal that he had told the story years earlier in the presence of Foster, and the truth of it had been admitted. He did not hide his feelings about the deceased man: 'He was no friend of mine. In 1828 and in 1829 he gave me all the opposition he could in Clare.'

O'Connell could be very sensitive to examples of ingratitude. On one occasion he did a service for a man, who promised him that he would be 'eternally grateful'. 'Don't pledge yourself too strongly, my good Sir,' joked O'Connell, 'I am quite convinced that you entirely mean, *at present*, what you say. But mark my words: you will yet attack me, and *bitterly*; and you shall be welcome so to do!' And so it came to pass, with O'Connell being attacked, 'and the realisation of the prophecy gave no surprise to its author, and caused no feeling in his mind beyond that of indulgent pity'.[27] Similarly, over a period of time he helped a young barrister establish himself, but later the barrister did a deal with the government and received a colonial appointment in return for a promise to attack O'Connell. When the attack came O'Connell was not too surprised. 'It was but natural that he should do so,' said O'Connell. 'Did I not give provocation? *Did I not do him a service?*' But, whatever about his studied nonchalance, incidents like these hurt O'Connell deeply. His son later revealed that 'no man ever felt unkindness, ingratitude, betrayal, more keenly and more painfully'.

In 1837 there was violence on the streets of Dublin when the trade unions clashed with the employers and O'Connell became embroiled in the conflict.[28] The unions wanted to secure fixed wages, limit the number of apprentices, and prevent the employment of workers who were not union members. There were a series of strikes, and 'violent assaults were committed on masters and men who refused to yield to the demands of the unions, and trade was, in consequence, much disturbed'.[29] O'Connell sided with the employers, and at a meeting of one union he denounced the violent tactics which were being used and called for a peaceful resolution of the issues. He also became chairman of the Anti-Combination Society, which was formed in the interests of the employers. The unions had always been among O'Connell's greatest supporters, and by siding against them he 'not only risked his popularity, but his very life'. Whenever he walked the streets he was 'hooted and assailed' and 'made the mark for every insult by the workmen of Dublin'. A public letter to the *Freeman's Journal* in January 1838 demanded to know the benefits of emancipation: 'Has it given a loaf of bread to any of the thousand starving families of the poor operatives of this city?'[30] Stung by the criticism, O'Connell addressed a meeting of the unions, and risked genuine physical danger. Bravely facing the mob, he insisted that he had never asked anyone to follow him, and demanded to know, 'Am I not old enough, or am I to be told that this is Irish respect? Or have I no tradesmen of Dublin to stand round me?'[31]

At the height of the conflict, O'Connell's meetings were broken up by organised mobs, 'the most insulting language was directed against him, even threats of assassination were uttered'. It had always been said that O'Connell would sacrifice 'honour, consistency, and truth' for popularity, that he too 'dearly loved the applause of the multitude'. But, by standing against the workmen in this dispute, he showed that 'he would rather go out into the cold and the night' than offend 'his sense of right and justice'.[32]

A poor law bill for Ireland was introduced in the Commons on 1 December 1837, but it was only on 9 February 1838 that O'Connell rose to oppose it. Explaining that he had not the 'moral courage' to do so earlier, he asserted that the law was a 'delusion' which would result 'in greater misery and more dissatisfaction' and that it afforded 'less relief than it inflicts injury'.[33] However, his efforts were in vain and the bill passed on 27 July.

On 21 February 1838 O'Connell finally got to meet Queen Victoria, when he was presented to her at St James's Palace. This followed a special request from the queen to meet him; in her diary she admitted that he was 'the only person who I was very anxious to see'.[34] She described him as 'very tall, rather large' with a 'remarkably good-humoured countenance, small features, small, clever blue eyes, and very like his caricatures'. Following protocol, O'Connell kissed her hands when he was presented to her. He was well aware of her interest in meeting him, and took it as a sign that she was 'determined to conciliate Ireland'.[35] The next day the queen wrote to her uncle (the man who had defeated O'Connell to become king of the Belgians!) and told him that she had greeted O'Connell 'with a very smiling face—he has been behaving very well this year'.[36] She admitted that it was 'quite a treat for me to see him, as I had long wished it'. From the very start of the reign, O'Connell had an intense devotion to Victoria, the lonely widower finding in the youthful queen the representation of everything he admired about monarchy in general and womanhood in particular. He never wavered in his belief that the queen would bring about justice for Ireland, and his romantic idealisation of her grew stronger every year.

O'Connell also saw the queen at a 'splendid entertainment' in the apartments at Kensington Palace which was hosted by the duke of

Sussex. 'The little lady honoured me with a good stare,' O'Connell joked afterwards.[37] At this meeting the duke of Sussex slapped O'Connell good-naturedly on the back, and asked him, 'How are you, Dan my boy?' Sussex was the brother of the late Kings George IV and William IV, but, although a liberal, he was disliked by O'Connell because of his treatment of his son, Augustus Frederick D'Este. D'Este was considered illegitimate because his parents' marriage was declared invalid under the Royal Marriages Act and, although his father acknowledged him, it hurt deeply. From about 1825 he was mainly confined to a wheelchair, suffering from multiple sclerosis, and he is considered to have left the 'earliest clinical account' of the disease.[38] Throughout his life D'Este was deeply upset about his failure to be recognised as legitimate and he campaigned intensely for a peerage, but it was never granted. Whenever he saw him, O'Connell always addressed him as 'your royal highness', and believed that he was 'perfectly well entitled to that designation'.

On 23 September 1838 O'Connell was granted a singular honour by Pope Gregory XVI. This was the privilege of a portable altar, something normally only granted to a head of state, which meant he had the right to have Mass celebrated and the sacraments dispensed when away from home. Earlier in the year the pope had granted O'Connell and his family two indulgences, as well as one for any person who prayed at O'Connell's oratory at Derrynane. O'Connell had first requested the privilege of a portable altar in 1837, but it was refused because of concerns in Rome that O'Connell was too unorthodox in his religion. O'Connell was hurt, and sent a message that his 'submission to the authority of the church is complete, whole, and universal'.[39] But there were occasional tensions between O'Connell and the Catholic church in Ireland. For example, in 1838 there was a damaging dispute with Archbishop Murray over the national education board. The Rev. John Miley, curate at Marlborough Street in Dublin, issued a public letter dated 12 October 1838 defending O'Connell and rejecting any attempt to find a new leader.[40] It marked the beginning of a close relationship between the two men, and Miley became O'Connell's spiritual advisor and a trusted friend for the remainder of his life.

Repeal continued to dominate O'Connell's thoughts. The problem was that 'The O'Connell Tribute' was falling, and he wondered if his popularity would survive his involvement in so many compromises.[41] Everyone thought he should be able to secure whatever they wanted, and disappointment bred resentment. For example, the grocers in Ireland were angry with him for not doing enough to repeal an unpopular piece of legislation concerning retail of spirits. In reality, O'Connell had arranged numerous meetings with government officials and had used 'argument, entreaty, and any influence' he possessed. 'The shameful *disregard*' of his efforts by the grocers, and similar disappointments, made him think about retiring from politics. But one thing sustained him: '*we must Repeal*'. 'The enmity to the Union was my first effort, it will be my last.' He was confident that someday he would succeed, 'idle as it may seem', and he revealed that 'I *live for the Repeal*'. But his spirits were beginning to fall, and he admitted that he was 'heart-sore at many disappointments'.

To try and cement the alliance with O'Connell, especially now that that a monarch was on the throne who did not hate him, on 17 June 1838 the government decided to make him its final offer. There was some talk of making him chief baron, but O'Connell made it clear he would not accept it. The lord lieutenant, Lord Mulgrave, then sent for him and let him know that there would be no difficulty in making him Master of the Rolls for Ireland, 'and in fact he offered it'.[42] This time there was no royal opposition, and the offer had been cleared with the queen beforehand. Unlike her uncles she had no problem with giving office to O'Connell and, when she was asked, twice, if she had any objections she said she had 'none whatsoever, and therefore think it is [better] left to ministers to offer it, or not, as they may think fit'.[43] This was the one position, apart from chief secretary, that O'Connell really wanted, and he was sorely tempted to accept. It would resolve his financial problems, and give him the recognition and status he had always wanted. But it would also remove him from the frontline of political activity, and mean the end of independent agitation. Indeed, this was the very strategy of the Whigs, and Melbourne told the queen that it was hoped the offer would satisfy O'Connell and his party, 'and get him out of the way'.[44] Melbourne was convinced that even the Tories would not object too loudly as they would be equally 'glad to have him out of the way'.

The offer was a very tempting one to O'Connell, sixty-three years old and beginning to tire of the challenge of leading a national movement. 'Let me see, now,' he told his close friend, William O'Neill Daunt, 'there would not be more than about eighty days' duty in the year; I would take a country-house near Dublin, and walk into town' and spend the

rest of the time at Derrynane.[45] He was also attracted to the idea of
being idle in the month of April, 'just when the jack-hares leave the
most splendid trails upon the mountains'. 'In fact, I should enjoy the
office exceedingly on every account', but, he concluded, only 'if I *could*
accept it consistently with the interests of Ireland—but I cannot!' And
so, after much internal turmoil, O'Connell turned down the offer. As he
admitted afterwards, 'The die is cast. *I have refused office . . . My heart is
heavy but I have made this sacrifice.*' He was guided by a number of
things. The first was his belief that he could not accept any office while
Ireland was so troubled: 'I nail my colours to my country's mast.'[46] The
second was the memory of his late wife and the fact that she would have
disapproved. He admitted that his heart was 'sad at the sacrifice I now
make'. But he was reassured when he thought of '*her* memory' which
'casts a protection about me which will prevent me from abandoning
my struggles for Ireland save with my life'. He was melancholy with the
thought that '[i]f SHE was alive I should have my reward and my
consolation'. And so he resolved to continue as before. He admitted that
he was 'perhaps a fool', but he had not 'the heart to desert Ireland'.

It was now time to consider reviving the agitation for Repeal. To this
end he organised a new organisation, the Precursor Society, which was
launched in Dublin on 18 August 1838. Rather than being a Repeal
society, O'Connell insisted it was in fact the reverse.[47] Meeting at the
Corn Exchange, the home of agitation for O'Connell, the society aimed
to secure serious reforms in Ireland and thus make Repeal unnecessary.
Among the most important of his complaints were partisan judges,
jury-packing, 'the odious tithe system', municipal reform, an extension
of the franchise, and an end to 'Orange domination'.[48] And so he called
on even the enemies of Repeal to join it and 'consolidate the Union'.
Unfortunately, few people understood what the society was about. The
story was told of an English traveller who asked a Dublin car-driver
what the object of the society was, and was told, 'Pray-curse, sir! Why,
to pray curses on the enemies of Ireland, to be sure!'[49] But O'Connell
knew what he was doing. He realised that it would be dismissed as a
Repeal society, and that nothing would be done for Ireland. Thus its
opponents would 'ultimately drive not the "Precursors" but the people
to Repeal'. 'How little they know of human nature,' he laughed, and
especially of Irish human nature, and he made a prediction about the
'magic power of "Repeal" on the Irish mind'. He also made a solemn

promise that Repeal would be carried. 'Laugh at me now', he insisted, but someday people would 'recollect my prophecy'.

Peter Purcell, 'an opulent stage-coach proprietor', was a key figure in the new organisation.[50] He and O'Connell soon developed a close friendship. But tensions soon began to emerge. Purcell wanted to change the name of the Precursor Society to indicate that it was some kind of national movement. O'Connell refused, insisting that the name 'National Association' be reserved for the agitation of Repeal. He believed that it would be 'a practical blunder to call that national whose efforts may induce us to acquiesce in being merely a province'.[51] Despite Purcell's best efforts, O'Connell refused to budge on the issue. 'Fie upon it!' he declared. 'Our present struggle is not national; it is only "precursor" of nationality or of continued provincialism.' And he believed that it 'will, shall, and must precede Repeal agitation if justice be refused'. Fearing that the Precursor Society would be declared illegal, O'Connell dissolved it on 18 December 1838, reforming it immediately under a new constitution that could not be challenged.[52]

On 5 January 1839 a scandal engulfed the society, and O'Connell suffered one of the greatest betrayals of his life. He had spent the day with Purcell at the Corn Exchange, attending various committee meetings, and afterwards they walked arm-in-arm in friendly conversation back to O'Connell's home at Merrion Square. O'Connell begged Purcell to join him and his family for dinner, but Purcell excused himself and the two men 'parted at the door as friends part, who expect to meet next day'.[53] There was some time before dinner, so O'Connell entered his study, where he picked up that day's *Freeman's Journal*. He began reading it and was astonished to find a letter from Purcell exposing financial irregularities in the Precursor Society and threatening to resign unless they were resolved. Purcell had discovered that the funds of the society had been lodged in O'Connell's name in the National Bank, and implied that O'Connell had turned a political movement to his own pecuniary advantage and had used 'the garb of patriotism' for his own ends. Demanding a full investigation, Purcell called for the money to be placed in the hands of publicly appointed treasurers.

This unexpected attack hit O'Connell like a 'thunder-clap'. An hour later, when a family member called him for dinner, he was still in the study, 'the newspaper hanging from his hand, not a limb changed from its position; his eye mournfully fixed—in no unconsciousness, but in the deep, mute agony of a wounded heart'.[54] He agreed to open the accounts for inspection, and Purcell hired a city magistrate and a bookbinder to assist him. The book-binder was there to examine whether there had been a fraudulent insertion of new pages as part of a cover-up. No evidence of corruption was discovered. O'Connell attempted to keep Purcell on board but it proved impossible to prevent a split. By making the matter public Purcell had damaged the credibility of the society and the members voted to expel him. The incident left O'Connell much shaken, and his family considered it 'a severe blow indeed'.

The rumours of financial irregularity gave a license to those who wanted to attack O'Connell. On 17 January the *Dublin Monitor* published a long editorial denouncing the whole affair, and reminding readers that O'Connell had behaved in the same way in the 1820s with the funds of the Catholic Association, '*not one shilling of which has ever been satisfactorily accounted for*'.[55] In the House of Lords on 5 February 1839 the duke of Wellington took the opportunity to abuse O'Connell, virtually accusing him of plotting an insurrection, and making reference to the money which was 'deposited in his "private bank", ultimately to be deposited in his private pocket'.[56] With his loose approach to financial matters, O'Connell was always vulnerable to such charges. It was not that he was dishonest; it was just that he never understood the dividing line between the public and the private. The treasurers in the Precursor Society intervened and vouched for the funds that were in O'Connell's keeping, but the fact that he had decided to rest the money in his account, and in his own bank, reflected badly on him. There was a justification: if the society was declared illegal then the money could not be confiscated if it was in O'Connell's account. But it did leave him vulnerable to these allegations. O'Connell never changed in his practices and he did the same thing with the funds of the Repeal Association in the 1840s. The Precursor Society failed to gain any momentum and O'Connell dissolved it on 2 September 1839.

Postal reform was a key issue for O'Connell and Gladstone later remarked that he was probably one of only a handful of people to recognise its importance at the time.[57] On Thursday 2 May 1839 a deputation from the city of London uniform penny postage committee, accompanied by some 150 MPs, including O'Connell, were received by

Lord Melbourne. There were a number of speeches. The room was packed, so O'Connell stood on a chair and made a special appeal on behalf of the poor Irish in Britain who were cut off from 'home, kindred, and friends' by the prohibitive postage rates.[58] Responding, Melbourne praised the speeches and, in particular, the eloquence of O'Connell. Five days later, however, his government resigned. This followed concerted opposition to the bill to suspend the constitution of Jamaica for five years, with William Smith O'Brien one of the Irish MPs who broke ranks and voted against the government.

O'Connell feared the return of a Tory ministry, and admitted in private that he had never 'felt so uneasy and unhappy'.[59] However, the 'Bedchamber Crisis' saved the ministry. Peel made it a condition of taking office that the queen dismissed some of her household ladies because they were Whigs. The queen refused, and so Peel resigned his commission to form a government. Melbourne and the Whigs returned to power. O'Connell was delighted, and it increased his affection for Victoria: 'Hurrah for the darling little queen! . . . She has shown great firmness and excellent heart.'[60] When the queen married later in the year O'Connell celebrated the news and wished 'the dear little lady every kind of happiness'.[61] In years to come, he continued to cherish the way she had thrown over Peel, believing that her conduct deserved 'immortal praise'. On 10 June 1840 an attempt was made on the lives of Victoria and Albert by a deranged youth called Edward Oxford who fired two shots at their carriage.[62] O'Connell was deeply relieved that this attempt failed, and not just because of his affection for the queen. He recognised that if it had succeeded the most repressive policies would have been introduced, and 'the horrible fate of Ireland' would have been 'a persecution of blood'.[63]

The abortive change in parliament caused divisions in the Tory ranks. The spoils of office had already been divided up, and many were upset at what they were going to receive. For example, Alexander Perceval, MP for Sligo, was only offered the governorship of Trinidad, and O'Connell joked that it was 'clear he would kill himself in three months drinking *sangaree*, a favourite beverage in the West Indies'.[64] Every man who had not been promised something became 'a declared enemy'. 'In short', O'Connell laughed, 'the mere approach to office has created one hundred divisions in their party.' Queen Victoria held a ball on 10 May, which O'Connell attended. 'She was in great gaiety and good humour,' he noted, 'remarkably civil to all the Liberals, the reverse to the Tories.'

Increasingly O'Connell began to worry about his leadership and the challenges to it. A major irritant was William Smith O'Brien, MP for Limerick. In private he was rude and impudent to O'Connell; in public he was not to be trusted. O'Connell considered him 'an exceedingly weak man, proud and self-conceited and, like almost all weak men, utterly impenetrable to advice'.[65] He investigated ways of having Smith O'Brien deselected at the next election, revealing that he was so unreliable, 'You cannot be sure of him for half an hour.'

O'Connell was also forced to recognise that his alliance with the Whigs was coming to an end. He had never been particularly welcomed by them, and as time went on was increasingly shunned. Even Melbourne made little attempt to establish a relationship, once remarking that if O'Connell could be invited to a dinner then you might as well invite anybody.[66] When Francois Guizot, the French historian, orator and future prime minister, was appointed ambassador, the only person that he wanted to meet in London was 'the celebrated Irishman Daniel O'Connell'. However, he discovered that O'Connell was rarely invited to any of the official events, and he had to arrange to meet him at a small private dinner.[67] During the dinner O'Connell spoke of the progress the temperance movement of Fr Theobald Mathew was making in Ireland: 'the drunkards were disappearing by thousands', and he predicted that it would lead to 'more refined manners' among the population.[68] Guizot wondered whether this was 'a mere puff of popular humour, or a lasting reform'. O'Connell replied gravely, 'It will last; we are a persevering race, as are all who have suffered much.' After dinner it was mentioned that some important political and church figures were about to arrive at the house for a reception, and O'Connell got up to leave so as not to embarrass his hosts. But he was persuaded to stay, and he remained, 'with visible satisfaction, not unmingled with pride'. Guizot left the reception at around midnight, the first to go, and he left O'Connell 'surrounded by four cabinet ministers, and five or six ladies of rank, who listened to him with a mixture, somewhat comic, of curiosity and pride, or deference and disdain'.

'I *was* the happiest of men.'[69] The death of O'Connell's wife weighed heavily on him. He believed he would 'never again know happiness' and every day convinced him 'more and more of that fact'.[70] Slightly misquoting Alexander Pope, he spoke of 'the aching void left craving at my heart'.[71] There were also concerns about his family. His daughter Betsey Ffrench suffered from depression, renounced her faith, and began exhibiting symptoms of mental ill-health. He called it 'the severest blow' he had ever experienced, and spoke of the 'mental agony' he endured as he struggled to help her get better.[72] Pleading with her to seek religious instruction, he begged her not to give in to despair: 'despair is your danger'. He asked her how she could think that 'the God who, in the lingering moments of the cross, shed the last drop of his blood for her, is a tyrant, or that he does not love her?' And he advised her to look after her family and children, taking her mind, 'without bustle and violence, from the thoughts that make you unhappy to your domestic occupations'. He sent her money so that she could take a holiday in France, and told her that it would kill him if she did not take his advice.[73] 'I see your case clearly', he revealed, 'and it breaks my heart to think of it.'

Burdened by private grief and public regret, in the autumn of 1839 O'Connell was at the lowest point of his life. His attempt to win 'Justice for Ireland' had failed, and his popularity in Ireland had suffered as a result of the association with the Whigs. 'The O'Connell Tribute' seemed in terminal decline, his finances were a mess, his friends were deserting him, and, worst of all, Repeal was as far away as ever. Without his beloved wife to sustain him, O'Connell's natural ebullience slowly gave way to despair. It was his sixty-fourth birthday on 6 August 1839 but O'Connell did not feel like celebrating. Instead, he thought about retiring from politics completely, and spending the remainder of his life in quiet, contemplative prayer. He gave serious thought to withdrawing to Clongowes, the Jesuit-run college, for 'a period of retreat to think of nothing but eternity'.[74] Following that, he would spend the remainder of his days in 'the solitude of my native mountains', and wait for death, 'a change which may be postponed but is inevitable'.[75] He did not think he would have to wait long, for he did not see how he could 'long survive the blow I apprehend from the desertion of me by the country at large'.[76]

Depressed and dejected, O'Connell spoke often of the intense 'mental agony' he experienced at this time. Convinced that the country had grown tired of supporting him, he admitted that 'it weighs heavily upon my heart and interferes with my health'. It was a '*painful, painful* subject' for him. As he revealed to P.V. Fitzpatrick, his closest remaining friend, 'I am, I confess, very unhappy . . . I am indeed unhappy.'[77] Consumed by self-doubt and self-pity, he could not help asking, 'What shall I do?' O'Connell blamed the collapse of his popularity on a number of things. The main reason was the lack of 'prominent, or glaring success [which] has weakened the tie of affection Ireland has cherished for me'. After close to forty years in the service of Ireland, he was only surprised that he had managed to remain popular for so long. He was willing to keep going if 'Ireland thought fit to support me', but he thought it was 'plain I have worn out my claim on the people'. O'Connell's great career seemed destined to end in failure. He felt incapable of resisting the onslaught of illness, 'the illness of despondency', and sometimes his hand started shaking when he attempted to put his thoughts down on paper.[78] As the year drew to a close he felt his prospects grow 'daily darker and more dark'.[79] And, for the first time in his life, he admitted that 'it is clear I have no one to blame but myself'.

PART II

Chapter 8

THE RESURRECTION OF O'CONNELL: THE CAMPAIGN FOR REPEAL, 1840–1843

'I was never more convinced of the necessity of a Repeal of the Union, and of establishing a national parliament on College Green ... The time is not far distant when the Union will be prostrate at our feet, and Ireland freed from her chains.'

(SPEECH OF DANIEL O'CONNELL AT A MEETING OF THE ANTI-TORY ASSOCIATION, 1834)[1]

With 'everything growing dark and dismal', his spirits low, and Ireland in a state of 'foolish apathy', O'Connell decided to begin a new campaign to Repeal the Union.[2] This campaign would take place outside of parliament and would try to copy the mass popular movement which had succeeded in winning Catholic emancipation. The same venue—the Corn Exchange—was chosen for the meetings, but just as in the early 1820s the mood of the country was apathetic and few people attended.[3] At the first meeting of the Repeal Association on 15 April 1840 only about fifty people attended, 'a discouraging display of empty benches'.[4] The very idea of Repeal, it seemed, 'had lost its potent magic'. Monitoring events from London, Robert Peel would later dismiss the Repeal movement as 'a failing concern'.[5] The journalist Leigh Hunt derisively compared the Repeal cry to the cry of the Derrynane beagles. But O'Connell was delighted with this comparison, noting that 'my beagles never cease their cry until they catch their game'.[6]

All but the most loyal of O'Connell's followers were convinced that his powers were on the wane. His speeches at the Association were dull and repetitive, and despite some 'happy touches of humour', were 'often tame and tedious'. It was only when a new wrong was to be denounced, or when O'Connell was personally attacked 'by an opponent worthy of an answer', that the 'born orator awoke'.[7] Then the old fires were rekindled, 'the mobile face, gleaming with humour or blazing in wrath, the well set head, and iron jaw, the towering figure . . . furnished a picture never to be forgotten'. But these days were far too infrequent. Whenever a success was achieved O'Connell would announce that it was 'a great day for Ireland', and the phrase became so overused that 'great days became too numerous for the most patriotic calendar'. O'Connell was at his best when he combined 'close vigorous logic and scathing indignation'. But deprived of any challenges, and with his own morale low, he often resorted to a set speech on 'the natural resources and picturesque scenery of Ireland, the hundredth repetition of which was a trial to human patience'.[8] For more than a year O'Connell failed in his attempts to rally popular support for his cause. 'The people continued apathetic, and the middle class stood apart,' there was little church support, and many in private mocked his efforts.[9] But O'Connell was not to be put off. 'As soon as the people begin to find out that I am thoroughly in earnest, they will come flocking in to the Association,' he insisted.[10] 'My struggle has begun', he revealed, 'and I will terminate it only in death or Repeal.'

O'Connell's key lieutenants were a small group of family and friends. Thomas Steele was the 'Head Pacificator', the man who maintained order at the meetings and who was sent to whatever part of the country disturbances were taking place. Born in Co. Clare in 1788, he was a Protestant who had inherited a large fortune from his uncle but had squandered it in various quixotic schemes. For example, he purchased a warship and set out to aid the liberals in Spain in the 1820s, though he arrived too late to provide any real service. A Cambridge graduate, he was an engineer of some ability and experimented with submarine illumination, as well as attempts to improve the navigation of the Shannon.[11] Steele had joined the Catholic Association in the 1820s and had become a key disciple of O'Connell. During the Clare by-election in 1828 he seconded O'Connell's nomination in Ennis, and went on to play a central role, with his unique personality a key part in O'Connell's success.[12]

The centre of Steele's life was O'Connell, whom he called his 'mighty leader'.[13] It was said that as long as he could be near O'Connell he would never be unhappy, and he 'could willingly die for Mr O'Connell as well as for his country'.[14] Indeed, he often boasted that if O'Connell asked him to sit on a mine that was about to explode he would do so without any hesitation, and no one doubted his sincerity. At a Repeal meeting in Tralee in the winter of 1840 an elderly harpist, dressed as an ancient bard, played in the cold for O'Connell. Betsey Ffrench, O'Connell's daughter, was moved by his forlorn and miserable appearance and asked Steele to do something for him. Steele agreed and went over to speak to the man, but did not give him any money. When asked what he had done for the man, Steele beamed. 'I have made him immortal,' he said, 'By virtue of my office as Head Pacificator of Ireland, I have constituted him O'Connell's chief musician.'[15] 'Oh, run off, Tom,' laughed O'Connell, taking some money from his pocket, 'and give the poor bard a crown.'

Only once did Steele and O'Connell fall out. The source of the quarrel was a young girl Steele met on the street in Ennis whom he immediately fell in love with. O'Connell advised him against pursuing the relationship, citing the extreme age gap, as well as the fact that Steele did not know the girl, and warned that it left him open to ridicule. Steele was deeply hurt and declared that he could no longer serve a man who did not understand him, and who had not appreciated the object of his affection.[16] For the next few months Steele retired from public life completely, until finally O'Connell persuaded him to meet. O'Connell had been deeply hurt by the estrangement and reconciled with Steele 'in a manner that poor Steele never spoke of afterwards without tears in his eyes'.

By the 1840s Steele had become a figure of fun. In his adventures he had lost most of his teeth and suffered from imperfect articulation as a result. This meant that whenever he spoke he tended to cover his listeners in spittle. In addition, 'Honest Tom', as Steele was known, was often mocked for his unblinking devotion to O'Connell. The younger members could never understand his usefulness and dismissed him as a 'semi-lunatic'.[17] But there were stories which vindicated the trust

O'Connell placed in him. During the Whiteboy violence of the early 1830s he was sent to resolve the problem, and he succeeded in quieting and disarming the people. In the summer of 1843 it looked like more violence would erupt when the government withdrew the mail coach contract from the man who held it. This caused great unhappiness and an angry mob 'threatened to bring the public peace into considerable danger'.[18] Steele set out with a single green twig as an emblem and completely pacified the mob, and the scene of the riot was in an instant changed into one of perfect repose, 'of the most complete tranquillity'. It was precisely because there was something 'exaggerated and fantastic' about Steele that meant he was so effective: 'popular audiences do not dislike melodrama'.[19] He wore a faded blue military uniform, and spoke 'a language which could only be matched in the romances of knight-errantry'. But the younger members grew impatient listening to his extended monologues, believing that at a time when the fortunes of the country were at stake, he was wasting their time 'haranguing in language fit for the mouth of Garagantua'. James O'Connell was once asked why his brother had appointed such a man to be his Head Pacificator. The embittered younger brother replied, 'Pray, who the devil else would take such an office?'[20]

In the 1830s it had been predicted that O'Connell's eldest son, Maurice, would become his political heir. He was 'frank, courageous, fond of enjoyment' and his enthusiasm made him 'the darling of the young men of the national party'.[21] But his bad marriage wrecked his life, and he lacked the emotional maturity to become a notable figure. His place was taken by his younger brother John, who was a trained barrister, though he did not practice. John was small and slight, and was very unlike his father, his strength being in statistical calculations rather than oratory.[22] Desperate to succeed his father as leader of the people, he revelled in the name of 'Young Liberator', which was bestowed on him, without ever being earned, in the 1840s.

The real genius behind the scenes of the Repeal Association was Thomas Matthew Ray, its secretary. O'Connell discovered him in the Trades' Political Union and, recognising his organisational abilities, head-hunted him for the Association. He rarely spoke, but was always active behind the scenes, and he was the person who turned O'Connell's instructions into reality. Completing the staff were William Joseph O'Neill Daunt, O'Connell's private secretary, and two journalists, John Gray, the editor of the *Freeman's Journal*, and Richard Barrett, the editor of the *Pilot*. Barrett had started as a Tory journalist, spending much of his time abusing the Catholics, but eventually he offered his services to O'Connell and became a supporter. When O'Connell was once told that he had made a 'precious bad bargain', he admitted, 'Devil a worse, but he was of use at the time.'[23]

The arrival of a group of young and energetic figures into the Association provided some much needed vitality. These included Thomas Davis, the brilliant young writer who had been auditor of the College Historical Society in Trinity College Dublin; John Blake Dillon, a Roscommon lawyer; and Charles Gavan Duffy, the editor of a provincial newspaper in Belfast. Dillon and Duffy would together found the new newspaper of the movement, *The Nation*, in 1842. These men acted almost as a kind of civil service for O'Connell, researching information, preparing papers, and organising events for him. By the winter of 1844 O'Connell would be referring to this group as 'Young Ireland' and, although there was later some dispute about whether this was a name they called themselves, it was certainly one they were happy to use.[24] O'Connell delighted in entertaining these men with stories from his younger days, such as how he had challenged John Keogh for leadership of the Catholics, or how he had met his childhood hero, Henry Grattan, when Grattan was in his old age, and the 'secret wonder and contempt' which the vigorous young man had had for the 'dilapidated patriot'.[25] The irony was not lost on his younger listeners, who saw the older O'Connell in exactly the same terms as the dismissed figures of Keogh and Grattan. The arrival of these talented younger members opened O'Connell to questioning and criticism.

O'Connell had never been good at dealing with opposition, but as long as the difference of opinion did not threaten his dominance he dealt with it 'with a certain humorous forbearance'.[26] However, once it became dangerous 'he broke into a cold scornful rage which was likened to the boiling surge of a northern sea'. One observer felt that he was 'often bitter and unscrupulous, but never malignant in his quarrels'.[27] Those who supported him were flattered and praised, and country gentlemen who joined the Association were praised indiscriminately. O'Connell's overblown compliments soon became much caricatured. A story was often told of him proposing a country gentleman for membership in these terms: 'I have the distinguished honour and satisfaction of moving that we enrol among our members my esteemed friend the worthy and patriotic Mr . . ' And then turning to his secretary and whispering, 'What's his name?'[28]

There was always a blind spot when it came to Ulster and the Protestants of Ulster. O'Connell never really understood the people, or their traditions, and his few attempts to reach an understanding failed as a result. The most famous example was his ill-judged trip to Belfast in January 1841 when he had reluctantly accepted an invitation to speak by the local Repeal organisation. Beforehand O'Connell had received warnings that Orangemen intended to ambush him on his way there, and he devised a stratagem to outwit them. He contacted the innkeepers on the road from Dublin ordering post-horses for 18 January, and then ordered some more for two days earlier under the name of C.A. Charles, a Dublin ventriloquist.[29] The ruse succeeded, and he arrived in Belfast on the evening of 16 January without incident. Massive Orange demonstrations were organised to protest against his visit and a large force of police and soldiers was required to guarantee his safety. The windows of his hotel were broken by stones, and O'Connell was left in no doubt of the opposition to his campaign. Dr Henry Cooke, a Presbyterian minister, challenged 'the invader' to a public debate, but O'Connell refused, fearing mass violence. Instead he mocked his opponent as 'Bully Cooke, the cock of the north'.[30] He joked that 'Daddy Cooke' was 'a comical fellow' because he invited him to a debate in the most insulting terms, and was then surprised when he refused. 'What a way of coaxing me to do the thing! Why he'd coax the birds off the bushes!'

A Repeal dinner was held on 18 January, with a public meeting the next day in front of the Linen Hall. A crowd of about nine thousand people gathered to hear the speeches, but only one third were supporters of Repeal. The rest shouted and jeered throughout, for example, giving 'Three cheers for Ellen Courtenay', and calling out 'No surrender' and 'No pope'.[31] The smaller crowd of supporters responded with cries of 'Dan O'Connell for ever' and 'Hurrah for Repeal'. O'Connell was defiant throughout, throwing off his green cloak and revealing his Repeal frock-coat, with its white velvet collar and Repeal buttons. This just provoked the crowd further, and the shouts and hisses drowned out most of his speech. The speech itself was a trenchant attack on the Union and the corruption which had accompanied it, and a powerful call for toleration and understanding between Catholics, Protestants, and Presbyterians. O'Connell called on everyone to disperse peacefully after the meeting concluded, and then he handed over to the chair, Robert McDowell. At a public event that evening there was so much stone-throwing that O'Connell had to be given a police escort back to his hotel. He was relieved to escape Belfast the next day in one piece.

Responding to the visit a few days later, Cooke challenged the version of Irish history which had been presented by O'Connell. In his speech, O'Connell had spoken of three periods of Irish history since the Reformation, and had insisted that Catholics had not persecuted Protestants in any of those times. But Cooke believed that a fourth period of Irish history should be mentioned, 'the glorious era of the reign of King Dan himself'.[32]

In July 1841 O'Connell lost his seat for Dublin in the general election. The Whigs were also ejected from office, with a Tory ministry formed under Robert Peel. The alliance with the Whigs had long ceased to bring benefits to either side, and was effectively over, but the return of the Tories was another serious blow. Following his defeat in Dublin, O'Connell was returned for both Co. Meath and Co. Cork, and he decided to sit for Co. Cork as he began working on new ways to promote Repeal and create an impression in the capital. The recent Municipal Reform Act for Ireland had opened the offices of Dublin corporation to Catholics and O'Connell decided to take advantage of this change in the system. In October he decided to run for lord mayor of Dublin, which required returning an O'Connellite majority to Dublin corporation. The election on 25 October was a massive success, with forty-seven supporters elected out of a total of sixty. On 1 November the corporation met at the City Assembly Room in William Street. Alderman Isaac Butt proposed Sir Edward Borough for lord mayor, and attempted to argue that O'Connell was disqualified from consideration because of his position as leader of a national party. Alderman Boyce then enquired how O'Connell, if he was elected lord mayor, would act upon the Repeal question, stating that the answer would decide how he voted. O'Connell replied that although a Repealer, and 'to my last breath a Repealer', as lord mayor no one would 'be able to discover from my conduct what are my politics, or of what shade are the religious tenets I hold'.[33]

O'Connell was elected without a division and 'a peal of the most tremendous applause burst upon the entire meeting'. O'Connell immediately assumed the chair as lord mayor to prolonged cheering. Promising to set 'a glorious example' of how Irishmen of all different political principles could work together, O'Connell 'proceeded to speak exclusively on business', pausing only briefly to put on the crimson velvet robe of office. That evening, O'Connell appeared at a window of the corporation in his robe and cocked hat and the sight of him, 'enrobed in the official paraphernalia, the spoils won from prostrate Orangeism, was a signal for a vociferous cheer of the most intense delight'.[34] O'Connell engaged in banter with the crowd, asking if they recognised him and if the hat suited him. The men threw their hats in the air, and one was heard to shout, 'He's the finest lord mayor we ever saw!' Later in the night, O'Connell addressed the crowd which had gathered outside his home at Merrion Square. He told them that 'a great revolution' had been completed that day, and that it was only a matter of time before he was elected to serve them in an Irish House of Commons. 'I am now the guardian of your rights,' he declared, as he called on them to abstain from violence and from drinking, because he was now their chief magistrate. For the first two months of his year-long term O'Connell chose to live in Merrion Square, preferring its comforts to the Mansion House, which was considered to have 'defective accommodation'.[35] When he finally made the move, many Orangemen mourned that their 'sacred citadel of sectarian and political ascendancy' had fallen.

O'Connell took his responsibilities as lord mayor seriously and was determined to act completely impartially so that his term could be seen as a symbol of how things would be under an Irish parliament. Every Thursday he held a weekly court at Green Street as chief magistrate. One of his first cases, on his very first day, was a complaint made by a servant against a priest for unpaid wages. O'Connell sided with the servant and joked afterwards that he appreciated the irony that he had been forced to decide against a priest on his very first day.[36] O'Connell was very much his own man, and insisted on running the court his own way. One day he had to adjudicate between the competing claims of a Mr Kenny and a Mr MacNamara. O'Connell was unimpressed with both men, attacking Kenny for making 'a rigmarole speech in reply to a case which hadn't yet been made', and slating MacNamara for being 'wholly unintelligible'. In another case, when a Mr Burke replied angrily to a question about whether he had ever kept accounting books, O'Connell interrupted him and said, 'I'll tell you what you'll keep. You'll keep your temper.'[37] Burke continued to respond angrily to even the most innocent of questions, prompting O'Connell to joke that Burke was the type of person who if asked if he wanted something to eat 'would break out into a passion'. In 1844, when O'Connell's friend Charles Bianconi was elected mayor of Clonmel, he wrote to O'Connell asking for advice. O'Connell replied that the best thing was to 'act upon your own sound common sense and do not look into any law book'.[38]

The formation of a new government in Britain also meant the appointment of a new lord lieutenant for Ireland. The arrival of Lord de Grey, an opponent of reform, meant that the lord mayor would have to call on him and pay his respects. O'Connell made his feelings clear in public: he was acting only in his official capacity as lord mayor. In a wonderfully insulting speech at the Corn Exchange, he said that he neither respected nor disrespected de Grey. Rather he believed that he was 'a good-humoured, good-natured, good-for-nothing kind of private gentleman!'[39] At the *levée* a few days later, O'Connell approached the throne, bowed, and then left.

Determined to reduce the amount of jobbery when it came to corporation positions, O'Connell made a point of resisting the claims of some of his Repeal supporters. In December he objected to a motion from Councillor Callaghan, a Repealer, who was looking to get his son appointed junior counsel to the corporation. But his supporters were reluctant to pass up the spoils of office. When it looked like he would be defeated, O'Connell threatened resignation, announcing that '[h]e had, he perceived, sat too long in that chair'.[40] There were loud cries of 'No! No! No!' and great confusion. O'Connell revealed that he had prepared notice of his resignation, and insisted that unless the rebels backed down he would leave not only the chair, 'but the assembly also'. His opponents conceded the point and a counter-motion was passed by acclaim begging O'Connell to remain in office.

O'Connell was a master of the political gesture. When it was announced that he would attend Mass on New Year's Day in his official capacity, he was attacked by the pro-Orange Dublin newspapers and reminded that there was a penalty of £100 for any Irish official attending Catholic worship in his robes of office. On the day, O'Connell travelled to the cathedral in the state coach, wearing his scarlet robes, gold chain, and cocked hat, and was followed by a large procession of people. But when he reached the door he made a big show of taking off his robes, hat, and chain, saying with a laugh, 'The lord mayor may be a Catholic, but his robes are good Protestants.'[41] When the 12 July celebrations approached, O'Connell ordered that the statue of William of Orange on College Green should be painted bronze, so that it would look orange and would not have to be decorated, thus reducing the risk of violence. But O'Connell also proved a master of detail. Without any help, he drew up a complete water-pipe bill in twenty-four hours, ensuring that it could be sent to parliament in time.[42] He also set up and chaired committees on finance, law, property, and water to improve the conditions of ordinary Dubliners.

Towards the end of his one-year term as lord mayor, O'Connell was faced with 'a Herculean task'.[43] The burgess roll of Dublin required revision, meaning that a new list had to be prepared of who was eligible to vote and sit on juries. Failure to complete the task on time would mean that the existing list, favourable to the Tories and excluding many supporters of reform, would remain in place. The problem was that there were 18,000 names on the burgess roll and their claims required investigation within fifteen days. According to the statutes the task had to be completed by midnight on 15 October, and failure to complete the revision on time would leave the franchise unchanged. O'Connell returned to Dublin from Derrynane at the end of September determined to succeed. Bets were taken that he would be unable to complete the task on time, but he just laughed and said, 'We'll try it, at any rate,' before setting to work, 'jesting, quizzing, and punning' to break the monotony of the job. For example, when a Mr Stanley Ireland presented himself as a claimant for the franchise there were objections because of an unpaid water-pipe tax. However, when it was discovered the tax had been paid, O'Connell joked that this 'was a great day for Ireland'.[44] Another time, O'Connell hurt the feelings of a Mr Carew Smyth by entering his name as 'Smith'. O'Connell joked that 'he would not knock out his *i* to please him'. Smyth kept complaining, until finally O'Connell relented. Apologising for having caused any unhappiness, O'Connell said to loud laughter, 'We will knock out your *i*, then, since you desire it.'

O'Connell worked for nine hours on the rolls every day for the first two weeks, and for fifteen hours on the final day, 15 October.[45] As the midnight deadline approached various attempts were made to distract and interrupt O'Connell. Opponents would shout, 'Time's run out,' or 'Lord Mayor, it's two minutes past twelve o'clock.' But O'Connell refused to be distracted and kept working on the lists, marking off names, and glancing occasionally at his watch which lay on the table before him. In the final period he allowed several Tory claimants to go on the list without examination, recognising that to miss the midnight deadline would cancel out all the good work which had been done. At five minutes to midnight O'Connell stood up and announced that the last name on the list had been reached. 'The announcement elicited a burst of astonishment and applause, from foes as well as friends,' who were amazed that he had achieved in such a short time what English revision courts had so often failed to do.[46]

During his lord mayoralty, many people took to visiting the Mansion House to see O'Connell. One day, when O'Connell was particularly busy, a man came in and apologised for not having visited before. 'Say nothing about it,' said O'Connell, 'I look on it as a very great kindness when people don't visit me.'[47] On another occasion, a servant announced that there was a man outside who said 'his business is to make his bow to his lordship'. 'Augh!' said O'Connell. 'Tell him I am quite satisfied to accept his bow where he is.'[48] His term of office coming to an end, O'Connell joked at a meeting of the Repeal Association that in two weeks he'd have 'the privilege of knocking down any man who calls me "My Lord"'. On 1 November O'Connell left office, and there was a civic procession in his honour, with O'Connell travelling in the old glass coach used for these occasions.

On 15 October 1842 the first edition of The Nation, the newspaper of the Repeal movement, was published. The paper combined articles on politics with stirring poetry, and played to the talents of Charles Gavan Duffy, who edited it, and Thomas Davis, who wrote much of the best material. O'Connell was suspicious from the start of the ambitions of the paper, and kept a close eye on its contents. For his part, Davis was unhappy with O'Connell's aggressive language at meetings of the Repeal Association, for example, his contemptuous description of Wellington as 'a screaming coward and doting corporal'.[49] In the thirty-fourth issue of The Nation Davis pointedly defended Wellington as 'that gallant soldier and most able general'. The *Pilot* continued to be O'Connell's mouthpiece and there was increasing tension and rivalry between the two papers.

As tensions grew, O'Connell began mocking the pretensions of *The Nation*. At one meeting of the Repeal Association he made reference to 'the poor rhymed dullness' of the paper, a slight which was not well received by the younger men. Recognising that the mood of the meeting was against him, O'Connell was forced to backtrack and praise the quality of the published poems and songs. None the less, Charles Gavan Duffy was upset by the regular criticism and asked a friend, 'Is O'Connell jealous of *The Nation*?' 'Jealous of *The Nation*,' the friend replied, laughing, 'why, he's jealous of Brian Boru!'[50] A poem published in *The Nation* on 1 April 1843 proved surprisingly controversial. It was soon reprinted in a small collection of poems, *The spirit of the Nation*. Entitled 'The memory of the dead', but known to future generations by its first line, it asked,

> Who fears to speak of Ninety-eight?
> Who blushes at the name?
> When cowards mock the patriot's fate
> Who hangs his head for shame?

The poem was as much an attack on O'Connell as it was on anyone else. Not surprisingly, therefore, he hated the poem, which was 'in direct opposition to his feelings'.[51] For him, the 1798 Rebellion was a model of what should not happen, and he detested the uncontrollable violence which had been unleashed. The success of the poem, and the rise of *The Nation*, contributed to his anxiety as he plotted a way of winning Repeal through peaceful means.

During this period O'Connell worked intermittently on a projected two-volume memoir of Ireland, though in the event only the first was completed. Rather than being a history, it was really a skilful brief, setting out the case against British rule in Ireland. Anticipating the critical reviews in the British press, O'Connell boasted that he had 'never hit the rascals right in the face till now'.[52] After working on the book, on and off, for more than two years, he finally published it as *A Memoir of Ireland, Native and Saxon* on 1 February 1843. The book was dedicated to Queen Victoria, 'queen of Great Britain *and of* Ireland',

and it took as its inscription the lines of Moore, 'On *our* side is virtue and Erin/On *theirs* is the Saxon and guilt'. Some weeks passed and the book was not reviewed, and O'Connell began to worry that it would sink without trace. But, almost at once, the *Warder* attacked the book for its 'impotent anger', the *Spectator* denounced it, and *The Times* declared that it combined intellectual imbecility with diabolical wickedness.[53] O'Connell was delighted that the book was finally making an impression, and reminded his friends, 'See, I told you I never hit the scoundrels right in the face until now.' He had never let criticism bother him too much. Indeed, Henry Brougham once said that assaults on O'Connell produced as much effect 'as paper pellets thrown at the hide of a rhinoceros'.[54]

By the spring of 1843 the Repeal Association still appeared almost as moribund as ever. There was some progress. *The Nation* had published twenty issues and was building a respectable readership, and regular meetings were being held throughout the country to discuss repeal. But although the weekly rent had started to rise the Association remained in debt, and could only raise about £60 every week. Little heat was being generated by the project, and all attempts to excite real public interest had foundered. Nevertheless, despite all the evidence to the contrary, O'Connell declared confidently that 1843 would be the Repeal year, and this claim seemed further evidence that he 'too often mortgaged tomorrow for the benefit of today'.[55]

It was then that O'Connell hit upon a masterstroke. He announced his intention to bring all his arguments in favour of Repeal before the chief representative body in Ireland, Dublin corporation. His successor as lord mayor, George Rose, objected on the grounds that it was a political topic, but as the corporation had already given its support to the Afghan war, this objection was ignored. O'Connell proposed a motion 'that a petition should be presented to parliament from the corporation of Dublin for the Repeal of the Union between Great Britain and Ireland' and Tuesday 21 February was set aside for this to be discussed. However, even then, there was little public excitement on the subject.[56] As the day approached, O'Connell asked for a week's postponement. His opponents gloated, seeing this as evidence of disarray and confusion. Alderman Isaac Butt, who had planned to oppose the motion, complained loudly that he had remained in town, at much personal inconvenience, to speak. The twenty-nine-year-old Butt was the Whatley professor of political economy at Trinity College Dublin, as well as a junior barrister, and had been the secretary of the Conservative Association in 1840. Many believed that O'Connell was afraid of having his weaknesses exposed. And some even speculated that O'Connell had postponed the debate to try and get Butt out of town. The reality is that this was all part of O'Connell's tactics, to create interest in the subject and make his opponents complacent. As he admitted to a friend, 'I know not whether it is exactly fair to play off a ruse in a grave political matter like this, but I find my postponement of the debate has produced exactly the results I anticipated.'[57] Anti-Repealers began saying that he was shrinking from Butt, Repealers kept insisting that he 'wasn't a bit afraid of him', but both sides were talking about the matter, thus building up public curiosity 'to a point of intensity' as 'the great day' approached.[58]

On Tuesday 28 February 1843 the motion was finally brought before the Corporation, in what turned into a three-day debate on the subject. It took place in the City Assembly House, a circular building with the seats arranged as if it was a parliamentary chamber, which was packed with interested observers. 'Even the recess under the canopy which covers the lord mayor's chair was as crowded as the body of the house', as people on both sides strained to hear what was said.[59] O'Connell opened the debate and spoke for four hours and ten minutes on the first day.[60] It was some time since he had delivered a great speech and few believed he was still capable of one. The wand of the magician seemed not only withered but broken. In this speech O'Connell had to confront not only his most bitter opponents, but also the fading confidence of his own supporters, and, perhaps, his own doubts and fears. From the moment he began speaking his listeners were startled by the combination of vicious logic and suppressed rage. This was a rare example of the boxer growing younger in the ring. O'Connell was not only displaying all the energy of his younger days, he was deploying new material in a dramatic and calculated way. In the fires of this speech the campaign for Repeal was forged anew. At one point O'Connell demonstrated his lifelong commitment to the cause by reading extracts from his very first public speech, his speech against the Union in January 1800, when 'as a young advocate he rose in the presence of armed soldiers to denounce the project of a Union with England'.[61]

Reviewing the history of Ireland, from 1782 to 1800 and from 1800 to the present, O'Connell demonstrated that the Union had been a disaster for Ireland. But he declared that the Irish parliament was not dead, only asleep, and that 'they were that day sounding the trumpet of its resurrection'.[62] Perhaps the strongest part of the speech was when O'Connell began discussing the corruption that had accompanied the passing of the Union. These facts were not new, but 'the skill and passion of the orator invested them with the charm of novelty'. He denounced the 'corruption, bribery, force, fraud, and terror' which had accompanied the Union and asked his listeners not to profit from that illegal compact.[63] Lord Byron had talked of 'a union between the shark and his prey', and O'Connell insisted that the relationship between Britain and Ireland had become that 'of master and servant, shark and prey'.[64] 'The effect was immediate' and men who had previously opposed the discussion of the Repeal question began to wonder if 'a compact so obtained could stand'. In his peroration O'Connell denied that an Irish parliament would lead to a Catholic ascendancy, insisting that 'the age of persecution' had passed. It was left to the young Protestant orator Isaac Butt to respond to O'Connell. His speech, however, was not a success and was notable for the frequent admissions that O'Connell was right in places. During the speech O'Connell repeatedly exclaimed, 'I never made so unanswered a speech! Why, he doesn't even try to make a case!'[65]

On the third day, Thursday 2 March, O'Connell dominated the floor. He answered every argument, he replied to every question, and he displayed a complete mastery over the issues involved. At times funny, at times theatrical, O'Connell was at all times in command. At one point he quoted from one of Thomas Moore's melodies the lines 'Oh, where's the slave so lowly/Condemned to chains unholy', to loud cheers. Silencing the crowd, O'Connell proclaimed, in an emphatic voice, 'I AM NOT THAT SLAVE. I will never submit to it.'[66] The reaction was incredible. The audience was shaken by the emotional charge of the moment, energised by the passion of the declaration. It was as great a performance as O'Connell had ever given. Afterwards he turned to his friend, O'Neill Daunt, and told him with mock-seriousness, 'I don't think you could have done that quite so well.'[67] When it came to a vote, O'Connell's motion was passed by 41 votes to 15. The first victory for Repeal had been won.

The corporation debate re-energised the Repeal movement and turned it into a national movement. Sections of the middle class, which had previously remained aloof, conceded the merits of an Irish parliament, and more 'men of social or political mark' joined the association in three weeks than had in the proceeding three years.[68] The Association was open to men, women, and children, and each upon joining could become an associate, a member, or a volunteer, with a separate card for each. The member's card 'was adorned with the ancient national flag, "The Sunburst", and a modern flag displaying a shamrock inscribed "Catholic, Protestant and Dissenter" on leaves issuing from a common stalk. On each corner of the card was printed the name of a great battle won by the Irish, with the date of the event.'[69] To the right and left were columns listing the resources and wealth of Ireland, but ending with the refrain 'And yet she has no parliament.'

The first meeting of the Association after the Corporation debate was the very next day, Friday 3 March. The chamber was packed and O'Connell rose to the occasion, delivering a speech which even the more critical Young Irelanders believed was 'worthy of a national leader'.[70] 'We had a glorious three days of it,' O'Connell announced to the gathering, and no one doubted him.[71] Ascendant once again, O'Connell was determined to emphasise his commitment to peaceful means in pursuing his objectives. He revealed that although he possessed 'a mighty influence' over the people, he would never allow a violent mandate to 'issue from his lips'. Noting that 'soon I must leave this fleeting scene', he promised that he would never 'imperil my immortal soul' to win glory or power. At this point O'Connell 'appeared deeply affected'. Vowing that 'not for all the universe' would he 'consent to the effusion of a single drop of human blood, except my own', he insisted, 'Any other man's blood I dare not spill.' In this speech, O'Connell paid a surprising tribute to Isaac Butt which proved remarkably prescient. O'Connell revealed that he had followed Butt's reply with 'a microscopic eye' and had noted that Butt never said anything which precluded him from being a friend of Repeal in the future.[72] This led him to declare that Butt was 'in his inmost soul an Irishman' and to great cheers he predicted that 'we will have him struggling with us for Ireland yet'.

The great room of the Corn Exchange, on the second floor, was where the main issues were debated, in a large chamber that could fit close to 250 people. In the middle of this chamber there was a deal table, about three feet broad and ten feet long, where the newspaper reporters were seated. The members of the Repeal Association sat on benches on each side of this table. At the upper end of the table there was a chair of unpolished wood for the president of the meeting. On this chair was attached a green flag, which had the word 'Repeal' inscribed in gold letters. Behind it there was a large banner with the legend 'Property has its duties as well as its rights'. A white cloth was nailed to the wall on the right of the chair on which was written in black letters, 'Let no country strong enough to be a nation remain a province'. At one end of the room there was space for the public, who paid a shilling for admittance and who were obliged to stand, and above them there was a seated gallery which was reserved for women.[73] At the back of the room there was a prominent banner, with an inscription in green letters, surrounded by green laurels, which declared, 'The people who do not desire to be their own law-makers deserve slavery.' And on another wall there was a green banner with an inscription in gold letters, 'The man who commits a crime gives strength to the enemy.—Daniel O'Connell'.

Many meetings had their share of drama. For example, there was uproar at one meeting when Thomas Steele rose to claim that O'Connell's watch had been stolen from his pocket while he had been passing through the crowd. Immediately there were cries of 'Lock the doors! Send for the police!'[74] The doors were barred shut. O'Connell was deeply upset, revealing that it was 'an old family timepiece' and he would not have lost it for £500. The meeting resumed, and O'Connell delivered a strong attack on Wellington and Peel. But before he was finished there was a disturbance at the door, which was opened to reveal a police inspector. Forcing his way to the front, the police inspector carried a gold watch in his hand. 'It was found, sir, after you left home,' he revealed, 'under your pillow in your bedroom.' There was much laughter in the hall, and O'Connell joined in the fun. One woman shouted out, 'Ah, Liberator, darling, sure no one would rob you.'

The Repeal rent was £259 the week after the corporation debate, and rose to £366 the following week.[75] The increased income dragged the Association out of debt and O'Connell immediately began planning the construction of a new building, on the same site as the Corn Exchange, large enough to accommodate three thousand people. O'Connell was insistent that the building would make an excellent temporary House of Commons, while the old chamber in College Green (owned by the Bank of Ireland) was undergoing the necessary alterations to convert it back into a parliament.

Disturbed by the rapid success of the Repeal Association, the prime minister, Robert Peel, made a speech in which he threatened that civil war would be preferable to the dismemberment of the empire.[76] O'Connell responded in a thrilling speech at the Association, declaring that he belonged to a nation of eight million, with a further million Irish in England, and that while they would not begin a rebellion, neither would they back down. And he wondered if Peel had the courage 'to begin that strife against Ireland'. With this speech, 'O'Connell had again become a great power'.[77] Many of those who listened, especially the younger members, believed that O'Connell was now prepared to fight if it came to it, and there was a growing confidence that the question would soon be settled one way or another.

Caricature of Daniel O'Connell attempting to take his seat in the British House of Commons in May 1829. (*Getty Images*)

O'Connell addressing the crowds from the balcony of his house on Merrion Square. (*Courtesy of the Glasnevin Trust*)

Drawing of Daniel O'Connell making his maiden political speech, January 1800, a speech which he referenced throughout his career, including in the great Repeal speech of 1834. (*Courtesy of the Glasnevin Trust*)

Painting of the British House of Commons, with O'Connell featured. (*The National Portrait Gallery, London*)

Lithograph of Daniel O'Connell. (*Getty Images*)

Painting of Daniel O'Connell touring the country in the Repeal Year, 1843. (*The National Gallery of Ireland*)

Drawing of Daniel O'Connell addressing the crowd at the first monster meeting at Trim, Co. Meath, on 16 March 1843. (*Getty Images*)

KING O'CONNELL AT TARA.

Caricature of Daniel O'Connell at the monster meeting at Tara, 15 August 1843. (*Getty Images*)

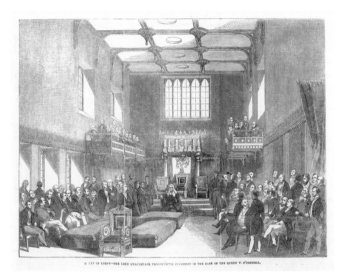

The trial of Daniel O'Connell, January–February 1844. (*Illustrated London News Ltd / Mary Evans Picture Library*)

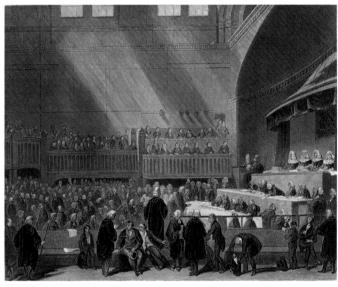

Daniel O'Connell leaving the hall of the Four Courts following his conviction in February 1844. (*Classic Image / Alamy*)

Engraving of Daniel O'Connell walking home following his release from prison on
5 September 1844. (*The Bridgeman Art Library*)

NIGHT-SCENE IN A DUBLIN-STREET.

Scene in Dublin on the night of O'Connell's release from prison. (*Getty Images*)

THE PROCESSION PASSING THE BANK.

Triumphant procession of O'Connell around Dublin to celebrate his release. (*Illustrated London News Ltd / Mary Evans Picture Library*)

Daniel O'Connell in his triumphal carriage addressing the people. (*Getty Images*)

Charles Gavan Duffy
(1816–1903), the editor of
The Nation newspaper.
(*Getty Images*)

Thomas Davis (1814–1845), leading figure in the Young Ireland movement. (*The Bridgeman Art Library*)

Daniel O'Connell on his final voyage to the continent, March 1847. (*Courtesy of the Glasnevin Trust*)

DANIELI · OCONNELLO
VINDICI · ILLI
IVRIVM · CIVILIVM · ATQVE · SACRORVM
HIBERNIAE · SVAE
QVI · QVVM · ROMAM · ITER · HABERET
HIS · IN · AEDIBVS · CESSIT · E · VITA
IDIBVS · MAIIS · AN · M · DCCC · XLVII.
MONVMENTVM · PECVNIA · COLLATII · FACTVM
ANNO · AB · ORTV · EIVS · C.
M · DCCC · LXXV.

Memorial marking where Daniel O'Connell died in Genoa. (*Courtesy of Dr Daragh O'Connell and Dr Nora Skrabanek*)

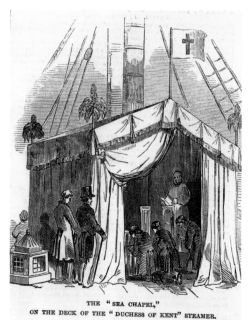

The 'Sea Chapel' on the *Duchess of Kent* steamer which brought O'Connell's remains back to Ireland. (*Courtesy of the Glasnevin Trust*)

THE "SEA CHAPEL," ON THE DECK OF THE "DUCHESS OF KENT" STEAMER.

INTERIOR OF THE "SEA CHAPEL."—THE O'CONNELL FAMILY RECEIVING THE REMAINS.

The O'Connell family receiving the remains of Daniel O'Connell. (*Courtesy of the Glasnevin Trust*)

The tomb of Daniel O'Connell at Glasnevin Cemetery, with the inscription behind: 'My body to Ireland, my heart to Rome, my soul to Heaven'. (*Courtesy of the Glasnevin Trust*)

The O'Connell Monument at Glasnevin Cemetery. (*Courtesy of the Glasnevin Trust*)

The funeral of Charles Stewart Parnell in October 1891 with the statue of O'Connell behind. (*Courtesy of the Glasnevin Trust*)

A photograph of the O'Connell statue on O'Connell Street, pre-dating the destruction of Nelson's Pillar. (*The National Library of Ireland*)

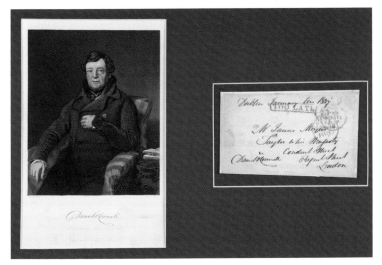

Portrait of O'Connell and copy of his signature. (*Courtesy of the Glasnevin Trust*)

DANIEL O'CONNELL.

THE CHAMPION OF LIBERTY.

Lithographed by Raffe   Entered according to act of congress in the year 1847, by Hoffy, in the Clerks Office of the district Court of the Eastern district of Pennsylvania   Printed by Wagner & McGuigan

Pub.ᵈ Sep.ᵗ 1847, by HOFFY, at N.° 26, South 3.ᵈ S.ᵗ Philadelphia.

Daniel O'Connell, 'The Champion of Liberty'.

Chapter 9 ∾

'THE MOSES OF IRELAND' AND THE YEAR OF REPEAL, 1843

'By the force of his own personality he led Ireland to St. Stephen's, almost as much as Moses led the children of Israel to Mount Sinai.'[1]

(W.E. GLADSTONE ON DANIEL O'CONNELL, 1889)

On 2 January 1843 O'Connell announced that 1843 would be the Repeal year.[2] Many mocked his presumption and few believed his bold prediction. The strategy was to have public outdoor meetings in almost every county. Rather than relying on newspapers and pamphlets to bring the message of Repeal to the country, O'Connell would speak directly to the people, giving everyone an opportunity to hear him speak on the subject. The risks were enormous. Would people turn up? If they did, could the crowds be controlled, or would violence and rioting take place? And did O'Connell, now in his sixty-eighth year, have the energy and enough of his old oratorical powers to undertake such an exhausting mission? Between March and October he spoke at thirty-one major outdoor meetings, and after all of these was called upon to give a speech (and sometimes two or three) at the public dinner which followed. In the same period he also attended thirteen meetings of the Repeal Association, as well as a number of smaller county meetings.[3] His son John calculated that O'Connell had travelled over five thousand miles to agitate during these months.

O'Connell later admitted that these seven months were 'the most anxious period of his life'.[4] Even though he had 'unbounded confidence in his influence for good over his countrymen', he was all the time filled with concern that something might go wrong and give the government an excuse to use force. What he was trying to do was translate his successful Clare campaign of 1828 into a national campaign, and terrify the British government into conceding Repeal by showing that he controlled the people. Even though O'Connell insisted he would never resort to violence, the spectre of violence was always left hanging in the air. At these meetings O'Connell called on the people to be ready to act if he called on them again, a threat to the government as well as a display of strength.[5] Nevertheless he always followed this up by insisting that he would never need to make that call, for Repeal would be secured peacefully. In the meetings of the Repeal Association he routinely repeated his key political principle, that 'a revolution would be too dearly purchased' if the cost was 'one drop of blood', and that 'in his time, and while he lived' the only blood spilled would be his own.[6] He was attempting to withstand any attacks from without, while all the time resisting the equal and opposite pressure from within.

It was a potentially treacherous course, made more dangerous by the boast of O'Connell's friends that he had 200,000 fighting men ready to respond to his command.[7] One danger was that the government would overreact and declare the meetings illegal or, worse, unleash the army against the crowds. Government spies were sent to all the meetings, to observe, report, and collect evidence against O'Connell and the other organisers. O'Connell welcomed them to the meetings and always made sure they were given places near the front to take their notes. Sometimes, however, he could not resist a joke at their expense, and would give his speeches in Irish to bewilder them. The presence of these reporters explains why any attacks on the British army were immediately corrected. For example, at a meeting of the Repeal Association on 29 May, O'Connell repudiated a report in the *Freeman's Journal* which quoted him as making reference to 'the ruffian soldiery of Britain'.[8] Knowing that such a claim could and would be used against him, O'Connell insisted that such a charge was false, and he praised the army for its conduct and discipline. The other danger was that the crowds would become so excited by the impassioned oratory that they would resort to violence, provoking a riot or, worse, a rebellion. But the temperance movement of Fr Theobald Mathew gave O'Connell confidence. It allowed him to assemble a voluntary police, which insisted on calling itself 'O'Connell's Police', to supervise all the events and make sure there were no problems, and he trusted this force because its members had taken the pledge. Large parts of the country had been transformed by the temperance movement, and O'Connell became convinced that the people could now be mobilised for a peaceful crusade which relied on 'moral force'.

The first public meeting took place in Trim, Co. Meath, on 16 March 1843, and was attended by thirty thousand, according to the government's own figures. O'Connell's speech used elements from his great Repeal speech of 1834, and it was clear to his listeners that this was the O'Connell of old, with his powers restored. At a banquet for the leaders afterwards O'Connell spoke of 'the multitudes that surrounded me today', and he asked the men of Meath, 'Are you slaves, and will you be content to be slaves?'[9] Answering his own question, he revealed, 'I shall be either in my grave or a freeman . . . for I am tired of remaining under submission to others.' He then pointed to the women in the room, and said that they were too good-looking and too pure 'ever to be the mothers of slaves', and he revealed that the time had come when Ireland must decide whether to be free, or 'consent to crouch for ever beneath the feet of her tyrants'.[10] Reviewing Irish history, he said that too many battles had been lost because the Irish had abandoned the field too early. And he promised them that he would 'never relax in the battle till the victory is mine'. The British parliament, he insisted, could not be relied on for anything except injustice, and he declared that the people must decide whether they were for Ireland, or against O'Connell, for there was nothing in between. During this period the Repeal rent, which was averaging £300 a month after the Corporation debate, began to grow in geometric proportions, reaching a high point of £14,000 in the summer as Repeal fever swept the country.

Despite approaching his sixty-eighth birthday at the start of the campaign, O'Connell was like a man reborn. A visitor to Ireland at this time described him as 'large, strong, broad shouldered, full-chested' with a head that was suited 'perfectly to his colossal figure'.[11] But it was also noted that 'in moments of repose there seems to impend over him an oppressive languor—perhaps as a result of his present labours— perhaps of his years'. However, as soon as he rose to speak 'all his face and person are lighted up with his innate spirit' and his 'vigour and power burst forth in every movement'.

At a meeting of the Repeal Association in May O'Connell addressed the speech by Peel which had threatened civil war as a more preferable alternative 'to the dismemberment of this empire'.[12] O'Connell was furious and delivered one of his most aggressive speeches, speaking 'in tones that thrilled his audience'.[13] It was in this speech that he announced that he belonged to a nation of eight million people, with a further one million Irish in Britain. And he returned the threat to Peel by challenging him to risk a contest with such a number. 'We will begin no rebellion', O'Connell insisted, 'but I tell him [Peel] from this place that he dare not begin that strife against Ireland.'

This was the speech which determined the character of the contest for the Young Ireland faction. They began to believe that O'Connell would meet unconstitutional force with open defiance, and merge his moral force with physical force if challenged. O'Connell encouraged such a belief in his speeches, to excite his own supporters, to terrify his enemies, and to add an undercurrent of danger to the movement. But O'Connell's constant references to peaceful methods, and his insistence that violent resistance would never be necessary, showed that at heart he had not changed from the man who won Catholic emancipation in the 1820s using exclusively peaceful methods.

Repeal meetings were held in Limerick and Sligo, but the next big meeting was at Mullingar in Co. Westmeath, which was attended by an estimated one hundred thousand people. In his address O'Connell was cautious, revealing his opinion that Wellington and Peel would show their teeth but not bite, because 'the object of Repealers was legitimate and their means peaceful and lawful'.[14] At the banquet that evening he became more aggressive, saying that if the Repealers were attacked by the government, despite not breaking any law or constitutional principle, then 'our patience will become exhausted and human nature would call for a more steady resistance'.[15] Two days later, at a meeting at the Corn Exchange, O'Connell went further, saying, 'We won't go to war, we will keep on the legal side. But if others invade us, *that* is not civil war.'[16] The government looked into ways of banning the meetings and suppressing the Repeal Association, and decided to dismiss any magistrate who attended any public meeting. This only alienated more people, and many young lawyers, such as Sir Colman O'Loghlen, joined the Association as a response to the high-handed methods of the government.

On 21 May O'Connell addressed a meeting at Cork, with an estimated half a million people attending according to the government. As he often did, O'Connell evoked the spectre of rape to terrify the women in the crowd and fortify the resolve of the men. He imagined a young Irish emigrant in England being told the news that his father had been murdered by a dragoon, his mother shot by a policeman, and his sister 'now a wandering maniac', adding, 'I will not say what happened to her.'[17] Such descriptions were brilliantly effective at creating an emotional response which could then be channelled and controlled. At the banquet afterwards O'Connell spoke of his pride that the weekly Repeal rent had risen to £694, and that he was confident it would 'close on a thousand, and perhaps more'. Upon hearing this a man shouted, 'More power to you.' 'More power to Old Ireland,' O'Connell replied, 'that is power indeed.' Addressing the fears that Britain might attempt to send troops to quell the meetings, O'Connell insisted that 'they will not attempt to bully us . . . They shall not attempt to massacre us.'[18] 'We are safe', he revealed, 'because "Ireland reposes in peace".'

The meetings, dubbed 'monster meetings' by correspondents to *The Times*, soon developed a momentum of their own. On 18 May O'Connell travelled in his private carriage from Limerick to Charleville in Co. Cork and all along the route he was met by people who stopped what they were doing to 'greet him heartily'.[19] It took half an hour to pass through the town of Bruff, because the crowds were so great, and O'Connell went through the triumphal arches which had been formed in every quarter. 'Every window in the town was occupied by ladies' and a reporter admitted that 'the cheering and waving of handkerchiefs in honour of the Liberator was beyond description'. It was estimated that 350,000 people had gathered at Charleville to hear him speak, and the streets were so packed that O'Connell chose to address the crowd from his carriage rather than on the platform. Afterward the Repeal warden for Doneraile presented O'Connell with £10 for the Repeal rent, and O'Connell joked that '[w]e shall never again call in dingy, dirty Doneraile, but in future it shall be brilliant Doneraile!'[20] From there O'Connell went to Cashel in Co. Tipperary, and then on to Co. Longford. The Longford meeting on 28 May was attended by somewhere between 60,000 and 100,000 people. Eight temperance bands were in attendance playing music, and the main platform had a banner which read 'Ireland for the Irish, and the Irish for Ireland'. In his speech, O'Connell declared that they would not break any laws, they would not resort to violence, but (and here he slapped his breast warmly to enormous cheers) if they were to be attacked, then 'who will be the coward? We will put them in the wrong, and if they attack us then in your name I set them at defiance.'[21]

For the next meeting at Drogheda on 5 June the streets were decorated with green boughs, and there were flags with various mottos. One of them had the inscription 'We are Irishmen, determined to be free—we are nine millions'.[22] This was to paraphrase O'Connell's great claim that the eight million people on the island of Ireland, and the one million Irish in Britain, could not be silenced. Another flag was inscribed 'A population of nine millions is too great to be dragged at the tail of another nation'. From Drogheda O'Connell made his way to Kilkenny for another meeting, and then on to Mallow, Co. Cork.

The baiting of the British government reached its zenith at Mallow on Sunday 11 June. Between three and four hundred thousand people attended, and twenty-six temperance bands entertained them. It had been reported that the cabinet had met a few days before to discuss the state of Ireland, and rumours circulated that the monster meetings were about to be declared illegal. Indeed, unknown to O'Connell, the British cabinet was meeting that very day to discuss whether to ban any discussion of Repeal whatsoever.[23] The army had been called out to monitor what was happening, and it seemed as if the meeting would be put down by force.[24] As O'Connell later explained, 'Aye, in Mallow things looked more threatening; they were ready to bring their horse, foot, and artillery on us, but in that very Mallow I hurled at them my high and haughty defiance.' 'The Mallow Defiance' was to become a key part of the Repeal legend, with O'Connell declaring afterwards that 'they could not conquer the Irish people. They admitted the truth of the assertion, and they neither attempted to conquer or delude us.' Faced with the threat of suppression, O'Connell decided to raise the stakes at Mallow, and make his most explicit assertion of Irish rights.

Before the meeting O'Connell was unusually preoccupied. A journalist, Maurice Lenihan of the *Cork Examiner*, noted this, and asked Steele if there was any problem. Steele discussed the rumours that the meetings would be suppressed, and explained, 'Our next move may be to take to the field.'[25] O'Connell noticed Lenihan and asked him to tell all the reporters to be 'very particular in taking down every word I speak today'. And he promised that something important would either be said at the meeting or at the dinner afterwards. At the meeting O'Connell said nothing controversial. In fact, he made sure to proclaim the loyalty of the Irish people, 'the finest people on the face of God's earth'. He also delivered a generous tribute to the British army, 'the bravest in the world'.[26] However, in a clever attempt to create disaffection, he unfavourably contrasted the promotion prospects of these same soldiers with their counterparts on the continent. In a stirring conclusion, O'Connell declared that Ireland 'would no longer submit to be branded and vilified by the Saxon'.[27] He promised that '[he] was counsel for Ireland, and the people were his clients, and if they acted on his advice, their country would soon be free'.

About six hundred men attended the dinner afterwards, and the gallery of the hall was filled with women. Here O'Connell decided to make his stand. A singer was performing before the speeches, and O'Connell asked him to sing one of his favourite songs by Thomas Moore. This was the song which contained the lines 'Oh, where's the slave so lowly/Condemned to chains unholy', which O'Connell had quoted at the corporation debate on Repeal. When the singer completed the verse, O'Connell jumped to his feet and extended his arms and exclaimed, 'I am not that slave!' It was a carefully staged moment and it jolted the audience into action. His cry was taken up by the audience, who rose to their feet and began shouting, 'We are not those slaves! We are not those slaves!'[28] As Oliver MacDonagh has shrewdly noted, 'O'Connell the revivalist' was 'the precipitator of something not unlike the conversion experience'.[29]

Beginning his speech, O'Connell declared that he was sick of speechmaking: 'The time is come when we must be doing. Gentlemen, you may soon learn the alternative, to live as slaves, or die as freemen.' Raising the recent discussions of the cabinet about what to do with Ireland, he repeated his insistence that 'as long as they leave us a rag of the constitution we will stand on it. We will violate no law, we will assail no enemy,' but they would defend themselves if attacked. A man shouted, 'We are ready to meet them.' 'To be sure you are,' replied O'Connell, 'do you think that I suppose you to be cowards or fools?' In a skilful demonstration of the Irish people's loyalty to the crown, he revealed that following any war, once they had defeated their enemies they would place the sceptre in the hands of Queen Victoria, 'whose conduct has ever been full of sympathy and emotion for our sufferings'. According to Lenihan, every sentence in the speech was greeted with 'frantic shouts'.

'Are we to be called slaves?' asked O'Connell aggressively. He suggested that the Irish might be sent to the West Indies as slaves, and reminded his audience of the 80,000 Irishmen who had been sent to Barbados as slaves by Cromwell. This allowed him to denounce Peel and Wellington as modern Cromwells, for attempting to make slaves of the Irish nation. But he insisted that they would never trample on him or, if they did, 'it will be my dead body they will trample on, not the living man'. In a particularly dramatic and emotional passage, he spoke of Cromwell's atrocities in Ireland, for example the three hundred women in Wexford who 'prayed to Heaven for mercy, and I hope they found it', because when they 'prayed to the English for humanity' they were 'collected round the cross of Christ' and slaughtered.[30] This produced an incredible sensation in the hall, with cries of 'Oh! Oh! Oh!', and some of the women in the gallery began screaming in terror. But O'Connell assured the women that there was no danger of this happening again, 'for the men of Ireland would die to the last in their defence'.[31] This produced a standing ovation for O'Connell, with wild cheering that lasted for several minutes. O'Connell reminded them, 'We were a paltry remnant in Cromwell's time; we are nine millions now!'

O'Connell then boasted of the fact that he was the only man 'living or dead' who had 'enjoyed forty years uninterrupted popularity and confidence'.[32] A man shouted that he hoped he would enjoy twice as many more. But O'Connell replied, 'No, that cannot be,' and he said that the time would soon come when he would go 'before my God, to answer for all the acts of my public and private life'. O'Connell admitted that he had been called a coward many times in the House of Commons, and it was 'a hard name to bear with'. But he revealed that those men were safe to call him it, 'for it was a punishment that I deserved'. This self-recrimination produced cries of 'No! No!' Referring to his fatal duel with D'Esterre, O'Connell accepted that he deserved punishment for having 'violated the law of the great God'. But he warned 'the enemies of Ireland' that they were mistaken if they thought he would be afraid to sacrifice his life for 'so righteous a cause as that of my native land'. 'What is life to me?' asked O'Connell. 'My heart is widowed, and I am a solitary being in this world.' As he discussed the memory of his wife, O'Connell became deeply affected, and many in the audience began weeping in sympathy. O'Connell ended his speech to tremendous cheering as he spoke of the hope that he would meet his wife again in 'a better world'.

The speech immediately became known as 'The Mallow Defiance' and was read, recited, and studied all across the country. To many it was a call to arms, daring the British to attack, and confirming that the Irish would respond with force. The Repeal Association commissioned John Hogan, the celebrated Irish sculptor, to make a massive marble statue of O'Connell, inscribed with the challenge to the government 'They may trample upon me, but, if they do, it shall not be on the living man, but upon my dead body.' The British government hesitated, unsure of what to do, and the immediate crisis passed. The Repeal Association was not suppressed, but O'Connell recognised that the gamble had been too great, and he never again resorted to such aggressive language.

After Mallow, O'Connell made his way to Ennis, Co. Clare, for another meeting, and then on to Athlone, Co. Westmeath. The Athlone meeting on 18 June attracted between forty and fifty thousand people who all gathered to hear 'The Coming Man'.[33] A German visitor, Jacob Venedey, who had made it his mission to attend as many meetings as possible, noticed that the prevailing fashion in Ireland was for men to wear grey coats, while the women preferred scarlet dresses. Venedey was impressed to see that very few were drinking, everyone seemed to be a teetotaller, and was told that 'factious fights' had disappeared with the passing of drunkenness.

There was an incredible stillness at the ground, until finally O'Connell arrived in his carriage and the crowd rushed to greet him. There then rose a cry such as Venedey had never heard before, hats were raised in the air, and shouts of 'Hurrah! Hurrah! Hurrah! Long live O'Connell! Long live the Liberator!' Venedey was in awe of O'Connell, 'the man whose necromantic power' had circled the crowd around him.[34] O'Connell descended from the carriage and made his way to one of the platforms, a path clearing before him. A seat was brought for him, and Thomas Steele held a standard over his head, which served as a shade to protect him from the rays of the sun.

As the speeches began there was a loud crashing noise. One of the steps on the platform had collapsed, but the crowd, fearing that the meeting was being raided by soldiers, began to panic. Thomas Steele turned to O'Connell and whispered, 'It is nothing—you need not fear.' 'Fear! Fear!' answered O'Connell, 'with so proud a glance, and in such a rebuking tone' that Venedey was in no doubt that 'nothing could be more strange to the mind of the Irish Agitator, than the thought of fear'.[35] There followed a number of speeches, until finally O'Connell was called upon to address the crowd. Venedey was unable to describe the reception, which was unlike anything he had ever seen in his life. During the speech an unruly horse broke loose and the people around it began to panic and run, and 'in an instant, a great portion of the congregated mass was in flight'. The noise was like the 'rapid advance of a heavy body of cavalry' and people remembered that the garrison at Athlone had recently been strengthened. 'Stand still!' demanded O'Connell, whose 'thunder-like tones came pealing over the multitude'. The panic ended as abruptly as it had begun. People stopped running and followed O'Connell's command. Venedey later wrote that it was 'as if fate had put the power of his word to the test, and wished to demonstrate that it was omnipotent'.[36]

In his oration O'Connell praised the people for the magnificent demonstration of moral resolution and physical power which they had exhibited. He noted the date and reminded his listeners that it was the anniversary of the battle of Waterloo, a battle won by Irish soldiers and valour, and he insisted that the Irish were as brave wearing grey coats as they were wearing red. After attacking Peel, he asked the crowd whether they could keep a secret, and he joked that it was 'a secret that I tell you in the deepest confidence, and I think there are enough of you here to help me to keep it'.[37] There was much laughter and a man shouted, 'More than enough!' 'Well then', said O'Connell, 'you must know that honest Bobby Peel has told a lie.' Peel had claimed that Queen Victoria had declared against Repeal, but O'Connell insisted that this was untrue. More than once, he revealed, she had reproached Peel for making claims on her behalf, at which a man shouted, 'I wish a crow picked Peel's eye's out.' O'Connell replied in a flash, 'I wish a crow came and stuffed your mouth with potatoes!' and this was 'an observation that excited the most uproarious laughter'.

Discussing the government's latest policy of conciliation, O'Connell declared that there would be no conciliation until he saw a parliament in College Green. He quoted the *Morning Chronicle*, which claimed that there would never be an Irish parliament unless England was too weak to resist. 'What a temptation is this,' said O'Connell, 'to offer up a prayer, after every mass on Sundays, that England may become weak.' He also criticised the building of a large new prison in Ennis, Co. Clare, which he said had become unnecessary, especially since Fr Mathew had visited the town. O'Connell asked if there were any teetotallers in the crowd. There was a cry of 'High for Fr Mathew' and 'thousands upon thousands of labour-hardened hands' were raised. 'Oh!' sighed O'Connell to much cheering, 'In that cry there is Repeal.'

O'Connell was determined to make his feelings on violence clear. He admitted that the gathering was large enough to throw all its enemies into the River Shannon, 'if you thought it worth your while to begrime its waters with them'. But, he declared, 'that you will neither wish nor will to do'. To general applause he announced, 'You will never again play into the hands of the Tories.' By keeping on a peaceful path, 'the day of our freedom' would draw near and Repeal would be secured. He reminded his listeners of the great victory which had been won in 1828–1829 and said 'the battle for Repeal' would follow the same plan that brought victory in 'the battle for emancipation'. In every speech O'Connell spent some time talking to the women in the crowd. This one was no different, and he called on single women to only marry Repealers.

A story was told from the Clare campaign. The men of Clare had taken a pledge that no whiskey would be drunk until the election was over and this promise had been followed very strictly. However a parish priest was still worried that the leader of the McNamara gang, 'a proud and passionate man', might be the cause of some violence. And so he sent for him and made him promise to abstain from whiskey and avoid any quarrels until after the election. 'Certainly,' said McNamara, 'provided no one strikes me a blow.' 'No,' replied the priest, 'that will not do. You must promise me not to strike any one, even though you yourself be struck.' At last, McNamara gave his word. When word of this circulated, some people decided to take advantage of the pledge. A man called Kingston called to see McNamara and asked him if he intended to vote for his landlord, Vesey Fitzgerald. 'No,' he replied, 'I mean to vote for Dan O'Connell.' 'You are a stupid fool,' said Kingston. 'You lie,' said McNamara, at which Kingston struck him in the face. McNamara was about to strike back, but he remembered his promise. So instead he made Kingston an offer. He would pay Kingston one pound, but only if Kingston struck him a second time after the election was over. Recognising the punishment that was in store, Kingston lost his nerve and rejected the offer, and he made sure that he avoided McNamara for the next six months.

The crowd at Athlone loved this story and cheered loudly. But there was a serious point for O'Connell. He declared, 'Thus did men conduct themselves to gain emancipation.' And so he called on the men of Ireland to '[t]ake a blow and bear it patiently, for the good of your country, until we have carried Repeal, and when you have it, you can pull a barefaced scoundrel by the nose!' There was general laughter, and O'Connell concluded by calling on the people to be united, and they would live to 'bless the day that God had made Ireland a nation. Hurrah, then, for the Repeal! Old Ireland and freedom for ever!'

After the speech, O'Connell returned to his seat like a boxer after a successful championship bout. Steele covered his shoulders with a cloak, while another man handed him a peach, 'out of which he took a hearty bite'. A third man presented him with an orange and, as he reached out to take it, he turned smiling to one of the bystanders and imparted some advice: 'To succeed with a multitude as a speaker, you must always say something that will excite their spirits and make them laugh.' There were other speeches after O'Connell's, but few people stayed to hear them, and by the end of the meeting only a small number of fanatical Repealers remained.

Afterwards O'Connell and the other speakers went to a house nearby where refreshments were served. He kept his cloak wrapped around him, as he now always did whenever he spoke in public.[38] O'Connell wrote some lines in the album of a female admirer and then had something small to eat, washing it down with a glass of champagne. That evening in Athlone town there was a large banquet for O'Connell, while a band played music. Venedey noted that 'the food and music were equally bad'. Few seemed to want to eat the food, and the covers were not even removed from a few of the dishes. O'Connell drank only water at the start of the meal, but later added a little wine to it, and Venedey would have been convinced he was a half-teetotaller if he hadn't seen him drink the glass of champagne earlier. Lord French gave a long and tedious speech, praising O'Connell's virtues, and O'Connell was observed laughing and then yawning 'awfully'.

Invited to speak, O'Connell delivered his second major oration of the day. He stood and, placing his left hand on his right breast, bowed, before addressing the gathering. He insisted that the day's demonstration had not been a compliment to himself; rather, it was a demonstration of national pride and determination. Their mission was 'to change a province into a nation'; it would give freedom to a nation and 'unfetter the slave, in order that he may, unbound, walk forth in the full dignity of man'.[39] To loud and continued cheering, O'Connell declared that he was proud to see that everyone had abandoned their own private interest so that they could be free, insisting that the alternative was death. This led to loud cheers and shouts of 'Freedom or death!' O'Connell addressed these cheers and reassured his listeners that they need not think of dying, 'for during my entire life I have always preferred one living patriot to ten dead ones'.[40] And he insisted that he had only introduced the alternative of dying as 'an oratorical phrase'.

Attacking the Act of Union, O'Connell denied that it had ever been a real union. Rather it was been 'a parchment, spider's web union' which had forced the Irish people into a state of bondage from 1801 to 1829. In that period O'Connell had been prevented from rising at the bar because he was a Catholic. It was a constant grievance, and was seen by his enemies as proof that personal ambition was at the heart of his campaign. He reminded his listeners of all that he had suffered in that period, because he was refused a silk gown, and he spoke of how he would return home from the courts, 'sick at heart, and disgusted in mind, when I reflected that it was not in my power to reach that promotion in my profession'. O'Connell ended the speech by predicting the coming of Repeal, and sat down 'amid thunders of applause'. Returning to his seat, he drank a couple of glasses of wine. A woman with a child was seated near him and during the dinner he played with the child. This was an age when few adults had much time for children, but O'Connell in his later years had an incredible rapport with the young. Before the speeches were over, O'Connell rose to ask for permission to retire early. This was readily given, and he stopped to kiss the child as he was leaving. This show of affection produced a visible effect, with people moved by O'Connell's demonstration that in private, as well as in public, he was the father of the nation.

Venedey concluded that despite his vanity, as evinced by the references to his own legal career and disappointments, O'Connell ruled over Ireland, 'as king never yet ruled over any country'.[41] He believed O'Connell had gained, and wielded, 'unbounded autocracy in Ireland'. But Venedey was concerned that there were but two roads open to him, one which led to the freedom of the Irish people and the other which would drag him to the place of execution. Leaving one of the meetings, Venedey noticed a group of beggars fighting over a sovereign which O'Connell had given one of them, but he could not understand their argument and was unsure whether they were fighting because each wanted his share, or because the money had extra significance as it had been given by O'Connell.

One of the organisers of the event offered to put Venedey up for the night, after learning that he had not secured accommodation. The man ran a general store, and had his daughter clear out a room for him. Venedey was the kind of man who fell in love very easily. When he saw the daughter he decided that he was 'in great luck' and was greatly taken by her 'dark hair [and] deep blue eyes', describing her figure as 'not very large, but stout, and yet finely shaped'. This 'Connaught beauty' had observed Venedey sitting across from O'Connell at the banquet dinner and this induced her to make every effort with his room. The next day they discussed O'Connell's injunction that the women should only marry Repealers, and Venedey became distracted by her 'rich kissable mouth'.

On 22 June O'Connell addressed the crowds at Skibbereen in Co. Cork and seemed determined to clarify, and perhaps contradict, 'The Mallow Defiance'. He declared that 'one living Repealer is worth a churchyard full of dead ones', insisting that he would rather live for Ireland than die for it. O'Connell would only lead the people so far, but no further. The point had been made to the British government and there was no need to labour it. The change of direction was noted, reluctantly, by his supporters. Revealingly, when Hogan finished his marble sculpture of O'Connell he was instructed not to put any quotation on the pedestal after all.

From Skibbereen, O'Connell travelled to Dundalk for the meeting on 29 June. Three triumphal arches had been erected in the town centre.

The one on the right was dedicated to Queen Victoria and had an oil-painting likeness of her, and the one on the left was for Prince Albert, and had his picture attached to it. The central arch was for O'Connell and on it was a piece of white linen, on which were written the words 'The Moses of Ireland, who has broken the strength of our enemies, welcome to Dundalk'. As he entered the town O'Connell was met by a large crowd. 'O'Connell stood erect in the carriage, and saluted the people on all sides.' Venedey noted that 'in every glance of his eye there was triumph, and the exhilarating feelings of joy'. And why not, thought Venedey: 'Who could, as he, this day say—"I am the man—Daniel O'Connell"'. The crowds opened before O'Connell and Venedey compared it to the passage of Moses through the Red Sea. Three marching bands accompanied O'Connell, but all were playing a different tune at the same time. One played 'God save the queen', another 'The garland of love', and the third 'Patrick's day in the morning'. Later in the day Venedey heard the bands play the tunes separately and they were so awful he decided he preferred 'the triplicated tune' when they were all played together.

The speeches at each meeting, Venedey noted, were always the same if studied in their entirety, but with occasional differences in delivery or tone, and sometimes new sections added for particular audiences. All the speeches owed much to the great speech in favour of Repeal in 1834, but as always O'Connell was trying to provoke a feeling with his oratory, rather than just convey ideas. It was clear from the beginning that the crowd in Dundalk had not taken the temperance pledge. Many had been drinking and the crowds 'rushed together in a disorderly manner—they pressed—they struggled through one another' and there was none of the stillness of the Athlone meeting. It was later revealed that Fr Mathew had never visited Dundalk.

Even the greatest orators struggle with a difficult audience. The crowd at Dundalk was impossible to please. For the first fifteen minutes 'the masses remained untouched', and Venedey noticed the 'dark cloud of dissatisfaction' gather on O'Connell's brow. To add to the pressure, the crowd was restless, shoving and pressing, and it looked like someone might get hurt. On a few occasions, 'a boy or a woman, in danger of being smothered, was raised out of the multitude and moved from hand to hand over the heads of the assembly'. Venedey was disturbed by the 'inattention and rudeness' of the crowd and thought that O'Connell should quickly bring his speech to an end. But O'Connell was determined to reach his audience. He kept lowering the tone of his speech, until finally he struck a note which met with approval. It was concerning the financial benefits that Repeal would bring, and O'Connell found that aiming at the audience's pockets was the best way of reaching their hearts.

O'Connell was playing with fire in this speech, admitting that he was almost tempted to hope that Britain would attack them, though he accepted that it was 'a wild and idle wish'.[42] And he set out his plan for convening a new Irish parliament of 300 members. Using the census of 1831, he argued that every town with at least 9,000 people should be given representation, and this, combined with the county members, would make up a parliament of 300. Each town would have to contribute £100 towards a Repeal banquet in Dublin, or risk having no representation in the new Irish House of Commons. This was a sly way of raising additional funds, as well as a way of gauging support for the scheme. O'Connell was confident that if this plan succeeded then Queen Victoria would call for the summoning of a new Irish parliament, and the Union would be dissolved.

When O'Connell sat down a man called O'Reilly attempted to challenge the objective of the meeting. This did not go down well, and O'Connell used the opportunity to mock him from his seat. At one point O'Reilly spoke of a relative he had lost, 'an only relative', and O'Connell told an anecdote from his bar days when a man had been indicted for the murder of his mother. The attorney general, attempting to show the crime in the strongest light, had described with horror how the man had killed 'his mother, the only mother he ever had', and so on, and the laughter became so loud that at last O'Reilly was reduced to silence.

There were also meetings of the Repeal Association to be attended. On 4 July O'Connell arrived at the Corn Exchange and was cheered as he entered the debating chamber. He was wearing a grey coat with a dark collar, and stood 'erect, unmoved, with the most perfect calm personified in his entire manner'.[43] Venedey believed he was like an 'unshakeable and immoveable rock, in the depth of a stormy, raging sea', at times 'half smiling and then again so serious, presenting an image calculated to inspire the deepest feelings of reverence'. Next to O'Connell sat his youngest son, Daniel O'Connell Jnr, who was described by Venedey as 'a well looking (perhaps too handsome), fair haired, young gentleman, with large moustaches, and wearing yellow dress gloves'. The younger O'Connell was acting as president of the meeting, while opposite sat John O'Connell, who was the secretary. The meeting lasted six hours and almost every function was conducted by the Liberator. 'He spoke, read letters, and then spoke again upon these letters,' he counted the contributions which had been received, and he discussed where the money had come from. Seeing him here, in the presence of the elite of the Repealers, Venedey believed that he was finally beginning to understand 'how unlimited was his greatness'. Even though he was a great orator, his oratory was just a means, not an end, and everything he did was directed at a higher purpose.

There were a number of letters from America and O'Connell suggested having a special meeting just for this correspondence because it was so important. He praised the way the Americans had 'gloriously won their freedom and independence' and noted that Britain had since learned her lesson. He was, critical, however of slave-owners, and announced that no money would be accepted from that quarter. And, to continued shouts of 'Hear! Hear!' and loud applause, he ended the discussion by noting that in this, 'the Repeal year', they would 'advance the next step for the abolition of the Union, in a legal and constitutional manner'.

After a few more letters were read, Thomas Steele stood to propose Sir James Graham as a Repeal warden. In his speech he went a little off message and attacked 'these two jackeens and diverting vagabonds—Wellington and Peel'. 'O'Connell smiled, but interfered,' and brought the discussion back to the business at hand. O'Connell was always monitoring what was being said, and intervened whenever the discussion was veering towards the inappropriate. Near the close of the day a Mr Burke began speaking about the Fourth Regiment of Dragoons, then stationed in Dublin. O'Connell interrupted him and said, 'Let the army alone.' Burke replied that he had 'no intention of saying anything, but what was in their praise'. 'Exactly so,' said O'Connell in response. 'Let there be neither praise nor blame; all we have to do is to leave the British army to its officers and its own discipline.' Venedey was astonished that O'Connell spoke close to a dozen times, and that despite his age he 'endured the heavy burden of the entire day'.[44] One speech in particular struck Venedey as strange.

O'Connell spoke of how the Repealers would bring their petitions to the next sitting of parliament in 1844, and Venedey wondered what this meant given that he had previously claimed that 1843 was to be 'the Repeal year'.

At a meeting of the Repeal Association on 7 August 1843, the editor of the *New York Herald*, James Gordon Bennett, arrived at the Corn Exchange with a letter of introduction for O'Connell. A path to the table was cleared for him, with people calling 'to make way for the American gentleman'. Upon being presented with the letter, O'Connell launched into a vicious attack on Bennett's character and career, declaring, 'We don't want him here.' He revealed that Bennett was 'precisely the very sort of man that I do not wish to see here, he is the publisher of the most vile paper that ever disgraced the press of any country'.[45] The crowd turned on Bennett and began abusing and jeering him as he slunk away. The next day, O'Connell informed the meeting that he could never consider himself a true friend of freedom if he allowed 'a dishonourable journalist to intrude himself upon me, without expressing my contempt for him'. The seemingly unprovoked attack on Bennett astonished the gathering, but there were a number of reasons for it, both personal and political. Never one to forget an insult, O'Connell had been an enemy of the *New York Herald* since 12 October 1838, when it had published an article on O'Connell's alleged infidelities. It advised O'Connell not to make a tour of the United States because he would leave 'his numerous children and concubines . . . fatherless and comfortless'.[46] And it quoted him as having boasted in public that 'he never spared a man in his anger nor a woman in his lust'. These were lines which had originally been attributed to King Henry VIII in Robert Nauton's *Fragmenta Regalia*.[47] One of the more lurid allegations was that O'Connell's wife, in order to shame him, had taken in six young women whom he had seduced and then discarded, and employed them around the house in various menial capacities.

Bennett was in France when the article was published and he later blamed it on a vindictive sub-editor after he discovered that O'Connell had read it. To make amends, he published an article praising O'Connell, but the damage was done.[48] O'Connell was not inclined to forgive the insult to him or that to his dead wife. In any case, he knew that the attack had been prompted by his constant attacks on American slavery. Bennett had become highly critical of O'Connell for his attacks on the slave-holding states, and, as a result, had done much to oppose the collection of money for Repeal in the United States. With the combination of a private grievance, and a public issue that O'Connell would not compromise on, Bennett became another victim of O'Connell's furious rage and calculated aggression.

Allegations of financial impropriety returned to distract O'Connell. An attack was made upon him at this time by the duke of Rovigo, a French nobleman who had settled in Co. Clare after he married a rich heiress. Rovigo accused O'Connell of using the money of the Repeal Association for his own purposes and of hiring his sons on a salary of £2,000. The allegation made no impression. There were a number of reasons. First, O'Connell was back to the zenith of his popularity, so any attacks bounced off him. But, more importantly, it was now generally accepted that O'Connell, for all his vices, was not avaricious, and that he was happy to spend his own money on his political activity. Finally, there was enormous sympathy for the fact that he had abandoned his lucrative legal career to become a full-time agitator. Therefore few had any doubt that he 'neither regards money, nor takes much trouble to get it, and still less, when he has it, to keep it together'.[49] O'Connell mocked Rovigo's pretensions, telling the story of a man who had once insisted that he was 'a born gentleman on his wife's side'. And so he taunted Rovigo for being 'a rich landed proprietor—on his wife's side!'

After some difficulty, Jacob Venedey arranged an invitation to join O'Connell's table for dinner. While waiting for O'Connell to make his way home he immediately developed an attraction to the wife of Morgan O'Connell, 'a lovely blooming daughter of Connaught'. O'Connell arrived, wearing a great coat with a black collar, with a blue cloak around him which he kept on during dinner time. He explained that he had developed the habit of keeping himself thus wrapped after speaking in public.[50] During the dinner he sat at the head of the table, 'like a colossus or statue of Jupiter, dominating all'. His daughter Betsey Ffrench sat on his right, and Morgan's wife on the left. It was a Friday so no meat was served, but there was 'everything else in abundance, the best wine, and the newest fruits'. O'Connell said little, apart from encouraging people to try a particular dish or wine. After dessert was served a number of O'Connell's grandchildren came in and each gave him a kiss. 'He then took his daughter by the hand, and held it in his for a short time; he gave the other to his daughter-in-law, and thus sat hand in hand with them.' Venedey was surprised by such a solemn moment at an otherwise informal meal. After dinner Venedey mentioned the irony that in Ireland everyone was trying to dissolve the Union, whereas in Germany they wanted to unite. Tea was served in the drawing room, but O'Connell retired to his study and then to bed. Venedey had made a good impression and was invited back for a second dinner. On this occasion, he was drawn into a conversation about Repeal. One of the guests commented on how difficult it would be to bring Britain to a compromise. But O'Connell answered that the winning of Catholic emancipation in 1829, 'even to the last hour of its passing, was so improbable, that nothing in England's conduct to Ireland could be despaired of as improbable'.[51]

O'Connell was kept particularly busy in July. At a meeting at Donnybrook in Co. Dublin, which followed a successful one at Galway city, he spoke of what 'a glorious sight' it was to see such a gathering, and he declared that 'we will have the country for ourselves'.[52] At the next meeting, at Tullamore in Co. Offaly, between sixty and seventy thousand people gathered from nearby and the neighbouring counties to hear O'Connell. When O'Connell arrived he noticed that an arch had been erected at the main platform which bore the inscription 'The Repeal of the Union, or the World in a Blaze'.[53] He was immediately disturbed, recognising that this slogan could be interpreted as an incitement to violence and used as an excuse to bring the meetings to an end. Steele was immediately dispatched to the organisers to tell them that unless the arch was removed O'Connell would not attend the meeting. The arch was pulled down. On 24 July O'Connell addressed a meeting at Tuam in Co. Galway, and at the banquet afterwards O'Connell declared that 'the strength of their enemies was shattered'.[54]

On 6 August a monster meeting was held at Baltinglass in Co. Wicklow. O'Connell reminded the gathering that they had lost their parliament by 'force and fraud' and promised them that 'Ireland shall be a nation'.[55] At this meeting O'Connell reminded his listeners of his motto 'Whoever commits a crime gives strength to his enemy', urging them to maintain their discipline and abstain from violence. One man shouted, 'We are determined to get Repeal, as we are all sober, and we shall not be put down as we were in 1798.' The only meeting O'Connell did not attend was the one at Clontibret, Co. Monaghan, which took place on 15 August, the same day as the massive meeting held at Tara.

In an article in *The Nation* on 12 August the peaceable nature of the crowds was discussed, 'the serious good temper, the absence of riot or vice', and the military-like discipline which was said to make all of these meetings 'a strange and formidable event'.[56] The government shared this point of view and, as in 1828, was disturbed that O'Connell's orders to assemble and disperse peaceably were being so rigorously obeyed. It feared that peace would only be maintained until the opportune moment to strike appeared, and it derived no comfort from the absence of violence.

While following O'Connell around Ireland, Venedey heard many of the criticisms and rumours about him. Some people accused him of being avaricious, while others said that he was in debt.[57] He was also said to be a coward, afraid of the battlefield. He was accused of being inconsistent, though the only changes Venedey noticed were the occasional changes of his blue frock-coat to a grey one. Venedey was blind to his defects, for there was some merit to this charge. Sometimes during his tour of the country, O'Connell praised Napoleon, and at other times attacked him, and in the same way he sometimes spoke highly of the Whigs, and at other times denounced them. But to Venedey this was nothing more than 'the blue coat yesterday and the grey coat today!' Friends of Venedey back in Germany wondered how a clever man such as O'Connell, without being a hypocrite, was able to take part in the antiquated ceremonies of the Catholic church. But Venedey had no doubt that O'Connell's faith was genuine. A man who had been friends with O'Connell in his younger days, but who was not a Repealer, told Venedey of the change that had occurred in O'Connell's character following his return to the Catholic faith. One day, the man was reading a book of philosophical questioning and recommended it to O'Connell. But O'Connell told him solemnly, 'I know the book, and will never again look at it. I have suffered enough from doing so. Since I have been restored to my former faith, I have enjoyed peace, and trust it will be allowed to remain with me.'[58] On another occasion the man found O'Connell, in his leisure hours, translating Arnauld's book on the infallibility of the Catholic church.

One of the largest Repeal meetings took place on 15 August, the feast of the Assumption in the Catholic liturgy and a strict holy day. The venue was the Hill of Tara, a place rich in symbolism and meaning in Irish history. It was there that St Patrick had preached to the kings of Ireland and converted them; it was there that the old high kings of Ireland had been anointed; and more recently it had been a battleground during the 1798 Rebellion. It was claimed at the time that a million people came to attend the meeting, and while it is impossible to be precise about the exact figure there is some evidence which can be studied. At the Cabra toll-house seven hundred cars (small carriages) and thirty-two coaches passed through that day on the way to Tara, at Phibsborough there were three hundred and twenty-one cars and sixty coaches, and at Blanchardstown there were three hundred vehicles. Forty-two temperance bands also went to Tara to play music during the day. The government estimated the crowd as being anything from one hundred thousand people to a million (Captain Despard, a magistrate who attended, calculated the figure at three hundred thousand), acknowledging that even the lowest figure made it 'a formidable event'.[59] Some people in Dublin went to it out of curiosity, treating it as a holiday. A few took their carriages as close as they could, without going further, just so they could tell people afterwards they had been there. Temporary altars were erected in the morning so that priests could deliver Mass in the open air. Almost forty Masses were celebrated in that way, each one having about a thousand in attendance. One observer described it as a 'strikingly impressive sight', with five or six Masses going on simultaneously a few hundred yards apart, and barely a sound to be heard except the 'low murmur of the voices of the officiating priests, or the tinkling of the tiny mass-bells'.

O'Connell attended Mass in Dublin and then had a massive 'agitation breakfast,' before setting out for Tara. The sun was shining, and all along the way he was greeted by people travelling to the event. He arrived to find a crowd larger than most of the previous meetings put together. It was, John O'Connell later thought, 'the crowning day' of his father's life.[60] He believed that on 'that day the star of his earthly destinies touched its meridian, that day his fortunes culminated, and the labours of his life met their highest earthly reward'.[61]

Addressing the multitude, O'Connell reminded his listeners that everyone had laughed at him on 2 January when he had announced that this would be the Repeal year. But he said that no one was laughing now, and '[i]t is our turn to laugh at present'.[62] Convinced that

Queen Victoria would call for a parliament in Ireland, O'Connell spoke of his hopes for the future. In a dramatic new policy, he called on the people to ignore the British courts of law in Ireland and submit to arbitrators that the Repeal Association would appoint to settle grievances without any expense. This was in response to the government's dismissal of magistrates who had attended some of the Repeal meetings, and was intended to demonstrate that the Union was void. At the banquet that night O'Connell asked the gathering, 'When I want you again will you come?'[63] The answer was 'The sooner the better.' O'Connell's idea for arbitration courts was something he had been thinking about for some weeks. On 17 August a subcommittee of the Repeal Association published a report on the subject, having devised 'a general system of arbitration throughout the country'.

On 20 August John O'Connell decided to organise an out-door *fête* in honour of his father, and help him recover from the exertions of all the monster meetings. The place chosen was Dalkey Island, a steep rock to the south of Dublin Bay, and Venedey was invited to join a group consisting of O'Connell's whole family (sons, daughters, brothers-in-law, and grandchildren), Thomas Steele, P.V. Fitzpatrick and his wife, and two other people. Seasickness prevented the group from making its way to the rock, so instead it was decided to have the festivities on the mainland. After a walk the guests had dinner and then Thomas Steele stood to deliver a speech. Referring to the old Dublin tradition of annually electing a king of Dalkey Island, until this tradition had been suppressed by the British government and made illegal, Steele asked the group to imagine that they were actually on Dalkey Island. This allowed him to arrange an election to choose a king. Morgan O'Connell proposed P.V. Fitzpatrick, who was elected on the spot and saluted as 'His Majesty'. In his acceptance speech, Fitzpatrick announced that he wished to appoint a prime minister and he named Daniel O'Connell. There was no dissent, and everyone drank a toast to the prosperity of the new government. O'Connell then rose and delivered a short speech, nominating Steele as lord chancellor, because he, 'of all present, and beyond dispute, knew not the smallest particle of law!' Steele accepted the office and declared that it was his intention to administer the law as badly as he possibly could, as befitted a real and genuine lord chancellor. O'Connell then appointed a court fool and a lord of the bedchamber, the latter being one of the younger guests who spent most of his time in bed. Venedey was appointed home secretary, precisely because he was a foreigner, and Venedey accepted in good humour, saying that he was a good choice because he would be leaving the country in eight days. One of the wives was appointed the war minister, and another commander-in-chief of the army. The wildest of O'Connell's grandchildren was appointed master of ceremonies, and a quiet young man, who never said anything, was named Speaker of the House of Commons. The new Speaker was called upon to make a speech and he won the loudest applause for his single sentence: 'Mum's the word.' Venedey, meanwhile, was once again taken by his 'Connaught beauty', almost certainly Morgan's wife, and he spent much of his time gazing into her 'two deep, deep dark eyes, whose bright flashes kindled up in my soul thoughts of the beautiful and the past'.[64]

In the middle of these games, O'Connell was asked his opinion of Fr Mathew's powers as a speaker. He revealed that he thought Fr Mathew was one of the best speakers he knew because in his speeches were found 'such simplicity, brevity, distinctness, poetic language, and striking imagery, conveyed in a manner so plain and comprehensible', that they were able to move all his listeners.[65] At nine p.m. the party broke up and the gathering decided to walk to the railroad at Kingstown and get the train into town. However, as soon as O'Connell was spotted a large crowd began following him and, before the party reached Kingstown, several hundred had gathered around him. One man shouted, 'Hurrah for Repeal, hurrah for O'Connell!' and 'thus the avalanche increased at every step he took, until at length it swept an overwhelming mass through the streets of Kingstown'.[66] One woman ran out of her house and asked, 'What is it?' When told that O'Connell was passing through the village she ran forward, jumping for joy, and cried out, 'For thirty years I have heard of him, and now at last I shall have the good luck to see him.' Everyone who had a hat waved it in acclamation. A young boy without a cap, who was running with the crowd, was told by another boy to shake his 'fist for joy, as you haven't got a hat'. Another woman standing at a door was heard to exclaim, 'May God's blessing be with him wherever he goes.' When they arrived at the railway station, Venedey turned to O'Connell and told him, 'In France, whenever the king wants a couple of hurrahs, he pays for them.' O'Connell replied that, for him, 'the people cheer for nothing', and while he was saying it 'there was expressed upon his features the deepest feelings of strong emotion, and intense pleasure'.

There followed more public meetings, first at Maryborough, Queen's County (now Portlaoise in Co. Laois), and then at Roscommon. At the Roscommon meeting on 20 August O'Connell called on the people to abstain from alcohol, insisting that there was not an army in the world which would be able to defeat an army of Irish teetotallers.[67] But O'Connell was also beginning to worry about the future. At the close of parliament Queen Victoria made a speech about the state of affairs in Ireland and it destroyed O'Connell's naïve hope that she might support his plans for an Irish parliament.

One day during O'Connell's absence from Dublin, a meeting of the Repeal Association was disrupted by a legion of Orangemen, led by the Rev. Tresham Gregg. They forced admission to the Corn Exchange, and stormed the great room upstairs, where they installed Gregg as chairman and passed motions denouncing 'Popery, Repeal, and Daniel O'Connell'.[68] However, one Repealer escaped and brought news of this invasion to the coal porters nearby, and they immediately came to the rescue of the Association, as they had many years earlier during the agitation for Catholic emancipation. The Orangemen were forcibly evicted. The new premises, named Conciliation Hall, finally opened in October 1843. Gregg and his supporters made a last attempt to disrupt proceedings at one of the first meetings there, but the coal porters were waiting and only the intervention of Thomas Steele prevented the porters from throwing them into the river, or delivering 'an exemplary *dusting* with the coal-sacks'.[69]

At a meeting of the Repeal Association on 4 September O'Connell announced that a great meeting would take place at Clontarf on Sunday 8 October. Clontarf was the scene of one of the most iconic battles in Irish history, when the high king, Brian Boru, won a great victory against the Viking invaders on Good Friday in 1014, but lost his life in the process. O'Connell announced that the speeches would take place 'on the mound raised to cover the bodies of the Danes who fell in battle there'.[70] And he attacked the government for the queen's speech at the close of parliament, accusing it of putting words into her mouth to upset 'the sensitive Irish mind'. In this speech O'Connell declared that he wanted 'no revolution', or if he did, only a return to former times, 'such a revolution as 1782 or 1829—a bloodless, stainless revolution—a political change for the better'.[71] O'Connell had been thinking of bringing the series of monster meetings to an end, convinced that they had made their point to the British government.[72] But the queen's speech changed everything and he immediately organised new meetings for Loughrea and Clifden in Co. Galway and Mullaghmast in Co. Kildare.

The Loughrea meeting took place on 10 September. The weather was terrible, with heavy rain all day, and O'Connell shortened the proceedings so that people could get away early. In his speech he announced that 'Connaught is doing well, right well' and spoke of his pride that 'Connaught is exhibiting a right noble spirit'. At the dinner afterwards O'Connell attacked the government for using the queen to attack the Repeal movement. He said 'they had but one arrow in the quiver—but one stone unflung—but one trick untried, and out they brought the queen. All Europe was to be astonished by the splendour of her speech against Ireland.'[73] O'Connell had been deeply hurt by the perceived betrayal of the queen, and was rightly determined to blame Peel for her intervention. 'Oh what a trick it was!' he exclaimed, comparing it to the 'scolding match between two fishermen in Billingsgate'.

At Clifden on 17 September O'Connell paid a special tribute to the women of Connemara. He said he had always believed that they were as good-looking as any in the world, and that this 'opinion has been abundantly confirmed by the beauteous scene I have beheld today'.[74] But he then posed a challenge to the men. He wanted to know if they were 'as brave and as Irish as the rest of the nation'. This secured him the unquestioning support of the crowd. Addressing the economic problems of Ireland, he blamed the lack of commerce and manufacturing on the fact that Ireland was 'governed by Saxons and not by Irishmen'. Ending his speech, O'Connell insisted, 'Force and violence are not to be used.' But if they were attacked, then 'woe to those who dare attack you'. At the banquet that evening O'Connell spoke directly to British ears. He declared that he had 'demonstrated that I have more men, more men of a fighting age (why should I not use that word) ready to stand by their country than ever evinced that determination before'. This force would never be called upon to attack, but it would be reserved for defence, and O'Connell dared Britain to 'attack us if you dare'. O'Connell repeated his hope that arbitration courts would be established throughout the country, meeting every Friday, so that 'disputes which now fester and rankle in a village will be settled amicably'. And he threatened that in this way half the business would be taken out of the British courts in Ireland. This would mean nothing less than the establishment of an independent Irish judicial system, but O'Connell defied the crown lawyers to find anything illegal in the plan. Returning to the idea of gathering 300 presumptive MPs in Dublin, O'Connell suggested playfully that these men would be meeting in Dublin 'by one accident or another'. Thus it could not be attacked as an illegal assembly, and O'Connell declared that this gathering would be 'ready to enter into immediate negotiation with the British minister, to show him the state of Ireland, to show him our further resources . . . To show him that we have physical power, and that if assailed, we will use it.'

O'Connell knew that the monster meetings must soon come to an end. He planned seven or eight more before the end of the year, but after that no more. They had served their purpose. They had been a 'demonstration of moral combination'; in other words, they had revealed 'the mighty giant power of the people of Ireland' and shown how disciplined and controlled this power was. A few days after Clifden there was a meeting at Lismore in Co. Waterford. Here O'Connell repeated his question, 'If you were wanted by me tomorrow would you not come?' There was tremendous cheering for several minutes. Then he asked, 'Let as many as would come at my call hold up their hands.' And it was reported 'a dense forest of uplifted hands waved to and from amid the most tremendous cheering . . . the scene was actually indescribable'.[75] Lashing out at the men who spoke of compromise, O'Connell insisted, 'They might talk of compromise. Compromise to the winds! He would have no compromise.'

The adulation of the past few months had clearly affected O'Connell. Perhaps this was unavoidable given the triumph of the monster meetings, especially as O'Connell was always vulnerable to anything which reinforced his massive self-image. He now spoke of how no man, except kings and emperors, had ever enjoyed as much popularity as him, and that even though, 'once or twice', he had been abused by 'some kings', he had never returned the compliment. The power he possessed, he said, was 'his vocation under heaven'. It was his way of 'working out his salvation' by 'working out good for his fellow man'.[76]

Perhaps the most controversial monster meeting to take place was the one on 1 October at Mullaghmast, Co. Kildare, which according to tradition was the scene of a notorious massacre of the Irish in the reign of Queen Elizabeth I. It was said that four hundred Irish chiefs were invited to a feast and brutally murdered, though by the 1840s many accepted this was 'a somewhat doubtful tradition'.[77] The government placed the attendance at the meeting at a quarter of a million, though O'Connell himself claimed that a million were present. Certainly it appears to have equalled Tara in size.[78] O'Connell arrived at two p.m., wearing the scarlet robes from his time as lord mayor. When he took the chair he was presented with a green velvet cap, shaped like an old Irish crown, which was placed upon his head.[79] The cap had a narrow gold band surrounding the upper part, 'thus, for all the world, resembling to the eye a crown'.[80] O'Connell said that he was delighted to receive such a gift, and promised to wear the cap for the remainder of his life. This was no idle talk, for it was a promise he kept, and the Repeal cap became a key part of his iconography.[81] To the government spies in the audience this was nothing less than a coronation, and in their reports to the government it was said that O'Connell had received a gold crown from the people and had placed it on his head. This was not an overreaction. For when John Hogan, the sculptor who designed the cap, presented it to O'Connell he was quoted afterwards as saying, 'Sir, I only regret that this cap is not of gold.'[82]

Standing upon the Rath, O'Connell declared that it was 'the precise spot on which English treachery, aye, and false Irish treachery too, consummated the massacre unequalled in the history of the crimes of the world'. There were numerous banners in evidence, ranging from 'Ireland for the Irish—the Irish for Ireland' to 'Remember Mullaghmast' and 'Ireland must be a nation'. The Repeal wardens were also in attendance, and these men had the title 'O'Connell's police' written on their hats. During his speech O'Connell said 'he was proud to see his own police there, and he hoped he would shortly see no other police in Ireland'. Surveying the crowd, he said that he felt 'more honour than ever I did in my life, with a single exception, and that related to an equally (if possible) majestic meeting at Tara'. And he repeated his demand that the people should commit not the slightest outrage, violation of the peace, or crime, so that the enemy had no power. Speaking as 'a constitutional lawyer', he declared his conviction that the

Union was 'totally void in point of principle and constitutional force'. Though it was supported by the force of law—the 'policeman's truncheon, the soldier's bayonet, and the horseman's sword'—it was not supported by constitutional right. Playing to the more aggressive instincts of the crowd, O'Connell admitted that he had 'physical force enough about me today to achieve anything', but he instantly qualified this by reminding his listeners that they knew 'full well it is not my plan'. He assured them, 'I won't risk one of you. I could not afford to lose any of you. I will protect you all, and I will obtain for you all the Repeal of the Union'. He pleaded with the people to follow his advice, promising that 'No man shall be fined, no man shall be imprisoned, no man shall be prosecuted who takes my advice.'[83] He told them of his plan to organise a new Irish House of Commons, admitting that it was only 'a theory', but 'a theory that may be realised in three weeks'. This theory was the old and now discredited idea that the queen might dismiss the government and form a new one friendly to Ireland, leading to a new parliament being formed in Ireland afterwards. O'Connell stated that Conciliation Hall would soon be open, and this could be used to temporarily house the new parliament. Discussing the 1798 Rebellion, he denounced it as an 'ill-organised, a premature, a foolish, and an absurd insurrection', though he did praise the brave and valiant men who had fought in it. O'Connell blamed the leaders of the rebellion, and traitors, for the failure, but he reassured the gathering that they now had a leader 'who will never allow you to be led astray'. The Union was also denounced as an act that was 'perpetuated in fraud and cruelty', 'an act of the most decided tyranny and corruption that was ever perpetuated'.

O'Connell asked if there were any teetotallers in the crowd. There were cries of 'Yes' and O'Connell declared that it was teetotalism which was repealing the Union. He admitted that he could not have risked bringing some large crowds together unless he had teetotallers for his police. At this the crowd shouted, 'We are all your police.' 'To be sure you are,' replied O'Connell, and he told them they would soon be 'the only police, by the help of God'. In a rousing peroration, O'Connell said that Ireland was 'a country worth fighting for', it was 'a country worth dying for', but above all, it was 'a country worth being tranquil, determined, submissive, and docile for' so that they would achieve their constitutional liberty. 'Let the English have

England,' he stated, 'let the Scottish have Scotland, but we must have Ireland for the Irish.'

A number of resolutions were passed at this gathering. Perhaps the most significant, in the light of subsequent events, was one which recognised

> [t]hat forty-four years of devoted and successful labour in the cause of his country have justly earned for O'Connell, the Liberator of Ireland, the unbounded confidence of the Irish people. And that we, relying upon his supreme wisdom, discretion, patriotism, and undaunted firmness, hereby pledge ourselves, individually and collectively, to follow his guidance under any and every circumstance that may arise; and come weal or woe, never to desert the constitutional standard of Repeal which he has raised.

This resolution had clearly been drafted with the blessing (and input) of O'Connell and was seeking to secure a guarantee that the people would not be diverted into another rebellion, and would follow O'Connell's 'constitutional standard' no matter what. At the dinner afterwards, O'Connell abused Wellington, joking that 'To be sure he was born in Ireland, but being born in a stable does not make a man a horse!'[84]

On 30 September an advertisement was published in *The Nation* which caused much alarm for the government. Under a heading 'Repeal Cavalry', instructions were given for those Repealers who planned to attend the Clontarf meeting on horseback.[85] They were instructed to bring 'a cockade and wand', and were given orders befitting a military regiment. O'Connell was furious when he read the advertisement. At the very next meeting of the Association, on 2 October, O'Connell announced that 'it ought not to have been printed'.[86] Rather than disavow it completely, he attempted to claim that the advertisement was really just trying to give safety instructions for men who were going on horseback to Clontarf so that no one was injured or trampled upon. As the meeting approached, the *Pilot* published a controversial article which challenged the idea that O'Connell was 'too old for the camp or the field'. It declared that O'Connell was 'of Herculean frame, buoyant in spirit, and youthful in constitution'.[87] And it noted that while

O'Connell was sixty-eight years old, Brian Boru had been eighty-eight when he won his great victory in 1014. 'This should serve to warn our rulers against wantonly attacking O'Connell,' it insisted. 'Clontarf— they should remember Clontarf!'

The British government had been monitoring the monster meetings since the beginning and now decided to act. The disturbing image of massive crowds all showing their allegiance to O'Connell was bad enough. But the idea of independent law courts and the plans for a new Irish parliament were just too much. For the government it was overwhelming proof that O'Connell was effectively declaring Irish independence, and was sounding the call for separation. The mention of 'Repeal Cavalry', which seemed to imply a martial aspect to the Clontarf meeting, was the excuse it needed to finally intervene. Peel decided to issue a proclamation cancelling the meeting, claiming it tended 'to overthrow the constitution of the British empire as by law established'.[88] But it was only after nightfall on Saturday 7 October, the day before Clontarf, that the proclamation was published in Dublin. A large army with heavy artillery was moved to Clontarf, ready to open fire if crowds gathered. And three gunships were moved into position, to command the area planned for the meeting. In addition, the 34th regiment and other regiments were sent to Dublin as reinforcements in case violence erupted.[89] O'Connell was faced with the most difficult decision of his life and one that was to define his legacy for all time.

He acted quickly. Although he felt the proclamation was illegal, he thought it still had 'a shred of legality', and he was insistent that 'the time for resistance had not come'.[90] He gave the order for the Clontarf meeting to be cancelled. In later years Young Ireland would criticise O'Connell for not 'raising the standard of revolt at Clontarf'.[91] However, at the meeting itself they went along with the decision to submit. Afterwards, Thomas Davis and his friends asserted that the power which they had helped to create was being 'recklessly squandered'.[92] But the decision was O'Connell's to make and he made it. Thomas Reynolds was at this meeting, and he turned to a friend and whispered, 'Ireland was won at Clontarf, and she is going to be lost at Clontarf.' O'Connell sent one of his most trusted followers, Peter Martin, a builder, to Clontarf to take down the platform and remove the materials. Twenty or thirty volunteers were ordered to go out in pairs around the county and send people home who were coming to the meeting. O'Connell also issued an address, which was posted all around the city, explaining his reasons for cancelling the meeting. It was later discovered that the government order suppressing the meeting had arrived in Dublin on the Friday, but had not been published until the Saturday. This led to suspicions that the Irish administration had been hoping for the people to assemble so that the meeting could be dispersed by force. O'Connell later stated that he had cancelled the meeting, not because he thought it was illegal, but because it would 'have inevitably ended in the slaughter of the people, and the plains of Clontarf ... would have been a second time saturated with blood'.[93] And he insisted that if he was forced to choose one act from his career that he would wish to be remembered for, then it would not be emancipation, but the decision to cancel Clontarf and prevent 'a collision between the military and the people'.

The split in the Repeal movement widened. In the next issue of *The Nation* Duffy revealed that not everyone supported O'Connell's decision, though he accepted that O'Connell was the chief and should be followed. Davis then took up the subject, saying that retreat was sometimes dishonourable, and perseverance was better than peace.[94] At the next meeting of the Repeal Association the attendance was so large that the meeting was moved to the theatre on Abbey Street. Everyone wanted to hear what O'Connell would say, but his defence of his actions satisfied few. He raised the idea of arranging simultaneous meetings around the country, a monster meeting of the entire Irish nation, to convince the British government that they could not be stopped. And he insisted that the plans for the independent arbitration courts and the revived Irish parliament would continue. According to Duffy, 'It may be confidently stated that O'Connell's course at this critical moment did not satisfy any considerable section of his supporters.'[95] This was probably accurate enough. For the first time, O'Connell's leadership of the Repeal movement was being questioned openly. A crisis appeared unavoidable until the government intervened to postpone the debate. On 11 October O'Connell was arrested on a number of charges, including conspiracy to excite ill will among her majesty's subjects and exciting disaffection among her majesty's troops. Remembering the show trials of 1798, O'Connell feared that he would be charged with high treason, found guilty, and hanged. He admitted that there was nothing for it but to make his confession, 'and prepare for death'.[96]

When he discovered that the prosecution would be for seditious conspiracy he was relieved. 'I do not think two years' imprisonment would kill me,' he told his son John. 'I should keep constantly walking about, and take a bath every day.'

Six other key figures were arrested alongside O'Connell: his son John O'Connell; his political aides, Thomas Mathew Ray and Thomas Steele; the editor of the *Pilot*, Richard Barrett; the editor of the *Freeman's Journal*, John Gray; and the editor of *The Nation*, Charles Gavan Duffy. It had been rumoured that some archbishops and bishops might also be arrested, but in the event the government just made an example of two priests, Fr James Tyrrell, who had been involved in the organisation and cancelling of the Clontarf meeting, and Fr Thomas Tierney, a man who had only ever attended a single monster meeting—and that was the Clontibert one, which none of the others had been at. Duffy later joked that of the seven men who had been arrested for conspiracy 'one-half had never seen Fr Tyrrell and three-fourths had never heard of Fr Tierney'.[97] Tyrrell had spent the entire night before the Clontarf meeting on horseback, telling his parishioners to stay away from the meeting, and he died shortly after his arrest.[98] The charges against Tierney were later dropped after the trial. In November the indictment was sent to the grand jury and the trial was set for January 1844.

Reflecting in later years on the decision to cancel the meeting at Clontarf, Duffy concluded that Peel had made as great a mistake as O'Connell. For he believed that 'the abortive insurrection of 1848, and the Fenian conspiracy which followed nearly twenty years later, were stimulated by a national pride wounded and humbled in 1843'. In the 4 November issue of *Punch*, a weekly illustrated magazine which had begun in 1841 and which mercilessly caricatured O'Connell, there was a drawing of 'The Irish Frankenstein'.[99] It showed O'Connell conjuring up the 'Repale' monster, and reflected British fears of the forces that were being unleashed in Ireland. Watching events in Ireland from London, the duke of Wellington was delighted that decisive action was at long last being taken. He was insistent that there 'must be no paltering or truckling with O'Connell' and that the opportunity must be taken to 'set him at defiance'.[100] For Wellington, there was only one thing to be done: 'we must now bring the rascals on their knees . . . and put them down'.

Chapter 10

THE TRIAL OF DANIEL
O'CONNELL, 1844

'What will be done with Mr O'Connell?'[1] According to Thomas Babington Macaulay, in a debate in the British House of Commons on 19 February 1844, this was the only question which people wanted the answer to, nationally or internationally. 'Go where you will on the continent, visit any coffee-house, dine at any public table, embark on any steamboat, enter any railway carriage' and, 'from the moment that your accent shows you to be an Englishman', the very first question asked was about O'Connell. Macaulay was not an admirer of O'Connell. He regarded the means he had used to try and win Repeal 'with deep disapprobation'. He considered it 'unfortunate' that so many people in the world admired him. But he recognised that O'Connell had attained a position in 'the estimation of his countrymen such as no popular leader in our history, I might perhaps say in the history of the world, has ever attained'. He was speaking after Daniel O'Connell had been found guilty in Ireland of conspiring against the state.

The trial of Daniel O'Connell, and the other seven men, began on 15 January 1844. 'The whole country was full of rumours,' O'Connell later said, with speculation rife that 'something dark and atrocious would come out' exposing a massive conspiracy to rebel.[2] Contributing to this febrile atmosphere was the attorney general, who boasted in advance of the trial that he would expose 'as wicked and foul a conspiracy as ever disturbed an empire'.[3] O'Connell had spent the winter at Derrynane, where he worked on his defence and relaxed by spending hours outdoors hunting. He was delighted to find that he had more energy than the young men who accompanied him, and boasted that he had more 'wind' than at any time in the past five years.[4] In his absence from Dublin he had been snubbed at the official dinner of the outgoing lord mayor, George Rose, who had toasted various dignitaries but had pointedly ignored his predecessor.[5] But O'Connell was more worried about his finances, as he struggled to pay his debts, and he recognised that he would need to 'resort to the tribute' to be secure.[6]

In the popular imagination, the arrested men soon became known as 'the traversers', after they had traversed the indictment. Two counsel and an attorney were assigned to each man, though O'Connell insisted on defending himself. The defence team included Richard Lalor Sheil (who defended John O'Connell) and Gerald Fitzgibbon (who defended John Gray), as well as, in a junior role, John O'Hagan, James Whiteside, and Sir Colman O'Loghlen. Some of the attorneys also had impressive reputations, for example, William Ford and Peter McEvoy Gartland, and collectively they became known as the 'Traversers' Brass Band'.[7] The crown prosecution was led by the attorney general, T.B.C. (Thomas Berry Cusack) Smith, the second son of William Cusack Smith whom O'Connell had long abused. Smith was said to suffer from 'sudden fits of irritability' which were blamed not on 'a bad disposition' but on 'bad digestion'.[8] Charles Gavan Duffy described him as having 'a certain prim dignity' in the law courts, but said he was 'so meagre, unwholesome, and ghastly that elsewhere he looked like an owl in the sunshine'. O'Connell called him 'Alphabet Smith' and cruelly described him as 'the vinegar cruet on two legs'.[9]

There were some surprises. Despite his performance at the corporation debate, Isaac Butt was not given a brief by the crown. Equally surprisingly, Robert Holmes, the brother-in-law of Robert Emmet, received one. Holmes had been a vehement opponent of the Union, and had been jailed at the time of Emmet's rebellion. Although now over eighty years old, he accepted the brief because he detested O'Connell. This was in part because of O'Connell's history of denouncing the leaders of the 1798 Rebellion as 'miscreants', and there had been many fierce clashes between them when O'Connell had been practising at the bar.[10] Holmes was known as 'the enemy of the Liberator' because 'he resented insults flung on the grave of his early friends'.[11] Leading out of this animosity, Barrett had abused Holmes in the pages of the *Pilot* in the early 1830s, and had been sent a challenge which he declined. Despite Holmes' history with O'Connell and Barrett he did not display any hostility during the trial, and his acceptance of the brief was soon forgiven by nationalists. The chief justice, Edward Pennefather (the brother of Richard Pennefather, who had acted as a model judge during the Doneraile conspiracy case), and Judges Burton, Crampton, and Perrin presided over the case.

The printed indictment handed to the grand jury in November had been almost a hundred yards long, delaying a decision for five days.[12] The indictment included the charge of simply attending the monster meetings, and the three journalists were charged with reporting the speeches which had taken place. O'Connell was also accused of delivering seditious speeches at the Repeal Association and, again, the other men were charged with attending them or reporting upon them. The attempt to organise the Clontarf meeting was also part of the indictment, as were various articles and poems published in the editors' newspapers. For the trial, these charges were distributed into eleven counts. The first and second counts accused the men of conspiracy 'to raise and create discontent and disaffection among the queen's subjects' and made reference to the monster meetings (which were described as 'demonstrations of great physical force'). These counts also accused them of attempting to create an independent judicial system, and efforts to 'excite discontent and disaffection' among the soldiers serving in Ireland.[13] The third to seventh counts were essentially restatements of the first two, though the seventh made a specific reference to the attempts to dissolve the legislative Union. The eighth, ninth and tenth counts referred to the attempt to create independent arbitration courts, which would 'diminish the confidence of her majesty's subjects in Ireland in the administration of the law therein'. The eleventh count was a general one accusing the men of conspiring to bring about 'changes and alterations in the laws and constitution of this realm as now by law established'.

The very complexity of the counts was to prove the greatest weakness of the prosecution. The individual counts were too similar, allowing for ambiguity and anomalies, especially if someone was convicted on some but not on others. The crown had attempted to construct a watertight case, but in doing so exposed itself to criticism if the verdict was challenged. Some of the crown decisions were ingenious in their deviousness. For example, the individual monster meetings were not described as unlawful assemblies, as this would have required trials in the counties where they took place. Instead a general conspiracy charge allowed the government, in the words of the *Quarterly Review*, to go 'fishing with a net', where previously it 'fished with a hook'.[14]

The result of the trial was rigged from the beginning. Everyone knew that everything would revolve around the selection of the jury. A panel of forty-eight potential jurors was to be chosen from the special jury list, and from these a jury of twelve selected. But the most recent version of the special jury list had been carefully drawn up so that it only contained 388 names, and some of these people were dead or incapacitated. This was a systematic attempt to exclude Catholics from the list, or Protestants who might be sympathetic to the accused. However, there were objections, and a revised and expanded jury list was drawn up by the Recorder of Dublin before the start of the trial. This time there were 717 names on it, including a number of Catholics. The traversers asked for permission to study this list in advance of the trial, and the request was reluctantly granted. They discovered that the list which had been submitted to the court had pages torn out, and the names of sixty eligible Catholics were missing.

The trial began at five past ten a.m. on 15 January and a jury was selected from the forty-eight names which had been drawn from the jury list. Of these, eleven were Catholics, and all of these were peremptorily dismissed by the crown. An exclusively Protestant jury was selected. It included eight men known to have voted against Repeal, including one man, Henry Thompson, a wine merchant from Eustace Street, who had spoken against O'Connell in public.[15] O'Connell's very first action was to challenge the jury list because of the sixty names that were missing.[16] There followed a long discussion on the point, and O'Connell's attorney, William Ford, grew increasingly impatient and exclaimed that there had been 'an infamous tampering with the list!'[17] The attorney general accepted the truth of the facts alleged in the challenge, admitting that some mistake had occurred, but denied that this in any way constituted a legal objection to using the reduced jury list. He was supported in this by the chief justice, who overruled the objection. Judge Perrin, however, voiced his doubts, and the court was adjourned for the day. O'Connell turned to another of the traversers and whispered that they were lucky the attorney general was only charging them with conspiracy, as the twelve men selected would have no difficulty in convicting them of the murder of 'the Italian boy'. (This was a reference to one of the most sensational English crimes of the 1830s, the murder of a young beggar who was killed to provide a body for London surgeons to dissect.[18]) When the court met on 17 January (officially the 'first day' of the trial) the twelve members of the jury were sworn in. Word soon spread around the world that 'the most eminent Catholic in the empire' was about to be put on trial 'in the Catholic metropolis of a Catholic country', and with not a single Catholic on the bench or on the jury.[19]

There was enormous public interest in the trial. A civic procession accompanied the traversers from O'Connell's house in Merrion Square to the Four Courts on the opening day of the trial, and barriers of solid oak had to be erected at the entrance to the court of queen's bench to keep people out. The attorney general stated the case against the traversers over the first two days, his speech lasting over eleven hours in total. He had promised in advance to reveal secret consultations with soldiers and foreigners, and evidence of a vast military organisation, but his speech was little more than a straightforward account of the events of the Repeal year.

Smith's delivery, 'drip, drip, like water from a rusty pump', became difficult to follow.[20] *The Nation* reported that many people became distracted. Two of the traversers began reading newspapers, one began copying documents for his defence, two wrote autographs in ladies' albums, one read a brief, two were absent from the court, while the audience ate sandwiches and chatted. The jury 'fiddled listlessly with their pens', while Judge Burton was even believed to have fallen asleep. At several points, Steele audibly contradicted some of the statements. Knowing how much Steele wanted to stand alongside O'Connell, the attorney general threatened to *remove* his name from the indictment if he did not remain silent. Steele did not say another word.[21]

For the next seven days witnesses were produced to prove facts which were generally accepted about what was said at the various monster meetings and banquets. O'Connell's hearing seems to have been failing, for on a number of occasions he called on witnesses to speak louder.[22] When one government spy reported on what he had heard at the monster meetings, O'Connell rebuked him, saying, 'Raise your voice, sir! The end of your sentences is always lost, for you let your voice fall so short, and so low, that no person can hear you.' On the sixth day of the trial selections of the report of the Repeal Association calling for 'renewed action of the Irish parliament' were read to the court, and O'Connell insisted on having the whole thing read into the record.

A magistrate who had reported on O'Connell's speech to the Longford meeting was destroyed on cross-examination by Fitzgibbon. It was claimed that O'Connell had made many significant pauses during his speech, but Fitzgibbon demanded to know how long the pauses were and what they signified. The magistrate became flustered and admitted, 'Of course, he was saying nothing,' which was greeted with loud laughter. Fitzgibbon asked him to recite the lines in question and include the relevant pauses, and then joked that 'we are putting you in a false position by asking you to imitate Mr O'Connell's manner'.[23] The magistrate confirmed that the countryside, on the advice of O'Connell, was very quiet. 'You were very sorry for that, I suppose?' asked Fitzgibbon sharply.

Tensions which had been building for some days exploded on the thirteenth day of the trial. While the judges and jury were taking a break for refreshments, a heated argument broke out between Fitzgibbon and the attorney general, and when the court resumed there was 'a hush of public expectancy and almost breathless silence'.[24] Fitzgibbon immediately rose and declared that he had been handed a note from the attorney general when he had entered the court. The attorney general said nothing, allowing Fitzgibbon to carry on, and Fitzgibbon emphasised that no matter what he said during the trial he retained the utmost respect for the men on the side of the prosecution. He then revealed the substance of the note from the attorney general: 'He tells me in that note that I have given him a personal offence and he calls upon me, if I don't apologise for it, to name a friend.'[25] There was a 'sensation throughout the court' as people digested the news that the attorney general had challenged the opposing counsel to a duel.

The attorney general rose and spoke in rather indistinct tone, calling on Fitzgibbon to set out all the facts in an affidavit. But Fitzgibbon replied that he would never do that, and he called on the judges to deal with the affair. The attorney general revealed that he had been offended by comments made by Fitzgibbon in court alleging that 'private and dishonourable motives' had influenced his conduct in the prosecution. In an elegant response, Fitzgibbon replied that he might have apologised if the matter had been raised privately with him, but not at the point of a gun.

Some minutes passed as the judges consulted with each other. The chief justice declared that they had been placed 'in a very embarrassing and perplexing position' and he rebuked the attorney general for allowing himself 'to be betrayed into such an expression of feeling'.[26] At this point the attorney general rose to interrupt the court and he offered to withdraw the hastily written note, though he noted the 'strongly irritated feeling I was under'. Fitzgibbon denied having cast any slur on the attorney general's character and then ripped up the piece of paper and 'flung the fragments under the table'.[27] The matter was allowed to drop.

On the fifteenth day of the trial one of the defence lawyers (James Whiteside) spoke of the events of the 1798 Rebellion. He revealed that the United Irishmen had 'a horror of public speaking' and had even displayed a notice at their meeting room, 'Beware of oratory'.[28] He joked that O'Connell was surely the last man to ever warn his followers to 'beware of orators'.

Defending himself, Daniel O'Connell spoke on the eighteenth day of trial. It was to be the last time he would ever represent someone in a court of law, and he was determined to make an impression. In tone and style he attempted to capture the fiery eloquence of one of his most famous cases, the Magee trial of 1813. There he had abandoned his client to launch a powerful assault on British rule in Ireland. Here he would do the exact same thing, abusing the jury and assailing the prosecution, as he looked to speak directly to the Irish nation and an international audience. Those who read the speech afterwards were hugely impressed. R.R. Madden, who was in Lisbon, described it as a 'stupendous manifestation of intellectual power . . . The speech is a monument which will never die.'[29] But those who heard it in the court recognised the evidence of decline. One of the junior defence lawyers, John O'Hagan, later said that O'Connell's powers of delivery were fading, 'the old fervour had departed, the old mastery was no more', and that there was evidence of the 'fatal disease' that would later kill him.[30] But in terms of the content the speech was a masterpiece, and there was enough of the old energy to transfix the attentions of the court. The speech took up all the business of the eighteenth day and remains one of O'Connell's greatest statements about British rule in Ireland.

O'Connell began by denying that he was his own client; rather, he claimed to be representing the Irish people: 'my client is Ireland, and I stand here the advocate of the rights, and liberties, and constitutional privileges of that people'.[31] He then spoke of the integrity of his purpose and the purity of his motives in trying to bring about a Repeal of the Union. He admitted that he could not 'endure the Union. It was founded upon the grossest injustice, it was based upon the grossest insult.' Rather than challenging the substance of what had been attributed to him at the various monster meetings, O'Connell declared that he was ready to avow and vindicate the comments. The only concession he made was to apologise for 'many harsh things said of individuals', and some 'clumsy jokes', but everything else he was prepared to justify.

The jury was not insulated from O'Connell's attacks. He said that they differed with him on two points. The first was on the question of the Repeal of the Union. The second was their religion. 'Not one of you would be in that box' if Catholic, he declared, and he boasted that he was 'that Catholic who was most successful . . . in putting down that Protestant Ascendancy of which, perhaps, you are the champions'. O'Connell admitted that he was in their power, but he said he wished he was rather 'in the power of jurors of honesty, and of integrity'. At a later point in the speech, he turned angrily to the jury, asking, 'What care I what your politics are? You'll answer before your Maker for the verdict you pronounce—I leave the responsibility to you.' And he declared that he was not only addressing 'a jury of Protestant gentlemen' but 'the kings and people of the universe', to see if the religious and political beliefs of the Catholics of Ireland would be dismissed as feeble and foolish.[32]

O'Connell's legal skills were as sharp as ever, and in much of his speech he attacked the prosecution on the grounds that would later be used to overturn the verdict. He called it 'a strange prosecution', in fact, 'the strangest prosecution that was ever instituted'. This was because it was not based on 'one fact, or two facts, or three facts', but rather on the entire history of the Repeal year. Enormous amounts of material had been presented to the jury, but O'Connell offered to guide them through it and distinguish what was important from what was not. For him, everything centred around the definition of the word 'conspiracy'. This was usually seen as 'a secret agreement among several to commit a crime'. But O'Connell reminded the jury that even the prosecution admitted that 'there was no privacy, no secrecy, no definite agreement whatever to bring it about. And, above all, there was no private agreement, no secret society, nothing concealed, nothing even privately communicated, there was no private information; nay, not one private conversation.' Instead everything had been 'open, avowed, proclaimed, published'. 'A secret conspiracy!' snorted O'Connell, 'which there was no secret about!'

Poking fun at the attorney general's speech, O'Connell noted that he had been 'eleven hours at it, eleven mortal hours'.[33] But where, he asked, was there evidence of conspiracy? Imitating the attorney general, he joked, '"Oh!" said he, "wait awhile, wait till I come to the close, and, when I do come to the end, go back to the beginning [laughter] and find out the conspiracy".' O'Connell accused the attorney general of having spent eleven hours 'throwing out that garbage to the jury'. And he summed up the prosecution's case as 'Here are the speeches and publications—now find out the conspiracy. The case is good enough for you to make out the conspiracy.'

O'Connell told the story of one of the jurymen who had acquitted Thomas Hardy of treason in the 1790s. When asked his reasons he gave, or so O'Connell claimed, the following speech: 'The counsel was eleven hours stating the case; there were eight or nine days occupied in giving evidence. Now I know that no man could be guilty of treason when the case could take up so many words, and such a length of time to prove, so I made up my mind to acquit.'

O'Connell insisted that if the attorney general had a real case he would have made it in an hour and a half at most. And if any real evidence existed then specific times and dates would have been given, which would have allowed O'Connell to find an alibi if he was innocent. Where, he asked, was all the evidence of 'dark and atrocious' deeds which it had been claimed would come out? O'Connell laughed that with all of the government's spies and informers it still had not been able to conjure a conspiracy into existence.

Reviewing his own career, O'Connell asked who could believe that he had entered into a public conspiracy, after all he ever said previously against illegal activities. And he wondered if anyone would believe that he would have risked 'the cause which is nearest to my heart', the 'darling object of my ambition', the Repeal of the Union. O'Connell discussed the jobs that had been offered to him over the years: a seat on the bench and the office of Master of the Rolls. He joked that it was still a matter of dispute whether he had refused the position of chief baron before it was even offered, which drew a laugh, but he said there was no question 'that I did refuse the offer of Master of the Rolls'.

O'Connell discussed the campaign to abolish the slave trade, and all that had been done to achieve it. He said that according to the attorney general's definition of conspiracy then all of these campaigners would have been arrested. 'Why was not [William] Wilberforce accused of conspiracy?' he asked.[34] And in the name of Wilberforce he called on the jury to dismiss 'every attempt to prevent the millions from seeking peaceably and quietly to obtain an amelioration of existing institutions'. Then discussing the 'conspiracy for the abolition of slavery itself', he rejoiced that he had been 'a sharer in that conspiracy'.[35] And referring to the great campaign for Catholic emancipation in the 1820s, O'Connell noted that despite the determined opposition of the then attorney general (an 'eminent lawyer' and the 'superior' of the present holder), there had never been any attempt to prosecute the leaders for conspiracy.

O'Connell did not deny that monster meetings had taken place and that 'people attended them in hundreds and hundreds of thousands', but he challenged the prosecution's claim that 'the magnitude of these meetings would alone make them illegal'. In a stirring defence, he said that not a single life had been lost at them, not a single man, woman or child had been injured at them. Nor had any property been destroyed. 'Oh, but I forgot,' he said, 'there was a policeman in coloured clothes who described a ferocious assault made by the people coming in from Carlow, which very nearly overturned the ginger-bread stand of an old woman.' The court erupted into laughter. O'Connell added that 'the amount of violence perpetrated was, not the overturning, but the nearly overturning, of a ginger-bread stand'.[36] However, if the people had really been incited into a rebellion, then he said they would not have been so well behaved and mothers would not have been as eager to bring their infants to the events. He quoted *The Times* as describing the Irish people as 'a filthy and felonious multitude', but O'Connell said that there was no other people on the earth who would have acted as well at such meetings.

O'Connell repeated 'the principle of my political career', that political changes were 'purchased at too dear a price if they could only be obtained at the expense of one drop of human blood'.[37] He said that this principle was known by all and that he had been fearless and unceasing in the repeating of it. Indeed, he said he could 'without vanity' assert that he was 'the first public man who ever proclaimed it'. Other politicians might say something similar, but always with a proviso about the use of physical force if it was necessary. 'It is my boast that Catholic emancipation, and every achievement of my political life, was obtained without violence and bloodshed.' The words were as much a rebuke to the people who had questioned his cancelling of the Clontarf meeting as a criticism of those who were accusing him of attempting to incite a rebellion.

Denying that he was someone who sacrificed principle for popularity, O'Connell referred to the events in Dublin in 1837 and 1838 when 'lives were lost in our public streets' and 'men were assaulted with such brutal violence'.[38] This was a result of 'a frightful combination' of the 'workmen and operatives of the city of Dublin'. O'Connell stated that he had come forward, 'publicly, single handed, and opposed them at the peril, not only of my popularity, but of my very existence'. At a meeting at the Corn Exchange his life had been threatened, and only the intervention of the police saved his life. But 'It was my duty to do it. I did not shrink from it.' And, as a result, those who had been most ferocious against him were persuaded to back down, and since that day 'not a single combination outrage has occurred in Dublin'. He also discussed his opposition to the poor laws, despite much criticism, because his conscience told him that 'the real nature of the provision makes more destitute than it relieves'.[39] Reminding his listeners that he had rejected money from the slave-owners in America, he said that he alienated them forever for the sake of a principle. Similarly he had alienated the Chartists, and politicians in France, because he had disapproved of their principles.

In the final part of his speech O'Connell delivered an attack on the Union, joking that he hoped, before he sat down, to have made everyone Repealers. O'Connell quoted the late chief justice, Charles Kendal Bushe, during the passing of the Union, who had declared that Britain had treated Ireland for six hundred years 'with uniform oppression and injustice'.[40] The crown lawyers were startled at this, but O'Connell assured them that these were not his words, but the words of recorded history. O'Connell also enlisted the words of the last Speaker of the Irish House of Commons, John Foster, and Lord Chancellor Clare, to show that Ireland had grown in prosperity from 1782 to 1800, and that legislative independence had been a glorious period in Irish history. In its place, the Union had brought nothing but debt and disaster to the Irish people. He then read his own maiden public speech, on 13 January 1800, to show that it was 'a fair epitome of all I have ever said since'.[41] O'Connell ended his speech by repeating his contention that he had acted 'in the open day in the presence of the government' to restore the Irish parliament. And he added that succeed or fail, 'it is a glorious struggle'.[42]

On day twenty-three, a Saturday, the jury retired to consider its verdict. At eight forty-five p.m. it was asked for its verdict, but it was not ready. Two hours passed and the attorney general was observed pulling out his watch and anxiously studying the time.[43] At ten forty-five p.m. the jury was called a second time. The foreman appeared and explained that the jury was confused about whether they had to give a verdict on every count. Judge Crampton informed him that a verdict of 'guilty' or 'not guilty' was necessary on each of the individual counts, and there needed to be a separate verdict for each individual traverser.

Shortly after, the foreman returned with the jury and handed a verdict to the clerk of the crown. On the first and second counts it had nothing to say, though it found O'Connell, Barrett and Duffy guilty on the third count. Crampton asked if there was 'no finding on that count against the others' and the clerk of the crown replied, 'No.' 'Then the finding is imperfect,' said Crampton. The foreman here interjected and said that the first count was too comprehensive. On the fourth count all seven of the traversers were found guilty; on the fifth count all of them except Steele were found guilty. There was no finding on the sixth count. On the seventh count all were found guilty except for Gray. There was no finding on the eighth or ninth counts. All seven men were found guilty on the tenth count. There was no finding on the eleventh count. Tierney was not found guilty on any count. Crampton ordered the foreman to take the verdict back, declaring that 'in the present state it is imperfect'.[44] He insisted that the jury had to deliver a verdict on each of the counts, or state clearly that it was unable to come to an agreement. The foreman was still confused and said, 'My lord, we thought that the first count was so comprehensive that it included everything.' Crampton agreed that 'the first count does embrace all' and called on them to 'retire for a few moments and arrange your verdict'. One juror spoke up and said, 'We are agreed on the first and second counts.' But another interjected, 'No, no, we are not.' The attorney general asked for an adjournment until the Monday, but the judges were anxious for a verdict and kept going. Shortly after midnight the jury returned. Asked if it had reached a verdict, the foreman replied, 'Not yet, my lord.' There was great laughter in the court and one judge reacted angrily, threatening to 'exercise the authority of the court' if someone was found 'committing a breach of order again'.[45] The jury retired for further deliberation. It was now five minutes past midnight. Once again the attorney general pressed for an adjournment, and one was finally granted until nine a.m. on Monday morning. The jury was ordered to be sequestered in the jury room over the weekend, with beds provided for comfort.

'The closing day of the monster trial' took place on the Monday.[46] From an early hour in the morning anxious crowds gathered in front of the court and along the quays. O'Connell arrived at eight fifty-five a.m. Judge Crampton announced that he had spent the break dividing the counts into various different issues to help the jury, recognising that many of the counts represented the same charges. The foreman of the jury admitted that he and his fellow jurors had done the same thing. The jury retired for a short time before returning with verdicts on all the counts and issues. On the first and second counts O'Connell, Barrett and Duffy were found guilty, omitting the words 'unlawfully and seditiously' before the words 'to meet and assemble'. All three men were found not guilty if the words remained. John O'Connell, Steele, Ray and Gray were found guilty on the first and second counts, omitting the words 'unlawfully and seditiously' before the words 'to meet and assemble' and omitting the words 'and to excite discontent and disaffection among divers of her majesty's subjects serving in the army'. The same men were found not guilty if the words remained. Fr Tierney was found guilty of the first part only of the first and second counts.

The verdict, in other words, was a mess. On the third count, O'Connell, Barrett, and Duffy were found guilty, with the remaining men found guilty only if certain words were removed from the count. On the fourth count seven of the men were found guilty, with Tierney only found guilty of part of the count. On the fifth count all eight men were found guilty. On the sixth to eleventh counts all the men except Tierney were found guilty. Following the usual practice, sentencing was postponed until the first day of the new term and the court adjourned.

Queen Victoria was delighted with the verdict. O'Connell had made much of his loyalty to the queen, and had long clung to the idea that Victoria would change her ministers and bring in a new government which was sympathetic to Repeal. But in private the queen had rejoiced at the arrest of O'Connell and, in a letter to her uncle, the king of Belgium, she declared that 'O'Connell's being pronounced guilty is a great triumph'.[47] Whatever hope for the future O'Connell had, it could not depend on the support of the queen.

The traversers were at liberty until the sentencing was pronounced. The Repeal movement now had to decide how to proceed. At a meeting of the general committee of the Repeal Association O'Connell brought forward two proposals. The first was to dissolve the Association and replace it with a new one which would be completely separate from any newspaper. The second was to abandon the arbitration courts. The younger members were horrified at both suggestions and there was more opposition than O'Connell was used to finding.[48] With the younger men threatening not to follow O'Connell, a compromise was reached whereby the arbitration courts would continue but would not be administered by the Association, the newspaper proprietors would resign from the Association, and the Association would continue. However, without the support of the Association, the arbitration courts had no chance of working and they soon died away.

The British parliament met on 1 February and the Whigs sensed an opportunity to attack the government. Charges were levelled about jury-packing during the trial, and the extraordinary circumstances of the attorney general's abortive duel. In the House of Lords the composition of the jury was defended by Lord Roden, who claimed it would have been impossible to have a fair trial if any Catholics had served on it.[49] On 13 February Lord John Russell introduced a party motion on the state of Ireland and delivered a stinging attack on the supposed benefits of the Union, and declared that Ireland was 'occupied, not governed'.[50] There followed a debate over nine nights on Irish affairs, though the subtext was who should be in power in Britain. It was here, on 19 February, that Macaulay delivered his great speech on Irish affairs. Perhaps the most important contribution was from Sir Thomas Wilde, who delivered the most damning criticism: 'Mr O'Connell has not had a fair trial.' T.B.C. Smith attempted to justify the jury selection on the seventh night, admitting that Catholics had been excluded from the list, but claiming that to have revised the list would have delayed the trial until 1845. The numbers, however, were with the government and a majority of ninety-nine voted not to consider the state of Ireland.

O'Connell decided to travel to London to take part in the debate. He was now at the height of his celebrity, and when he attended a meeting of the Anti-Corn Law League at Covent Garden he was applauded vigorously. Crowds waited to greet him at Parliament Street. Even Robert Peel was cheered by the gathering as he passed through, because, as he admitted himself, the majority had mistaken him for O'Connell.[51]

O'Connell's arrival in the House of Commons on 14 February created a sensation. The Irish MPs rushed to greet him, and the opposition applauded and cheered wildly. The MP for Belfast, David Robert Ross, was completing his speech and, seeing O'Connell, he asked, 'Let the House judge by the reception which the head conspirator has just met whether there be much cause for triumph. You may put that man in jail, but what will you gain?' In his own speech, on 23 February, O'Connell declared that he would not speak about himself but rather about Ireland, and he delivered a strong attack on British misrule in Ireland over the previous decades. Invitations soon arrived from all over the country, and he attended events in Birmingham, Manchester, Liverpool, and Coventry to enthusiastic receptions. A dinner in his honour was also held at Covent Garden Theatre.

Following a trip to the continent, William Smith O'Brien had re-engaged with Irish politics, and had joined the Repeal Association on 20 October 1843. Putting aside their differences in the past, O'Connell, preoccupied with preparing his defence, even appointed him his deputy. Tensions were never far from the surface. In April, O'Connell arranged to go to a dinner in his honour in Cork, arriving on the Sunday. But O'Brien objected, claiming that their Protestant supporters would be unhappy at having a political demonstration on a Sunday. O'Connell changed his plan immediately, to put O'Brien at ease, but he must have wondered why after so many years Sunday could no longer be a day for agitation.[52]

The traversers were meant to be called for sentencing on 19 April, but this was delayed while a motion was made calling for a new trial. The traversers were unsuccessful in this attempt, though a verdict of *nolle prosequi* was issued in the case of the Rev. Tierney, meaning that the charges against him were not pursued. It was announced that the sentencing would take place on the morning of 30 May. In advance of the sentencing, O'Connell issued an address calling on the people to stay at home and abstain from going near the Four Courts. He was anxious that no attempts be made to rescue the prisoners, and that nothing be done which might lead to violence. His instructions were ignored, as huge crowds gathered in the centre of the city to hear the verdict. But he was followed in spirit, and the crowds that gathered were 'orderly and self-restrained'.[53]

When O'Connell entered the court of queen's bench the crowded audience 'welcomed him with peals of applause which could not be repressed' and a large number of the barristers stood up to receive him, 'a deference ordinarily paid only to judges'.[54] It was an extraordinary tribute to the man who had been 'The Counsellor' for so many years and who would never set foot in a courtroom again. Judge Burton pronounced the sentence. O'Connell was given twelve months' imprisonment, fined £2,000, and ordered to present two securities of £5,000 for his good behaviour over seven years. The other traversers were sentenced to nine months' imprisonment, given £50 fines, and ordered to present securities of £1,000. William Ford was heard to ask, in an audible whisper, whether it was for preserving the country from civil war that O'Connell was required to give securities to keep the peace. And O'Connell himself commented to his friends that the only conspiracy he had been involved in was a conspiracy to prevent civil war.[55] It was revealed that the prisoners would be sent to Richmond Bridewell, and that they would be held in the sheriff's room until arrangements were completed to take them there.

'Thick flakes of snow' were beginning to fall outside, but they were ignored by the 'infuriated multitude' which 'surged through the streets of the metropolis' when they discovered the sentence.[56] O'Connell was led outside to the carriage of Colonel Browne, the chief commissioner of police, who was tasked with bringing him to Richmond. Fearing an angry mob, Browne took out a case of loaded pistols, cocked them, and placed them on his knee. When O'Connell saw them he smiled. 'A wise precaution', he said, 'but useless. If I were only to raise my hand you would be in eternity.' Later it was said that 'one word from O'Connell on that morning would have caused a revolution'. The army had been mobilised in case of trouble, and cannon had been placed at the thoroughfares, but these precautions proved unnecessary. O'Connell's instructions were obeyed.

It was one of the most remarkable days in the history of the capital. In particular, the reaction to O'Connell's short speech in the court was never forgotten by those who were there. After the sentencing was announced, O'Connell rose to speak, and delivered 'a few words with dignity and self-possession'. 'I will not do anything so irregular', he said, 'as to reply to the court, but I am entitled to remind Mr Justice Burton that we each of us have sworn, and that I in particular have sworn positively, that I was not engaged in any conspiracy whatsoever. I am sorry to say that I feel it my imperative duty to add that justice has not been done to me.' Upon hearing this, the younger barristers in the court raised 'a thrilling cheer for Repeal of the Union. It was taken up by the audience in the queen's bench, echoed in the great central hall of the Four Courts, and prolonged by the crowd who lined the quays into the heart of the city.' It was a cheer which carried the hopes, the fears, and the dreams of the Irish nation.

| THE PRISONER, 1844

Richmond Bridewell Penitentiary was an imposing stone building with 'a gloomy appearance which we usually associate with the idea of a prison'.[1] On the front of the prison was an inscription 'in conspicuous characters': 'Cease to do evil, learn to do well.' This was intended 'both as a rebuke for the past, and a warning for the future'. But if O'Connell had any fears about spending twelve months locked inside then he was soon reassured. The prison was under the control of Dublin corporation and instructions were given that every attention should be given to 'their distinguished countryman'.[2] The governor and the deputy governor were authorised to sublet their houses and gardens to the state prisoners, and members of O'Connell's family, and of the families of the other state prisoners, came to reside with them. The prisoners also brought their own servants and had no shortage of supplies. From the first day, 'presents of venison, game, fish, fruit, and the like began to arrive', as well as presents of linen and other luxuries. A confectioner sent the prisoners two gigantic cakes. A merchant sent seven musical boxes.[3] The prisoners decided to play all seven boxes together and were entertained by the resultant cacophony. Soon the prisoners found themselves 'established in a pleasant country house, situated in the midst of extensive grounds, bright with fair women and the gambols of children, and furnished with abundant means either for study or amusement'. The state prisoners became, in effect, a household of which O'Connell was the head.[4] Initially, O'Connell feared that while he was in prison the people might either rise up in rebellion or descend into apathy. But he was delighted that neither happened, and he rejoiced at 'what it is to have such a people to lead!'[5] Beginning to relax, and recover from the exertions of the past year, he soon admitted that 'we are quite gay and cheerful as larks'.[6]

Spiritual sustenance was also to be found. The Rev. Dr John Miley, the renowned pulpit orator who had defended O'Connell's leadership in 1838, accepted an invitation to serve as O'Connell's private chaplain during his imprisonment and provided much support. In addition, the Catholic bishops prepared a prayer 'beseeching God that grace might be granted to O'Connell to bear his trials with resignation, and that he might be soon restored to liberty for the guidance and protection of the people'.[7] This prayer was printed in a special prayer-book which became a popular seller in the country. The Catholic church also declared 28 July a day of solemn national prayer in honour of the state prisoners. Catholic colleges in France and Germany sent addresses to O'Connell, praising him for being 'the Catholic champion' and reminding him how blessed were those who suffered persecution for the cause of right. In addition, Belgian and Rhenish journals brought news of prayers for his deliverance which were being offered in churches from Ostend to Düsseldorf.

Each state prisoner had his own apartment in the official residence, and these were 'spacious and airy', 'nicely carpeted', with sofas and other pieces of furniture. 'No one could wish to live in better rooms.'[8] Friends could visit three days a week, on Mondays, Wednesdays and Fridays, but 'particular friends' were 'readily admitted' on any day. There were also gymnastic grounds where the prisoners could exercise and nearby a large mound, with a round glass house on the top, which served as an observatory. From this spot you could see a considerable portion of Dublin, and much of the south of the city. The prisoners called it 'Tara Hill', in honour of the great monster meeting of the previous year, the name coming from Thomas Steele. A bench in another of the gardens was named Mullaghmast. To amuse himself, Steele would defend 'Tara' with half a dozen picked men, against an equal number of opponents, and observers were impressed at how this man 'approaching sixty who was endowed with enormous strength' was able to hold his own against young men 'in the flower of manhood'.[9]

In prison O'Connell continued to rise early, usually getting up between five and six a.m. whatever the weather. When the clock struck seven a.m. he entered the chapel to attend Mass, and daily took communion. At eight o'clock he would return to his house, where he would take breakfast with the other state prisoners and then prepare his daily schedule. He exercised every day, 'alternately walking in the garden westward of the prison, and amusing himself with gymnastic feats in the grounds' at the east end of the building.[10] The prisoners breakfasted and dined together, 'but generally spent the evening apart with their personal friends, each prisoner having a separate sitting room at his disposal'.[11] During his imprisonment O'Connell decided to write his memoirs, and gathered together in his study all the books and journals that he needed for this purpose. But this 'History of his life and times' did not get very far. The steady stream of visitors interrupted any plans for study and seclusion. O'Connell drank alcohol rarely, usually having a single glass of wine at dinner in the evening, as much to put his guests at ease as for his own enjoyment. 'Whiskey punch', then very popular in Ireland, was avoided. Every night he retired to bed at ten p.m., 'no matter whose guest he may be, or who may be his guest'.

John O'Connell acted as a 'Master of revels' and to amuse the prisoners organised a production of *Julius Caesar*. However, no one was willing to play Cassius and so he persuaded his cousin, Maurice Leyne, to take the part. Leyne was not a prisoner, but willingly agreed to join the group. There he fell under the sway of visitors from the Young Ireland camp, and became their follower. Outside of prison, the meetings of the Repeal Association continued, with William Smith O'Brien serving as leader. However, the more radical elements began to worry that John O'Connell was determined to take over and run things from prison with the help of his brothers, and in August Thomas Davis began considering 'withdrawing silently from the Association' because of the actions of the younger O'Connells.[12]

As O'Connell was 'incomparably the greatest lion in his native land', every visitor to Dublin, whether from abroad or from any of the provinces, 'made it one of his leading objects to see Mr O'Connell, provided he could obtain the necessary introduction'.[13] One day a group of Americans visited O'Connell and suggested that he was probably more visited in prison than before. 'Yes,' replied O'Connell, becoming tired of all the attention, 'and *here* I cannot use the excuse of "*not at home!*"'.[14] Such was the traffic that O'Connell was forced to publish a notice in the newspapers announcing that no one would be admitted any day before noon or after four p.m., and certain days were excluded completely. But close friends and associates were welcome every day and the dinner table was never set for fewer than thirty people.[15] O'Connell's enemies were disgusted to hear reports of this benign prison life and complaints were made to the lord lieutenant. As a result, an order was given that admission would be subject to rules, and that large deputations could not be received. So, instead, deputations of civic functionaries visited individually, thus evading the new restrictions. Receiving one such address, O'Connell recounted everything he had done for Ireland, refusing office, honours, and money, and all the time praying, hoping, and watching for Ireland. But, he said, 'there was yet one thing wanted—that I should be in jail for Ireland'.[16] And he thanked his enemies for adding it to the list.

An artist's studio and a daguerreotypist's camera were set up in the grounds to produce 'multiple likenesses of the prisoners'. One portrait of O'Connell which was published at the time showed 'a man of vigorous frame and commanding presence', but one who had become 'depressed by age' and was 'beginning to be marked by decrepitude'. A young artist, N.J. Crowley, persuaded O'Connell to sit for him. Crowley produced an idealised version of O'Connell, as 'a tribune in the height of his vigour and inspiration', and it bore only 'a distant and fanciful resemblance to the original'.[17] Charles Gavan Duffy also sat for Crowley, and was drawn with 'a dreamy poetic head which might have passed for Shelley's' but which was very unlike the real thing. 'Is not that very like Duffy?' asked Crowley when he showed the portrait to O'Connell. 'Hmm,' said O'Connell, looking from the portrait to the original, 'I wish Duffy was very like that!'[18]

Every week the prisoners sent a bulletin on their status to the Repeal Association, where it was read by O'Connell's youngest son and namesake. The first bulletins merely discussed the good health of the prisoners, but they gradually developed into brief reviews of the public affairs of the week and, despite the regulations of the penitentiary, there was little doubt that 'the voice from the prison was the voice of O'Connell'. After a few weeks an idea was floated in some of the government papers that the state prisoners, with the exception of O'Connell, might be released as an act of grace.[19] But the men released a resolution declaring that they would reject any such offer and would remain in prison until O'Connell was freed.

James Grant, the author of some classic studies of the British House of Commons in the 1830s, set out for Ireland in 1844 and was determined to visit O'Connell in prison. He carried a letter of introduction from one of the parliamentary reporters, and had little trouble getting inside. The first person he met was Thomas Steele, and he was surprised to find him looking much better than he had ever seen him before. Steele was one of the most relaxed prisoners Grant had ever met, and Grant suspected that Steele had never been as happy in his life. It was not that Steele liked confinement; rather, he was happy to be suffering for his country, and 'above all, because he was suffering *with* O'Connell'.[20] Grant noted that it was 'a sober reality that the very ground on which Mr O'Connell treads is very dear to him'. And he was certain that Steele would have been the 'most miserable man in Ireland' if he had not been allowed to join O'Connell in prison. At Richmond, Steele refused to call himself a 'prisoner' and insisted on being called a 'convict'. Steele volunteered to take Grant to O'Connell. Grant wondered if the other prisoners were with him, but Steele corrected him: 'Convicts,' he said eagerly, 'call us convicts.' 'Would not patriots be a better term?' asked Grant. 'Oh no!' replied Steele, 'Convicts. Convicts, if you please!' 'Well then, convicts be it,' laughed Grant.

Grant met O'Connell in the large garden. There was a marquee near the north end which protected from the sun in the warm weather, and provided shelter from the rain the rest of the time. Like Steele, O'Connell looked better than he had for some time. And he admitted to Grant that he felt mentally as well as physically more relaxed. His mind, he revealed, was more at ease than it had been for some years. This was because of the stresses of the 'Year of Repeal', when he had feared that, at any moment, something could go wrong and the people might be massacred. During the visit a little boy came running up to them. 'Who do you think is that?' asked O'Connell. Grant admitted he had no idea. 'That', replied O'Connell smilingly, 'is Daniel O'Connell.' Grant paused for a moment and then remembered that O'Connell's grandson bore that name and, indeed, that he had recently become a subscriber to the Repeal rent. O'Connell stooped down and kissed his grandson. Grant fell completely under the spell of O'Connell and his account of the visit, published later in the year, was devoid of even the slightest criticism. He declared that there was not 'a fonder father than Mr O'Connell in her majesty's dominions' and that 'never did sons or daughters feel or manifest a more devoted attachment to a father'. An

indication of Grant's loss of perspective was the description of
O'Connell as 'a man of excellent business habits', who had always
managed his finances with success.

Relieved to discover that O'Connell was very easy to converse with,
Grant could not get over how relaxed O'Connell appeared in private.
He admitted that you would never imagine O'Connell had 'for the last
thirty years filled so large a space in England's and Ireland's eye, and in
the eye of the world'.[21] Politics was rarely discussed, and he was
astonished that it was possible to spend hours in his company without
realising O'Connell was 'the greatest political agitator which the world
has produced'. Grant was also impressed that O'Connell seemed able to
turn someone's violent prejudice against him into strong feelings in his
favour merely by talking to him.

In August it was rumoured that Queen Victoria was planning to visit
Ireland. If she did, it was believed that her first act would be to release
the state prisoners by an exercise of the royal prerogative. But O'Connell
was not pleased at the prospect and insisted that unless he was released
by a decision from the House of Lords, he would rather stay in prison
for the entire twelve months.[22] In fact, he was vehement that unless his
sentence was overturned he would not go out, 'unless he were literally
dragged out'.

It seemed everyone wanted to visit O'Connell, and during Grant's
time with him 'a great many persons called from all parts of Ireland,
and some from foreign lands . . . among them a number of ladies'.[23]
Catherine O'Connell (no relation) was one such English visitor who
was determined to see O'Connell in prison. On the first of many visits
she found him in a sunny garden, playing with children, with everyone
laughing and enjoying themselves. Dinner was also 'a very gay affair',
with a menu that was very unprison-like, consisting of some rarities of
the season which were offerings from friends and supporters.[24] But
despite the appearance of everything being happy, Catherine noted that
O'Connell's 'spirits drooped at times to the lowest state of
despondency'. Others also noticed O'Connell's occasional melancholy.
One day his son John made some remark about the gloomy high walls
which blocked the view of the countryside from the dining room. But
O'Connell replied that 'it would tantalize too much' to see 'the hills and
fields and sea coast, and to feel that you were debarred from the
freedom of walking among them'.[25] This, he said, would be 'a worse

affliction than to be deprived altogether of the sight'.

Trapped in this genteel prison world, O'Connell fell in love. The object of his affection was Rose McDowell, the eldest daughter of Robert McDowell, the Belfast Protestant who had chaired the stormy Repeal meeting in January 1841. She was twenty-three years old and had come to know O'Connell slightly, before his imprisonment, through Margaret O'Mara, the half-sister of Christopher Fitzsimon (who was O'Connell's son-in-law). In May, O'Connell had secured tickets for O'Mara and three female companions to a meeting of the Repeal Association at Conciliation Hall because 'Miss McDowell' had told him that O'Mara had expressed a wish to see it.[26] In June, Rose visited O'Connell in prison, accompanied by O'Mara, and once again she made a definite impression. He reported that she was '*one* of the most superior women I ever met, with intellect, sound judgment and fascinating sweetness'.[27] And he praised O'Mara for bringing her, admitting that she was 'indeed all you describe her, and more, both in head and heart'. O'Connell was anxious to see her again and begged O'Mara to visit soon with her, otherwise he feared he should 'never see her again'. Over the next few weeks Rose McDowell became a regular visitor.

O'Connell's interest in Rose McDowell was soon noticed and commented upon. Charles Gavan Duffy observed that O'Connell was 'labouring under the most distracting influence that can possess a man of his years', and cruelly, if accurately, described it as 'a passionate love for a gifted young girl who might have been his granddaughter'.[28] He later revealed that during the entire imprisonment O'Connell was 'an unsuccessful wooer'. The relationship was also discussed in public. *Punch* magazine claimed that O'Connell had become not only the victim of the blind goddess Justice but also of the blind god Cupid.[29] It seems O'Connell even proposed marriage, and was refused, but nonetheless persisted in pursuing her. It became a popular joke that O'Connell had gone to the Bridewell to find a bride. O'Connell's family was 'naturally alarmed', not only because Rose was so young, but also because she was a Protestant, and it was said that 'their feverish anxiety could not fail to react upon him'. In the event, Rose's insistence that she could not marry him settled the question, though it did little to restore the composure of O'Connell. 'In truth it left him discontented and perturbed in a high degree.' His correspondence with Rose McDowell was later destroyed by his friends at his own request, in an attempt to protect his reputation from this final affair of the heart.

In August it seemed that Britain and France would go to war. O'Connell guessed, probably accurately enough, that Britain would not declare war without releasing the state prisoners as it would need to recruit soldiers in Ireland. The source of the disagreement was French activity in Morocco as well as a bellicose French pamphlet proclaiming France's naval equality with Britain. The French bombarded Tangiers, and then Mogador, and it was feverishly speculated in Ireland that they would blow down the walls of Richmond prison when finished. O'Connell put up a map of the Mediterranean on the dining room wall, and every day the prisoners followed the progress of the French expedition. In the event war was avoided, as Britain backed away from a costly conflict with France.

In the meantime, an appeal was made to the House of Lords to overturn the verdict based on a writ of error. O'Connell had little faith that the conviction would be overturned, insisting that it was idle, 'quite idle to talk of it!'[30] Deciding on the case were the five law lords: Lord Denman, the lord chief justice who had defended Queen Caroline alongside Henry Brougham almost a quarter of a century earlier; Lord Lyndhurst, back as lord chancellor for the third time, the chief law adviser of the government and O'Connell's sworn enemy; Henry Brougham, now Lord Brougham, who had grown to hate O'Connell; Lord Cottenham, the Whig former lord chancellor who wanted to embarrass the government; and Lord Campbell, the former Irish lord chancellor who owed his promotion in part to O'Connell's patronage. The decisive voice was Lord Denman, who delivered a stunning rebuke to the Irish court on 4 September. He declared that if the practices which had been followed were allowed to continue then trial by jury in Ireland 'would become a mockery, a delusion and a snare'.[31] Sixty names had been improperly excluded from the list of potential jurors and Denman suggested that it was possible that the entire jury might have been selected from this number. Denman found numerous faults with the conviction. The defendants had been charged with different counts of conspiracy, not just one, and then had been found guilty of varying degrees of guilt on some of these counts. Denman was not really engaging with the substantive points of the trial—whether O'Connell or the others were guilty of conspiracy— rather, he found the easiest way to discredit the trial and overturn the result.[32] When the question was put for a vote three decided to overturn the judgment (Denman, Campbell and Cottenham) and the order was given for the traversers to be released.

On the evening of Thursday 5 September the ship carrying news of O'Connell's release reached Dublin. The traversers' attorneys had made flags in London, inscribed with the words 'Triumph of law and justice— the judgment reversed' and 'O'Connell is free', but the captain of the ship had refused to allow them to be unfurled. A large crowd had gathered at the pier at Kingstown, awaiting news, and when they spotted the attorneys waving their hats 'a cheer burst from the multitude, so vehement, so earnest, and so fierce, that in its excitement of exultation it pierced the ear as if it were a shriek'.[33] One of the attorneys shouted, 'O'Connell is free,' and 'the word "free" echoed back again in a hundred voices'. Once on shore, the attorneys unfurled the flags and their appearance was said by one reporter to have produced 'a magical effect'. With the white flags fluttering in the air, thousands of men, women, and children began to rush down to the pier. All throughout Kingstown men began waving handkerchiefs and hats, or lifting their hands in the air. At the railway station one of the engineers begged to be allowed put one of the flags on the engine, and thus the train carried the news that the traversers were free around the county.

All around Richmond shops were left unattended and houses empty, as crowds rushed 'to hear news about the Liberator'. Hundreds clamoured at the gate to see and greet him and one reporter heard many people refer to O'Connell by a new title, that of 'Our Own Father'. Messengers from the Repeal Association raced to be first to bring the news to O'Connell. Two were allowed entry into Richmond, and the younger man went ahead, shouting, 'I'm first! I'm first! I'm first!'[34] Throwing open the doors of the dining room, he continued to shout, 'I'm first! I'm first! You're free, Liberator, you're free.'[35] Sitting in his chair, O'Connell greeted the news of his release with absolute calmness. 'Bah! Not true! It can't be true!' he replied. 'But it *is* true, Liberator!' the messenger told him, showing him the placard which had been printed in London announcing the fact. He smiled as he read it, 'After all, this *may* be true.' The second man, William Ford, an elderly attorney, stumbled into the room and flung his arms around O'Connell, and kissed him, thanking God for his release. There followed 'a scene of unmingled joy' as people began shaking hands and embracing.[36] Thomas Cloney, one of the rebel leaders in 1798, who had been visiting the prisoners, sat down 'and cried like a child'. The deputy governor of the prison, an Englishman who had been a former valet of Peel, came in to congratulate O'Connell and was so overwhelmed with emotion that he rushed from the room, weeping. The governor, 'a large fat man with a red face', a high Tory, and a supporter of Peel's administration, was cheered loudly as he entered the room.[37] 'Evidently much excited, he kept saying, "Good God! Can it be true?"' He staggered towards O'Connell before falling exhausted into a chair, 'ghastly pale' and gasping for breath. The windows were opened so he could get fresh air and water was thrown on him. When he recovered he grasped O'Connell's hand and began sobbing, 'I come, sir, to congratulate you on what I heard.' O'Connell led the other prisoners on to the top of the prison and looked down on the immense crowd which had gathered. Spotting him, the crowd gave 'such an hurrah' as many had never heard before.

O'Connell was now free to do what he liked, and he gave instructions for those gathered outside to be admitted to the prison. Groups began entering Richmond until finally there was not enough room for everyone. O'Connell then walked down to the gardens as men, women, and children gathered around to touch his hand, pray for his welfare, and then move on. That evening O'Connell discussed his release with P.V. Fitzpatrick. In a tone of deep solemnity, he assured him that 'the hand of man is not in this'.[38] Rather, it was 'the response given by Providence to the prayers of the faithful, pious, steadfast people of Ireland'.

It was arranged that O'Connell would return home that night, but in the morning come back to Richmond so that a formal procession could celebrate his release. This was street theatre at its best, and O'Connell was determined not to miss the opportunity for a public demonstration of his popularity and his power. That evening O'Connell returned to his home in Merrion Square on foot. Thousands had gathered outside the prison, but the people grasped each other firmly by the hand, and made a space for him to pass through.[39] As he reached Harcourt Street the crowd was too large for him to go by road and he proceeded through the Green and on to Merrion Street. At Merrion Square it was estimated that fifteen thousand people had gathered, and when O'Connell placed his foot on the step at his house there was 'an outpouring of popular acclamation' which one reporter claimed never to have heard surpassed.[40]

O'Connell went inside and presented himself at the balcony of the house. During the brief intervals of silence he addressed the crowd: 'Why you seem ... [cheers]. It seems as if you are glad to see me home again [tremendous cheering and waving of hats].' He joked that he had not made a speech in three months, 'so my pipe is a little out of tune'.[41] There followed a moving description of 'the glorious meetings of 1843—they called them monster meetings'. He reminded them, 'No one was shoved, or crushed, or pressed upon,' and to great cheering he added, 'not a blow was struck, not a glass of whiskey drunk, not even an accident occurred'. They were, he boasted, gatherings which could have taken place in no other country except Ireland. O'Connell then asked the crowd to go home, for they would meet again the next day 'in peace and happiness. And I promise you we will have the Repeal.' Thomas Steele then came forward and cried out, 'Home, home.' The crowd dispersed, leaving the square silent except for the footsteps of casual passersby.

It rained heavily on Saturday 7 September. The weather was so terrible that a reporter believed it would be 'an act of madness to carry forth'. But the rain had little effect on the people who were determined to make their way to the prison. O'Connell had returned to Richmond at an early hour in the morning, in order to complete a novena for his release which he had begun a few days previously. After this, he enquired after all of the other prisoners in the jail, many of whom had been imprisoned for the non-payment of fines. Those who were believed to be of good character had their fines paid for them, and forty prisoners were released in this way. Some, whose release was only a few days away, chose to keep the money, but all were grateful for the gesture. At eleven a.m. the rain stopped and the sun began shining and thousands gathered to wait for O'Connell's emergence. Various representatives from the trades went to greet O'Connell, as did members of Dublin corporation and the lord mayor. A massive triumphal car, drawn by six white horses, arrived at the prison door ready to take O'Connell away. This car had three levels, 'rising one above the other, gorgeous in purple velvet and gold fringe'.[42] On the lowest level sat O'Connell's grandchildren, wearing green velvet tunics and caps with white feathers. On the middle level sat an old harper dressed as a bard. The highest level was for O'Connell and his chaplain, the Rev. Dr John Miley.

The crowds waited patiently, cheering and singing until two p.m., when the prison gates finally opened. It was said that 'the silence seemed to run with the rapidity of electricity along the line'. For five minutes there was complete silence, until O'Connell was led from the prison by William Smith O'Brien. 'A sudden cheer burst forth', but it was instantly suppressed, 'as if it was premature'. Men were seen to be struggling with their feelings as a 'low, deep, and thrilling murmur' passed along the crowd. The triumphal carriage was brought to the front of the prison and, as O'Connell climbed on board, there 'came forth a shout, so loud, so long, so vehement, and so enthusiastic, that even the man of firmest nerve must for the moment have felt himself shaken by it'. O'Connell was wearing his green velvet cap, and he took it off and waved it three times around his head. One reporter claimed that he had never seen a similar exhibition of popular enthusiasm, and some estimated that the crowd must have been half a million, though Charles Gavan Duffy believed two hundred thousand was a more accurate figure. From front to rear the procession extended for nearly six miles.[43] It made its way past the Four Courts, 'where the lists had been manipulated, the jury packed, and the illegal verdict found', and then Dublin Castle, 'where the blundering and defeated conspirators against Irish nationality were hiding their heads'. The procession then arrived at College Green, where the people hoped the Irish parliament would one day be restored. O'Connell stopped the car and rose to his feet, removed his Repeal cap, and pointed his finger, 'with significant emphasis,' to the portico. There arose a mighty shout. Again and again O'Connell repeated the gesture, and again and again the crowd raised their voices in 'deafening cheers'. It was described as 'the roar of the ocean, that proud shout of a nation's triumph and a nation's hope'.[44] The noise continued, one reporter said, until 'Echo herself was hoarse'.[45]

Arriving at Merrion Square, O'Connell again addressed the crowds from his balcony. He declared, 'This is a great day for Ireland [tremendous cheering]—a day of justice.' Discussing the cancelled meeting at Clontarf, he recalled that 'some of the minions of power laid a scheme to dye that day in gore—to deluge the soil with the blood of the people, but we disappointed them'. And to great cheering he insisted that it would be up to the Repeal Association to decide if the meeting should someday go ahead. This was just playing with the audience, for he then revealed his own opinion that Clontarf was no longer necessary, because its point had already been vindicated by the trials. 'But if we do not take that step, what are we to do?' he asked. 'I have a secret for you,' he answered. 'We will do everything that can be necessary to procure Repeal,' but everything would be proper and legal. He then made fun of the people who had said that he was no longer a lawyer, but had grown old and forgotten all his law. These people had taunted O'Connell for getting charged with conspiracy, after claiming for years that no man who followed his advice had ever been brought into jeopardy. But O'Connell insisted that he had been vindicated by Lord Denman's judgment and these people exposed as liars.

On Monday 9 September the Repeal Association met at Conciliation Hall. The place was packed, with thousands turned away, as everyone jostled to see O'Connell's triumphant return. A friend of O'Connell later said that his spirits had never been 'more elate, his step more elastic, his tone more exulting'. O'Connell spoke of his pride that the decision had been overturned 'on the merits', showing the injustice of the prosecution. And he defended Sheil from criticism that he had acted badly by accepting office from the government, admitting that although he had been annoyed with Sheil at the time, Sheil 'was one of those who can afford to be wrong once, for his country owes him a deep debt of gratitude'.[46] Concluding his speech, O'Connell boasted that he was 'in the midst of a people who love me and trust me, with more power in my hands than any monarch in Europe enjoys'. Here he was interrupted with vehement cheering and waving of handkerchiefs. He then revealed the secret of his success: he had always followed the law. In a dramatic defence of his strategy, and an explicit rebuke to those who wished for violent resistance, he repeated that 'no human revolution is worth the effusion of one single drop of human blood. Human blood is no cement for the temple of human liberty.'[47]

There were public celebrations all over the country, with bonfires blazing on 'every historic hill in three provinces and throughout a great part of the fourth' to telegraph news of the release.[48] In the towns there were illuminations (light displays) and musical accompaniments, but in no part of the country was there any complaint of insults or injuries. The peaceful demonstrations in honour of O'Connell were an 'unexampled spectacle of a whole people, in a delirium of triumph, maintaining moderation and courtesy'. The reporting of the release in the newspapers only added to O'Connell's reputation. It was said that his power had been increased, after he had 'trampled upon the government as he left the prison walls'. Or, as the *Examiner*, put it, he had 'first been made a martyr, and then a conqueror'.

DANIEL O'CONNELL AND THE CAMPAIGN AGAINST SLAVERY, 1829–1847

'There is a charm in the name Daniel O'Connell all over the universe . . . Mr O'Connell could do more for the suppression of slavery in the United States than any other man.'[1]

(JAMES CANNINGS FULLER, NEW YORK DELEGATE, AT THE
1ST WORLD ANTI-SLAVERY CONVENTION, JUNE 1840)

'The voice of O'Connell, which now shakes the three kingdoms, has poured across the waters as a thunder-peal for the cause of liberty in our own land.'[2]

(WENDELL PHILLIPS AT AN ANTI-SLAVERY MEETING IN
BOSTON, 28 JANUARY 1842)

In 1845 the great black abolitionist Frederick Douglass visited Ireland, as part of his campaign to raise support for the anti-slavery movement. He accepted an invitation from Daniel O'Connell to speak at Conciliation Hall in September and he looked forward to meeting Ireland's most vocal opponent of slavery. A great orator himself, Douglass was certain that the stories of O'Connell's ability were exaggerated, and he did not 'see how a man could speak to twenty or thirty thousand people at one time, and be heard by any considerable number of them'.[3] But as soon as he saw O'Connell in action, 'and heard his musical voice', he thought 'the mystery was solved'. Douglass was overwhelmed by O'Connell's oratory, which he 'never heard surpassed, if equalled, at home or abroad'. 'His eloquence came down upon the vast assembly like a summer thunder-shower upon a dusty road.'

With the affable arrogance that was characteristic of him, O'Connell introduced Douglass as 'the black O'Connell of the United States'. There was a loud welcome, and Douglass delivered a striking oration to the massive crowd which had gathered to hear him. In his own speech, O'Connell noted that as he hated oppression wherever it existed, 'my sympathy is not confined to the narrow limits of my own green Ireland'. And he declared that even though his attacks would bring an end to financial contributions from the United States, he did not care: 'he was the uncompromising hater of slavery wherever it was to be found'.[4] 'My heart walks abroad,' he announced, 'and wherever the miserable is to be succoured, and the slave is to be set free, there my spirit is at home, and I delight to dwell in its abode.'[5] Listening to these words, Douglass was moved by their power and intensity and he recognised that O'Connell could 'stir the multitude, at will, to a tempest of wrath, or reduce it to silence'. Afterwards, Douglass and O'Connell walked through Sackville Street and they were followed by a multitude of little boys and girls who ignored the visitor, shouting, 'There goes Dan! There goes Dan!' In later years, Douglass reflected on the fact that when O'Connell died it was a great blow to 'the cause of the American slave' as 'a great champion of freedom had fallen'. He regretted that O'Connell was succeeded 'by the Duffys, Mitchels, Meaghers and others—men who loved liberty for themselves and their country, but were utterly destitute of sympathy with the cause of liberty in countries other than their own'. And he quoted Mitchel, a great apologist for slavery and supporter of the Confederacy, who said that all he wanted upon arrival in the United States was a 'slave plantation, well stocked with slaves'.[6]

O'Connell's interest in the issue of slavery has been dated back to 1824, when James Cropper, a Liverpool Quaker merchant, visited Ireland to raise support for a proposal to undermine West Indian slavery.[7] But given that O'Connell had always equated the condition of the oppressed Irish with that of the slave (classical as well as modern), it seems certain that he would have developed views on the enslavement of Africans long before that. 'I am an abolitionist,' revealed O'Connell at a meeting of a London anti-slavery society in 1831, and it was a position he never departed from. He insisted he did not care whether it was based on 'caste, creed, or colour', he would 'enter into no compromise with slavery'.[8] In a public letter to his constituents on 8 October 1833, O'Connell explained his belief that 'slavery was a crime of enormous magnitude to be at once, unconditionally, and for ever abolished'.[9]

This was no empty rhetoric. At that time the West Indian lobby in the House of Commons had twenty-seven MPs, making it a significant interest. When the Catholic emancipation bill was passing through parliament in 1829 O'Connell accepted an invitation to speak at an anti-slavery meeting in London. Beforehand he was approached by a friend, the knight of Kerry, who was acting on behalf of the West Indian lobby group, asking him not to speak. But O'Connell refused to negotiate, insisting, 'I represent the Irish people here, and I will act as the Irish people will sanction. Come liberty, come slavery to myself, I will never countenance slavery at home or abroad.'[10] Afterwards, O'Connell worried that he had damaged the progress of Catholic emancipation, fearing that the twenty-seven MPs would vote against the bill. But he was relieved when they said they would not revenge themselves upon Ireland for his attack.

From the beginning, O'Connell's aggressive assaults on slavery in the United States drew attention. When O'Connell addressed that anti-slavery meeting in London in 1829 which so disturbed the West Indian lobby, he declared that 'of all men living, an American citizen who is the owner of slaves is the most despicable'.[11] In the same year he addressed the annual meeting of the Cork anti-slavery society and praised Simón Bolívar for his anti-slavery policies. He then contrasted Bolívar with his counterparts in North America and abused George Washington for owning slaves: 'America, it is a foul stain upon your character!' At the great anti-colonisation meeting in London in 1833, immediately after the passing of the British act abolishing slavery in the colonies, O'Connell admitted that he had often longed to go to America, but, 'so long as it is tarnished by slavery, I will never pollute my foot by treading on its shores'.[12] And he denounced the hypocrisy to be found in the Declaration of Independence, saying that the first line should read 'Liberty in America means the power to flog slaves, and to work them for nothing.'

These comments were, not surprisingly, controversial, and divided opinion in the United States. Even some opponents of slavery were uncomfortable with lectures from an Irishman about how they should live, and especially with the attacks on iconic figures such as Washington. But O'Connell was unrelenting. One day he was stopped in the House of Commons by an admirer from Alabama. O'Connell asked if he was a slaveholder and, when this was confirmed, he said, 'I beg to be excused,' and bowed and withdrew.[13] The story was widely discussed, and even Queen Victoria was told of it. At a London anti-slavery meeting in 1835 O'Connell claimed that recent death plagues in New Orleans were not surprising given the crime of slavery which many of its inhabitants countenanced. O'Connell was the recipient of the address of the Emancipation Society in the same year, and the speaker expressed a hope that 'some black O'Connell might rise among his fellow slaves' in the United States and cry, 'Agitate! Agitate!'[14]

Even during his whirlwind tour of Scotland in 1835, O'Connell found time to address meetings on the subject of slavery. At Glasgow he addressed the Emancipation Society and delivered a furious attack on the United States for its cruel laws. He boasted that he had 'given the Americans two or three hard thumps' in the past, and that they had paid him 'wages in abuse and scurrility'.[15] But he said he was happy they had done so, for he 'was accustomed to receiving such wages in return for his labours'. Americans were denounced as being 'traitors to the cause of human liberty' for allowing the sin of slavery. O'Connell revealed that it was a crime to teach a slave to read in the United States, and he asked 'were these laws made by wolves of the forest?' 'No,' he thundered, 'they were made by a congregation of two-legged wolves—American wolves—monsters in human shape, who boast of their liberty, and of their humanity, while they carry the hearts of tigers within them.' In a playful moment, he then asked everyone, the next time they encountered an American who supported slavery, 'to call out to him "Negro"'. There was much laughter at this, and O'Connell explained that 'what was sauce for the goose was sauce for the gander'. Within minutes he had the crowd in tears. He spoke movingly of the slave father returning home from the fields and shuddering when he saw his children because of the knowledge that they must inherit his misery. And he reminded them of the slave mother, who 'looks upon the child she has borne, and knows that she is but rearing the slave of another'. His closing words haunted his listeners: 'Instead of a blessing, she feels that in each child she has been visited with a curse.'

The future of Texas became a burning issue for O'Connell. His sympathy was with Mexico, a Catholic country which had abolished slavery, and not with the men who had broken Texas away from Mexico and established it as an independent, slave-owning state. In London in 1837 he denounced the men who had 'stolen, cheated, swindled, robbed that country, for the audacious and horrible purpose of perpetuating negro slavery'.[16] And he opposed any attempt to have Texas join the United States, recognising that this would bring an extra slave state into the union. Texans were dismissed as 'the gang of land pirates who have settled themselves on the Mexican territory', and he campaigned to ensure that Britain did not recognise the territory.[17]

O'Connell's attacks on the United States almost resulted in a duel. A major anti-slavery meeting was held at Birmingham on 1 August 1838 to celebrate the abolition of black apprenticeship in the West Indies (apprenticeship was an indirect way of continuing with slavery). In advance of the meeting, O'Connell called for the launch of a new crusade against slavery, attacking 'the vile union of republicanism and slavery', and expressing his hope that the day would come 'when not a single American will be received in civilised society unless he belongs to an anti-slavery union or body'.[18] At Birmingham, O'Connell was the final speaker, and his appearance was greeted with cheers and applause. Once again O'Connell attacked Washington for owning slaves and for waiting until his death before freeing them. Perhaps unwisely, he then launched into an attack on the United States' ambassador to Britain, accusing him of being a slave breeder, and wondering aloud whether it was 'possible that America would send a man here who traffics in blood?' Slave-breeding was a serious allegation at the time, far worse than simply owning slaves, for it suggested that owners treated their slaves like animals, encouraging (and sometimes forcing) them to breed and then selling the offspring for profit. It was a charge which struck to the heart of the slave-owners' attempts to portray themselves as kind-hearted and paternalistic, and thus was always rigorously denied, but the truth was that the reproduction and selling of slaves was an integral part of the slave system.

The ambassador in question was a wealthy Virginian landowner, Andrew Stevenson. He had been Speaker of the House of Representatives before his appointment in 1834 to the court of St James (an appointment which was only confirmed by the Senate in 1836), and he was enraged that he had been attacked so publicly. He immediately went to see an old friend who was visiting at that time, General James Hamilton of South Carolina, a noted duellist. Hamilton was asked to act as his second and arrange a duel with O'Connell. But Hamilton was anxious to learn how duels were arranged in Britain, and decided to consult with some other Americans who were also in London at that time. He was told that O'Connell should be given an opportunity to confirm or disavow the published report of the speech in the *Spectator* on 4 August. Acting on this advice, Stevenson wrote to O'Connell on 9 August asking him whether he had described him as 'a slave breeder—one of those beings who rear up slaves for the purpose of traffic'. O'Connell replied the very next day, claiming that having studied the version of the speech in the *Spectator*, he had no hesitation in saying that 'the paragraph you have selected is not a correct report of what I said on that occasion'.[19] And he insisted that having studied some other versions of the speech, 'as well as from distinct recollection', he was even more certain that the report was not correct. This was an ambiguous response, neither disavowing the controversial comments nor confirming the central allegation. Stevenson chose to read the response as a disavowal and decided to make the correspondence public, and he published the letters in *The Times* and the *Morning Chronicle* on 15 August.

Anticipating the publication of the letters, O'Connell decided to clarify in public what he had actually said. In a letter to the *Morning Chronicle* he revealed that the *Spectator* had made some mistakes in its transcription of his speech, and that the actual words were 'It is stated that their very ambassador here is a slave breeder, one of those beings who rear up and breed up slaves merely for the purpose of traffic. Is it possible that America would send a man here who traffics in blood? And who, if he does, would be a disgrace to human nature. I hope the assertion is untrue, but it is right to speak out.'[20]

The differences between this paragraph and the one in the *Spectator* were so minor as to be irrelevant. O'Connell claimed that he had made no apology, but had merely given a legally accurate response to Stevenson. Deciding to provoke Stevenson further, he went on to insist that, until slavery was abolished in the United States, 'no American slaveholder ought to be received on a footing of equality by any of the civilised inhabitants of Europe'. And he wrote movingly about the madness which mothers must feel when their children were taken away from them and sold into slavery.

Word of the dispute travelled across the globe. Some American diplomats rushed to praise Stevenson. Writing from the embassy in Paris, Lewis Cass praised Stevenson for having 'fairly put the braggadacio down'. J. Rudolph Clay, the American minister in Vienna, thanked Stevenson for having given 'that political Judas' a lesson he would never forget.[21] Stevenson waited some time before responding to O'Connell's justification, apparently because he was on holiday in Scotland, although this seems unlikely enough. On 29 October he wrote to *The Times* to deny that he was a slave breeder and to insist that no one in Virginia was one either. Rather, he claimed, O'Connell had invented the whole thing.

Having become involved in the controversy, General Hamilton was furious with O'Connell's behaviour, and believed that he had deliberately lied to extricate himself from his difficulty. He published a letter in the *Richmond Enquirer*, and other American newspapers, denouncing O'Connell's speech at Birmingham as a 'brutal outrage' on the United States and its ambassador. And he claimed that he would find a way to revenge himself on 'this Irish Caliban'.[22] This letter caused much controversy in the United States, with many people in both the north and the south disturbed by the violent language and the threats to O'Connell's life. Hamilton was forced to publish a clarification, and he defended his actions by saying that he had found evidence that O'Connell's speech was identical to what had been reported in the *Spectator*, but this was a hollow enough victory given that the central allegation was the same no matter what version was used. The abolitionist press in the United States wondered why Stevenson had not pressed the matter further; pro-slavery papers such as the *Richmond Enquirer* denounced O'Connell as 'a prejudiced and mad fanatic' who needed to be taught a lesson.[23] Many believed that Stevenson had demeaned the office of ambassador by engaging in the squabble, and one paper claimed he had made himself look like a fool by publishing the correspondence.[24]

The former president of the United States John Quincy Adams, who was now a member of the House of Representatives, would not let the matter rest. On 6 December 1838 he took to the floor of the House of Representatives to expose 'a conspiracy against the life of

Daniel O'Connell'.[25] He returned to this subject again in January 1839, denouncing the proposed challenge to O'Connell as 'a threat of assassination by one ruffian. That was a conspiracy.' The resolution which Adams proposed attacking Stevenson was defeated but the debate caused a considerable impression in the United States.

At the British and Foreign Anti-Slavery Society in 1840 O'Connell discussed the clash with Stevenson. He joked that Stevenson had tried to prove he was right by fighting a duel, and he insisted that he would never accept such a challenge: 'Nothing would ever induce him to commit murder. God had forbidden it and he would obey him.'[26] He taunted Stevenson with having first denied that he owned any slaves, but then later admitting that he indeed bought and sold slaves. Stevenson had insisted that no slaves were bred for sale in Virginia, but O'Connell quoted from William Jay's recent book, *A view of the action of the federal government*, which had been published in New York in 1839, and which showed that slave-breeding existed in Virginia and within twenty-five miles of Stevenson's home. O'Connell demanded that a slave owner should be treated as if he had the cholera or the plague, 'for there is a moral cholera and a political plague upon him'.[27] And he called on the people of Europe to say to slave-owners, 'Murderers, you belong not to us!'

The 1st World Anti-Slavery Convention was held at Freemason's Hall in London in June 1840. It was organised by the British and Foreign Anti-Slavery Society and attracted delegates from many parts of the world, including a number of female delegates from the United States. The presence of female delegates proved controversial. On its first day, on 12 June, the convention decided to withhold official recognition from them. Lucretia Mott, the Quaker preacher and reformer who would become one of the leading abolitionists, wrote to O'Connell to ask for his support.[28] O'Connell had missed the start of the conference and he admitted that when he first heard of the question of admitting female delegates he was not in favour.[29] But when he received Mott's letter he reflected on the grounds of the opinion he had formed, and found that 'it was on no better grounds than an apprehension of the ridicule it might excite if the Convention were to do what is so unusual in England'. He accepted that this was 'an unworthy and, indeed, a cowardly motive' and so he changed his mind. 'Mind has no sex,' he declared, and he came to believe that women should have the same rights and duties as men in the war against slavery. O'Connell's support for the female delegates was reported widely in the United States and 'created a strong feeling of regard and affection' for him.[30]

O'Connell's speech to the convention was one of his great orations. He was 'received with a storm of applause that almost shook the building to its foundations'.[31] This was the view of William Lloyd Garrison, a leading abolitionist in the United States who edited the newspaper *The Liberator*. He boasted afterwards that he had 'shaken hands with O'Connell repeatedly'. O'Connell made his usual criticisms of the United States, and he accused the founding fathers of lacking the 'moral courage' to abolish slavery.[32] Though he accepted that 'there exists not a braver people upon the face of the earth', he demanded them to prove it by abolishing slavery. According to Garrison, when O'Connell was afterwards confronted with the evidence of Irishmen who supported slavery in the United States, he 'indignantly exclaimed to my face . . . "Sir, they are not Irishmen! They are bastard Irishmen!"'.[33] Garrison would publish extracts from ten years of O'Connell's speeches on slavery in *The Liberator* on 25 March 1842. He believed that the speeches 'scathe like lightning and smite like thunderbolts' and he did not believe that any man 'in the wide world' had 'spoken so strongly against the soul-drivers of this land as O'Connell'.[34]

At this convention James Cannings Fuller delivered a notable tribute to O'Connell, and he pleaded with him to prepare an address on slavery for the Irish in America. Fuller had been born in Ireland, and had attended some of the Union debates before emigrating to the United States. To flatter O'Connell he claimed that his influence in the United States was greater than that of the whole convention combined.[35] O'Connell revealed that he already had such an address in mind, though he wanted to wait until after the 1840 presidential election before sending it.[36] This address, prepared with Fr Mathew, called on the Irish in America to unite with the abolitionists, and it was signed by sixty thousand Irish people before it was sent.[37] The address was read at a meeting in Boston on 28 January 1842 and Wendell Phillips, another leading abolitionist, spoke of his delight that 'the voice of O'Connell, which now shakes the three kingdoms, has poured across the waters as a thunder-peal for the cause of liberty in our own land'.[38] Fuller also addressed the meeting 'as an old countryman', and he observed that oppression had brought many Irish people to America, and that they must be as radical there as they had been in Ireland. Other Americans expressed their disapproval. John Joseph Hughes, the Irish-born Catholic bishop of New York, declared that the letter was either a fraud or an intolerable interference in American affairs. And many Irish-American newspapers also attacked O'Connell for sending the address.

A problem arose about what to do with contributions for the Repeal Association from America. Repeal Associations had sprung up across the United States, but many of them were pro-slavery.[39] At first, O'Connell was happy to accept contributions from these groups, suggesting that the best way of proceeding was to convince them in a conciliatory manner of the evil of slavery. But, in the spring of 1842, some abolitionists begged O'Connell to avoid such 'an unholy contamination'.[40] Even Garrison became critical of O'Connell, though he refused to disown him, and in private Wendell Phillips began referring to him as 'The Great Beggarman'.[41]

In 1843 the problem of the American contributions became decisive. At a meeting of the Repeal Association on 13 March a vote of thanks was passed to Robert Tyler, the son of the president of the United States, because of his public support for Repeal, which had included sending financial aid. James Haughton, a leading campaigner in Ireland against slavery, accused Tyler of being a slave-breeder and called on the Association to reject any money from such people.[42] On 3 April O'Connell assured Haughton that no conditions were attached to the money, and that therefore he was obliged to accept it even if it came from slave-owners. However, O'Connell became uneasy on the point, and soon afterwards decided to reject all monies from anyone who supported slavery.

On 10 May 1843 the Repeal Association heard an address from the Anti-Slavery Society of America. Responding to it, O'Connell boasted that he had 'never said a word of mitigation of slavery in my life' and would 'consider myself the most criminal of human beings if I had done so'.[43] There was 'tremendous cheering for several minutes' when he declared that 'every man [was] a faithless miscreant, who does not take a part for the abolition of slavery'. O'Connell then addressed the claims that slaves were treated worse because of the campaign of the abolitionists, as owners became more suspicious and more severe. He compared this to the claims of some men in the 1820s who said that

O'Connell's violent language was delaying the progress of emancipation. But, he said, 'I got emancipation in spite of them.' O'Connell imagined the slave-owners crying, 'Oh, it is not the slaves we are flogging, but we are flogging through his back the anti-slavery men.'[44] And he prophesised that slavery would never be abolished in America until 'some horrible calamity befalls their country'.

It was at this meeting that O'Connell announced a change in the Association's policy on receiving money from the United States. He declared that 'we do not want blood-stained money', and if that meant no more funds from the United States so be it.[45] The harshness of the language did indeed alienate opinion in the United States. O'Connell addressed this at a meeting of the Repeal Association on 6 August 1843. Just days before the monster meeting at Tara, he declared that he could never hesitate to oppose a 'system that would treat human beings as brute beasts of the field'.[46]

This was a time to address the internal and external critics who believed it was inappropriate of O'Connell to interfere in the domestic policy of another country by attacking American slave-owners. In his response, O'Connell stated that his 'entire life had been devoted to the individual, as well as the general liberty of mankind', and that because of this he had joined the Anti-Slavery Society as soon as he heard of it. In a dramatic declaration, he announced that if the Repeal of the Union depended on him changing his opinion on slavery, or even just suppressing his sentiments with regard to slavery, then 'I would never change the one, nor suppress the other.' No matter what the consequences, he insisted, 'I adhere to my opinions, and never shall I cease to pour out my entire heart and soul in reprobating, in calling down the curses of mankind upon that vile system.'[47]

Some abolitionists did not escape his censure. A number were attacked for their anti-Catholic prejudices, including William Lloyd Garrison, who O'Connell claimed was 'something of a maniac' when it came to religious subjects.[48] Garrison was deeply upset when he read these attacks and pleaded with O'Connell to let him know what he had done to offend him, but it seems the rift was never healed.[49] Nevertheless, when O'Connell died in 1847, his passing was mourned by Garrison, who admitted in private his 'many faults and failings', but recognised the 'feelings of gratitude and respect' which were owed to him.[50]

'A stout, thick-set Yankee', Dr Hare, visited Ireland at this time and tried to persuade O'Connell to relax his anti-slavery agitation.[51] Hare droned on about the fact that although he was not Irish he had once been in love with a young Irish girl, who had 'acquired a lasting place in his esteem'. 'O'Connell was desperately bored, but sustained the infliction with smiling resignation.'[52] Thinking he had made a good impression on O'Connell, Hare attempted to convince him that his opposition to slavery was injudicious. He told O'Connell that emancipation would produce a thousand evils and inconveniences, and that the subject was far too complex for someone not acquainted with American society. Claiming that O'Connell would think differently if he ever visited America, Hare reproached O'Connell for abusing Americans on the subject. O'Connell was not to be lectured. He told Hare that slavery was 'atrocious and abominable' and put America in 'a disgraceful and anomalous position'. Referring to a recent slave auction where a mother narrowly avoided being separated from her child, O'Connell vowed that he would never relax his opposition. Hare reminded O'Connell that America had inherited the slave system from the government of the United Kingdom. 'Aye, you got a *crime* from the government of Great Britain—a precious argument for retaining the crime,' replied O'Connell.[53] And he asked, 'Why, now, what do *I* care where you got your crime? *I* am not bound by the iniquities of the British government.' Hare attempted to assure O'Connell that he was not a slave-owner, merely someone who believed that O'Connell would spoil the abolition cause with his violent language. But O'Connell repeated his favourite story about how it was precisely his violent language which had succeeded in winning Catholic emancipation. Growing impatient, O'Connell rose and wished Hare a good morning. Hare rose reluctantly, and criticised O'Connell for getting involved in matters that were none of his business. 'You know,' Hare said as he prepared to leave, 'interference in another man's family matters is never well received.' Opening the door, O'Connell told Hare bluntly, 'I deny they are part of your family.' He bowed and wished Hare a good morning for the second time. 'But if you would only consider,' pleaded Hare. 'I wish you a very good morning,' said O'Connell firmly, and shut the door.

Many were concerned that O'Connell risked damaging the cause of Repeal by his inflexibility. A friend of O'Connell's pleaded with him at this time to be friendly towards the American slave-owners because they were so powerful. 'No,' replied O'Connell, 'what care I for the vagabonds were they twice as powerful?'[54] His friend then asked him to at least remain silent on the question, claiming that he injured '*our* question by mixing it up with the slavery question'. Again O'Connell disagreed. Virtues, he said, would be strengthened by being combined, and he insisted that 'it is *ourselves alone* must work out Repeal'.

Whenever the slave-owners attempted a defence they were denounced. Whenever they denigrated the black race they were attacked with a fervour and a ferocity that they were not used to encountering. In October 1843 a document from some supporters of slavery in Cincinnati was read at the Repeal Association. It contained the claim that 'the very odour of the negro is almost insufferable to the white' and insisted that 'the two races cannot exist together on equal terms under our government and our institutions'.[55] O'Connell raged in his response, denouncing the smell of white Americans, who offended with their 'overwhelming stench of stale tobacco spittle'. And he reminded them of the fact that many white Americans had fathered black children, through the rape and abuse of their slaves. It was at the close of this meeting that a young black man stepped on to the platform and, to much cheering, praised O'Connell for all he had done to help the lives of black people, claiming to have heard stories of his endeavours since he was a child.[56]

In 1843 O'Connell read Charles Dickens's *American Notes*, a non-fiction account of his travels in the United States, and was greatly moved by the section on slave auctions. Long an admirer of Dickens, O'Connell admitted that the chapters had given him 'a clearer idea of everyday life in America than I ever entertained before'.[57] Dickens was also well aware of O'Connell's campaigning against slavery, and used it in his novel *Martin Chuzzlewit*, which following serialisation was published as a novel in 1844. O'Connell is discussed in the section set in the United States, though he is not mentioned by name. When the eponymous hero attended a meeting of the Watertoast Association held at the National Hotel in the fictional 'Eden', he heard a number of speeches attacking 'the British lion'. He then learned that 'the Watertoast Association sympathised with a certain Public Man in Ireland, who held a contest upon certain points with England: and that they did so because they didn't love England at all—not by any means because they loved Ireland much'.[58] In the preface to the 1852 cheap edition Dickens revealed that what followed at the Watertoast Association was 'a literal paraphrase of some reports of public proceedings in the United States (especially of the proceedings of a certain Brandywine [Repeal] Association [of Delaware])'.[59] At the meeting in the novel, General Cyrus Choke read out a letter which was about to be sent to O'Connell, which included 'a contribution to the funds of your society'. However, during the speech a package arrived from England containing extracts from several newspapers, and when these were studied afterwards a change came over the general's face, 'involving such a huge amount of choler and passion, that the noisy concourse were silent in a moment'. '"My friends!" cried the general, rising, 'my friends, and fellow-citizens, we have been mistaken in this man.' 'In what?' asked the crowd. 'In this,' the general replied, holding up the letter he had read aloud a few minutes earlier: 'I find that he has been, and is, the advocate—consistent in it always too—of nigger emancipation!'[60] It is revealed that if O'Connell had been present at that time 'those sons of freedom would have pistolled, stabbed—in some way slain—that man by coward hands and murderous violence . . . They tore the letter, cast the fragments in the air, trod down the pieces as they fell; and yelled, and groaned, and hissed, till they could cry no longer.'

O'Connell's public declarations on slavery were a key factor in alienating the Young Irelanders. They believed that the Repeal Association should only address domestic, not foreign, affairs, and they were uncomfortable with the aggressive way O'Connell was alienating real and potential supporters in the United States. Duffy later wrote of how the time was not right 'for gratuitous interference in American affairs' and this was the general view.[61] The attacks on slave-owners in the United States was considered a 'wanton and intolerable provocation'. John Blake Dillon was furious with O'Connell's attacks on the United States in 1845 and reported to Thomas Davis on how 'everybody was indignant at O'Connell meddling in the business'.[62] 'Such talk', he declared grandly, was 'supremely disgusting to the Americans, and to every man of honour and spirit.'

But to black Americans O'Connell was not just a hero and champion; he was an inspiration. Charles Lenox Remond, another great black abolitionist, heard O'Connell speak at an anti-slavery event at

Exeter Hall in London in June 1840, and was profoundly moved by O'Connell's oratory. Reflecting on it immediately afterwards he declared that for thirteen years 'I thought myself an abolitionist', but that it was only when he heard that speech that he realised what being an abolitionist really meant. He said that 'every fibre of my heart contracted' when he 'listened to the scorching rebukes of the fearless O'Connell in Exeter Hall', and he praised his 'soul-stirring eloquence and burning sarcasm'.[63] Afterwards, when walking through London with Thomas Campbell, the Scottish poet, O'Connell was greeted by a free black man who took off his hat and thanked him for his work against slavery. In later years O'Connell enjoyed telling the story of Campbell's response. Campbell's 'poetical fancy was smitten' and he exclaimed with great fervour, 'I would rather receive such a tribute as that, than have all the crowned heads in Europe making bows to me!'[64] It was a response which reflected exactly O'Connell's own feelings and convictions.

Chapter 13 ❧

YOUNG IRELAND AND THE FALL OF O'CONNELL, 1844–1846

'Answer your enemies as I do mine—by redoubling your exertions for Ireland.'[1]

(DANIEL O'CONNELL TO CHARLES GAVAN DUFFY, N.D.)

Unable to prevent any longer the decline of his powers, O'Connell began to fail. Old age and creeping ill-health were already beginning to weaken him, and medical treatment did little to help. He underwent surgery for haemorrhoids, but a doctor later suggested that 'the operation caused a bacteraemia, whereupon organisms lodged in the frontal lobe of his brain'.[2] The death in October 1844 of his beloved grandson and namesake, who had spent so much time with him in prison, was a devastating blow, and was said to have 'all but crushed him'.[3] In addition, the great exertions of the Repeal year, the stresses of the trial, and the increasingly fractious relationship with the Young Irelanders all combined to further reduce his strength. The division in the Repeal Association, which made a split look increasingly likely, 'was a topic that evidently preyed upon his spirits'. A close friend observed that his appearance began to show, 'at last, the wear of years and labour. His step was heavy, and the vivacity of his manner had given place to an air of languor.'[4] O'Connell recognised the evidence of decline. Occasionally he would go over to a mirror, and sigh, saying, 'Well—I think I am looking very old and worn. I perceive the change very much. I think my face has got a very haggard look.'

To escape from the pressures of work, O'Connell took an extended break at Derrynane. A man who visited around this time noted, 'The life of O'Connell at Derrynane has always been that of an old clan chieftain.'[5] On Sundays at Derrynane the locals would gather for 'a game of hurling, or a dance' and sometimes O'Connell would come and watch, giving 'a livelier zest to their sport'.[6] There, wearing his green velvet Repeal cap with the gold band, O'Connell reminded his visitor of 'some old king in a German story'. The visitor conceded, however, that 'no old king in any German story ever occupied that position of importance, or exercised that moral influence which the Irish Agitator exercises at this moment'.[7] At nine a.m. every morning the bell at Derrynane rang for Mass and, 'for one hour, the whole place is as still as a tomb'. Breakfast was served at ten o'clock and then began the business or amusements of the day. 'Such is O'Connell at Derrynane.'

At Derrynane O'Connell was always able to find peace, and the rest allowed him to plot a new course for the Repeal movement. In October 1844 he sent a detailed letter outlining the future policy of the Repeal Association. There would be no more monster meetings, the idea of calling an Irish parliament was forgotten, and a proposal from the Federalists to create a subordinate legislature for local purposes was presented for consideration. To the younger members of the Association this suggested an abandonment of all that had been achieved in recent years and a return to the compromises of the 1830s. One summed up their position: 'though you are the leader, you shall not lead us to destruction'.[8] In *The Nation* O'Connell was accused of having abandoned the cause, further alienating him from the paper. O'Connell's enemies also taunted him with having failed in his stated promise during the Repeal year that within twelve months an Irish parliament would be sitting at College Green. The Federalism idea proved particularly controversial. But O'Connell was only testing the waters, and it remained nothing more than an open question for members to consider. He seems to have been moved to suggest the idea following a private meeting with Isaac Butt and some Liberals, where he was encouraged to believe that Ireland might be granted a subordinate parliament.[9] And yet he had mixed feelings. Indeed, he had ended his letter on Federalism by insisting that it was 'a mere question of time' before Repeal was won: 'Hurrah then, for the Repeal!'[10]

O'Connell returned to Dublin for the meeting of the Repeal Association on 25 November. His appearance was warmly received and he made sure his position was in no doubt by declaring that Federalism was not worth 'that', as he snapped his fingers.[11] O'Connell's floating of the Federalist idea, and then his abandonment of it, fatally undermined the Federalist cause. Years later, when one of their leaders was asked what had gone wrong, he replied, 'O'Connell jumped on our boat and sunk it.'[12]

In a clever attempt to neutralise clerical support for Repeal, the British government sent an envoy to the Vatican. The objective was to persuade the pope to issue an order calling on the Irish clergy to abstain from all political activity. The negotiations were successful, and the order was given, but its terms were interpreted so loosely by the Irish bishops that nothing changed.[13] Defeated, the duke of Wellington was heard to remark that O'Connell and his 'democracy' were 'too strong for the Roman Catholic nobility, gentry, and hierarchy, with or without the pope'.[14] In return, the Repeal MPs began staying away from Westminster, choosing to attend Conciliation Hall instead, and many politicians in Britain began to see the policy of abstentionism as a threat. One MP gave notice of a call of the House of Commons to compel the attendance of the Irish members, but O'Connell defied them to enforce it.[15]

This was a time of tension and turmoil. Religion was becoming a source of division. When Miley delivered a sermon on 8 September 1844 claiming that O'Connell's release had been secured, not by a decision of the law lords, but by the intercession of the Virgin Mary, Davis wrote an angry leader in *The Nation* asking whether O'Connell was ruled by 'superstition'.[16] Furious, O'Connell responded by mocking Davis's 'Protestant monomania'. In the aftermath of this clash, various attacks were made on *The Nation*, which was accused of being anti-Catholic in its outlook, and Davis and Duffy both believed the attacks were authorised by O'Connell. Although this was denied, the grievance festered.[17] The Repeal fund also became a source of contention. The problem was that O'Connell had exclusive control of the money, which rested in his bank account, with the reason given that it might be necessary to spend money on something that might later be found to be illegal. But the loose accounting procedures began to torture men such as O'Brien, Davis, and Duffy, who became increasingly suspicious of how the money was being spent.[18] However, they refused to make an issue of it, knowing that any hint of malpractice would destroy the Repeal Association.

The focal point for much of the trouble was not O'Connell himself, but rather his son John. Everyone could see that O'Connell was failing and this was as much a contest about who would succeed him as anything else. Young Ireland was prepared to put up with O'Connell's dominance, but it reacted badly to the increasing role taken by John. The younger men were jealous of the title he revelled in, 'Young Liberator', which, indeed, he had done nothing to deserve. And they reacted furiously to the 'fierce, offensive and dictatorial' tone which he began to take at meetings.[19] It became clear to them 'that the sceptre would pass from the house of Derrynane' and they blamed the attempt to found a dynasty for the eventual split.[20] Duffy, in particular, reacted badly to the 'dictatorship' of John O'Connell, who was accused of 'deliberately destroying the labour of years, and the hopes of a generation'.[21]

The '82 Club, a club based around a celebration of the winning of legislative independence in 1782, was founded in January 1845 with O'Connell as president. O'Connell had come up with the idea while in prison, and the hope was to bring Catholics and Protestants together in a way that the Repeal Association could not.[22] There were five vice-presidents and two secretaries, of whom four were Protestant, and at its public meetings any resolutions usually had both a Protestant and a Catholic to propose and second them. The first public banquet was held on 16 April 1845, the anniversary of Henry Grattan's famous declaration of Irish parliamentary independence. Close to a hundred men attended, all dressed in green, and the group included Thomas Meagher, John Mitchel, and Henry Grattan Jnr. There were toasts to Grattan and Flood, and the dinner ended with a toast to the arts in Ireland which was delivered by Thomas Davis.

All the time O'Connell was thinking of new strategies. He considered forming his own formal parliamentary party, committed to Repeal, and his constant refrain was the boast that 'with sixty-five members he would carry Repeal and restore the parliament to College Green'.[23] As a result, Peel's government decided to bring in various reforms in Ireland, in an attempt to undercut support for Repeal and weaken the position of O'Connell. The strategy, to a certain extent, worked, for it brought all the problems with Young Ireland to the fore. As Duffy later wrote, it 'compelled the young men to confront the greatest tribune of modern times in the arena where he had long been supreme'.[24] The breaking point came when an education bill was proposed, looking to set up third-level colleges throughout the country (what became the Queen's Colleges), which would be open to Catholics and Protestants. At a meeting of the general committee of the Repeal Association there was majority support for the measure. But O'Connell surprised many by denouncing the scheme. He believed that religious instruction was carefully excluded from the new colleges and that this was an unacceptable attack on the Catholic faith. It seems O'Connell feared the establishment of state-controlled education which would be anti-national and anti-Catholic, and saw the bill as a clever scheme to undermine his support in Ireland.[25] There followed a heated debate. Davis suggested keeping the controversy away from the next regular meeting of the Association, but O'Connell rejected this and declared his intention to raise the subject at Conciliation Hall. At the Repeal Association on 12 May O'Connell denounced the colleges as 'Godless', though he said he would abandon his opposition if the Catholic bishops approved of the scheme. O'Connell's preference was for specially designated Catholic colleges, with a Presbyterian one in Ulster, to match the Protestant college in Dublin. John O'Connell joined in supporting him, and this intervention, more than anything else, provoked Davis into preparing a response. During all of this period, William Smith O'Brien absented himself from the meetings, and it was believed that he 'intentionally shrank from any contest with O'Connell'.[26] All the time he followed a neutral course, neither siding with O'Connell nor with the Young Irelanders, but choosing to act as a kind of umpire, and hoping that his fear of conflict would be mistaken for independence of character. The report of the Catholic bishops added another twist. It resolved to support the bill provided certain amendments were made to protect the faith and morals of the Catholic students. This should have been enough to placate O'Connell. But he had gone too far to back down. At the next meeting of the Repeal Association on 26 May he declared that he was there to denounce the bill 'from one end to the other' and he refused any talk of compromise.[27]

A young man called Michael George Conway rose to speak. Conway had presented himself for membership to the '82 Club a few weeks earlier but had been blocked by the Young Irelanders. This was his revenge. In his speech he asked the audience not to 'yield up old discord or sympathies to the theories of Young Ireland' and he denounced the attempt to create a new ascendancy. The speech delighted O'Connell, who took off his cap and waved it repeatedly as he cheered each new attack.[28] To the Young Irelanders, this was a declaration of war.

Thomas Davis rose to reply. He began by saying that he had only a few words to say in response to the speech of 'my old college friend, my Catholic friend, my very Catholic friend, Mr Conway'.[29] Furious with the superior tone adopted by Davis, O'Connell immediately rose to interrupt and he asked Davis, 'It is no crime to be a Catholic I hope?' Davis was apologetic: 'No, surely no, for . . .' But O'Connell was not satisfied: 'The sneer with which you used the word would lead to the inference.' 'No! Sir, no!' replied a thrown Davis, who invited ridicule with his next line: 'My best friends, my nearest friends, my truest friends are Catholics.' He continued his speech, praising the merits of mixed education and defending the safeguards which would be put in place to protect Catholics. He was clearly shaken, for he switched sides halfway through his speech, and ended by denouncing the bill because there was no provision for the religious education of boys taken away from their homes, and because the government had the right to appoint and dismiss professors. Therefore he insisted he would 'give this bill in its present shape an unflinching opposition'.[30]

O'Connell decided to go for the kill. He noted that Davis had previously supported the bill and that it had been praised 'in a newspaper professing to be the organ of the Roman Catholic people of this country, but which I emphatically pronounce to be no such thing'. Not content with this attack on Davis and The Nation, O'Connell delivered a withering condemnation of 'the section of politicians styling themselves the Young Ireland party', accusing them of being 'anxious to rule the destinies of this country'. He said they were welcome to that name, for 'I am for Old Ireland.' Calling for 'this delusion' to be put to an end, he announced that 'Young Ireland may play what pranks they please. I do not envy them the name they rejoice in, I shall stand by Old Ireland.' And he concluded by saying that he had 'some slight notion that Old Ireland will stand by me'. When he sat down the 'consternation was universal'. Everyone realised that this marked the beginning of a bitter split which would never be healed.

O'Brien and Grattan apparently had a quick word with O'Connell, for he rose again in a few minutes and withdrew the name of 'Young Ireland', saying that he had heard it was disclaimed by those to whom it was applied. Davis rose to his feet a second time. He said he was glad to be freed of the assumption that there were factions in the Association and he spoke of his feelings of strong affection for O'Connell. Davis was not normally emotional or demonstrative, but the high tension of the meeting had got to him. He struggled to control his feelings, and then 'paused from emotion, and broke into irrepressible tears'.

For a moment there was an astonished silence. O'Connell rose to his feet and thanked Davis for the kind words, throwing his arms around him as he cried, 'Davis I love you.'[31] The men were reconciled, in public at least, and there was loud cheering and applauding at the meeting. One observer, however, was disgusted by O'Connell's theatrical display and described it as being 'more like the clumsy pantomime of an ox than any display of manly sincerity'.[32] Davis continued with his speech, saying that he and his friends had only ever opposed O'Connell 'when they were convinced in conscience that it was a duty to do so'. And, he said, 'he trusted their disagreement would leave no sting behind'.[33] But that day poison had been injected into the Repeal Association which was never fully removed. It seeped into the system and eventually proved fatal.

Before the end of the year Davis was dead. He contracted scarlet fever and died on 16 September. Some speculated that the clash with O'Connell had been a major factor in his quick decline, but Duffy accepted that this was unfair. He admitted that Davis 'bore away a wound which bled inwardly', but insisted that 'his nature was too robust to sink under it'.[34] Duffy was partly sympathetic to O'Connell, but saw him as 'an uncrowned king' who had come to equate his own interest with the national interest, and who began 'to treat dissent as treason'. The 'Scene' at Conciliation Hall, as it became known, divided opinion. Many believed that O'Connell had conjured an argument out of nothing, but rereading Davis's opening, and the repetition of the word 'Catholic', it is hard not to see it as a deliberate insult. Some of Davis' friends were embarrassed by his display of feeling, and angry that O'Connell's 'vulgar assault' had only drawn 'pearly drops' and 'quivering emotion'.[35] Even Duffy teased Davis about it, and the next time he saw him he sang the lines, 'We must not weep for you dear land, we must not weep for you!'

As part of a compromise deal, it was agreed that O'Connell and O'Brien would attend the House of Commons and demand amendments to the education bill. In June O'Connell travelled over to London, but he failed in his attempts to modify the bill and he returned claiming that it was as bad as ever. However, the Catholic hierarchy insisted on giving the bill a fair trial as it passed through parliament. During this period Davis admitted that his mixed feelings of admiration and censure for O'Connell were turning into 'genuine hostility' and he feared that O'Connell was trying to force him and O'Brien to secede.[36] Shortly before his death he described his relationship with O'Connell as simply that of 'great political friends'.[37]

Davis's death on 16 September led to a massive outpouring of grief. O'Connell was at Derrynane when he heard the news and he rushed to compose a public letter which was read at the Repeal Association; it was also published in the *Freeman's Journal*. In it, he paid a generous tribute to Davis, describing him as 'my beloved friend, my noble-minded friend'.[38] And he ended it by saying that he could write no more—'my tears blind me'. Of course, this was written for public consumption and O'Connell's private feelings on the death were not recorded. Certainly he had become increasingly irritated with the behaviour of the Young Ireland faction, and his feelings on the death of Davis were almost certainly tempered by all the bitterness of the past year.

O'Connell was more preoccupied with a controversy about his estates. In 1845 *The Times* commissioned Thomas Campbell Foster to visit Ireland to report on social conditions. His reports were, in general, fair, though O'Connell suspected that *The Times* was out to damage the Repeal movement and insult the Irish people. At meetings of the Repeal Association, O'Connell dismissed Foster as 'the gutter commissioner' of 'the infamous *Times*,' and accused him of being 'the traducer of my brave people'. Foster had foolishly made some negative comments about the appearance of women in Leitrim, and O'Connell seized upon this. 'Do you know what this gutter commissioner has also said?' he asked. 'He said that the Irish women are ugly!' There were cries of 'Oh!' and 'Shame!' 'He really did,' insisted O'Connell. Shouts of 'He's a liar!' filled the room. There were a number of women in the front row of the gallery, and O'Connell swept his hand towards them, joking, 'Heaven! How ugly they are!'[39] There were loud cheers. O'Connell said that he wished 'the ruffian was present today' to see 'that spectacle of female loveliness which now dazzles our eyes'. O'Connell did not relent in his attacks on Foster. At a subsequent meeting he claimed to have seen Foster in Limerick, and he joked that he 'really is not so ugly a fellow as I thought he was'. And he dismissed him as someone who would 'sink into his native insignificance, which God knows is low enough'.

Furious at these attacks, Foster decided to embarrass O'Connell by examining his estate in Kerry.[40] After collecting as much evidence against him as he could find, he denounced him for the squalor and misery of his tenants, and claimed that O'Connell ranked first among all those landlords who were a curse to Ireland, and that 'the most wretched tenants' in Ireland were to be seen on his estates.[41] Cahirciveen was described as 'dirty' and 'unpaved', and it was claimed that none of the windows had panes of glass. Foster was particularly scathing about the houses at Derrynane Beg, a particularly poor part of O'Connell's land, in the shadow of his own home, revealing that there was not a single pane of glass in the parish.

Responding to these charges, O'Connell joked that he wished Foster had 'as many pains in his belly' as there were panes of glass at Derrynane Beg. And he accused Foster of being so fond of lying that he could not tell the truth 'even by accident'. As for Cahirciveen, O'Connell was able to quote English authorities who described it as a town which 'bears all the marks of rapid improvement—the houses new and of handsome structure'.[42] He also revealed that he had spent £4,000 to provide it with a chapel, a residence for the priests, a convent, a girls' school, a boys' school, a bridge, and a quay. To answer these claims, *The Times* sent a second investigator, William Howard Russell, to Kerry, and he confirmed that at Derrynane Beg there was 'not a pane of glass, not a window of any kind in half the cottages'. But O'Connell was able to prove that the families at Derrynane Beg had been evicted from other estates, and that he had generously allowed them to settle on his land. Russell later conceded that the families at Derrynane Beg were indeed squatters, who had been evicted from other estates.

O'Connell had always been a benevolent landlord, giving his tenants the maximum amount of freedom to do as they wished, including the right to subdivide their land. This was one of the reasons he was so popular, but it also made him an easy target for cheap journalism. Other newspapers, even ones that were usually hostile to O'Connell, recognised that he was being unfairly treated and rushed to his defence.

The *Evening Mail* insisted that 'the management of O'Connell's property is excellent, and his tenants are comfortable and happy'. The *Morning Herald* accused *The Times* of 'hitting below the belt', and blamed its reporters for collecting 'the rancorous drivel of discontented tenants and servants and disappointed beggars'. As O'Connell and his family was able to refute the key charges the controversy died away, just as the greatest calamity in modern Irish history was about to hit the country.

1845 was the year when the potato blight first arrived in Ireland. Dublin corporation set up the Mansion House committee on 21 October to investigate the causes of the potato failure and, from the beginning, O'Connell took a leading role in its discussions. He demanded an immediate repeal of the corn laws, so that food could be imported as cheaply as possible. And he also urged the necessity of restricting the use of grain in brewing and distilling, and limiting the export of foodstuffs.[43] From the first signs of trouble O'Connell carried out intensive research on the subject, in an attempt to assess the scale of the crisis facing the country, and discover what relief measures should be implemented. O'Connell became convinced of 'the frightful certainty of an approaching famine' and he despaired because 'pestilence always follows famine'.[44] He recommended that the government adopt an energetic plan of works, giving employment to the labouring classes and then paying them in food as well money. Without this, he feared that it would be 'impossible to calculate the number of people that will perish in Ireland within the next twelve months of famine and pestilence'. However, his pleas were ignored, with the government choosing to send over its own scientific experts from England. At a meeting of the Repeal Association O'Connell raged at the painfully slow progress of the government's response. 'So', he exclaimed, 'we have got scientific men from England! Just as if we had not men of science in abundance in Ireland.'[45] O'Connell realised that the disaster provided further evidence of the need for a parliament in Ireland, but this was not the time for politics. Recognising the calamity that was about to face the country, he asked Fitzpatrick to postpone the annual tribute. And in a poignant address to the Repeal Association O'Connell even admitted that he would sacrifice Repeal if the choice was between it and keeping the people alive.[46]

To meet the approaching crisis, Robert Peel decided to repeal the corn laws. There was deep unrest within his own cabinet and, unable to command the support of his colleagues, he felt obliged to tender his resignation as prime minister on 6 December. William Smith O'Brien rejoiced at the idea of a change in government, believing that a new administration under Lord John Russell would help bring about Repeal. And he urged O'Connell not to make an issue of the corn laws and risk creating divisions in the Repeal Association.[47] The *Dublin Evening Mail* had recently made a reference to the rivalry between O'Connell and O'Brien, and claimed that the Repeal Association risked becoming 'O'Brienised'.[48] But O'Brien assured O'Connell that he had no reason to be jealous.

Neither the request about the corn laws, nor the comment about O'Connell being jealous, were likely to impress a man who saw himself as the central hero in the story of the Irish nation. O'Connell was furious, telling O'Brien that having spent 'fifty years of my life in agitation' he had never been jealous of any man.[49] And he rejected O'Brien's request to remain quiet on the subject of the corn laws. Despite the long years of conflict with Peel, and the prospect of a new government coming in, O'Connell was determined to put the interests of Ireland first. In the event, there was no change of government. Peel was recalled on 20 December after Russell proved incapable of forming a new government. O'Connell had been following things closely and had been told in confidence that Russell had failed because Lord Grey had refused to allow Lord Palmerston to become minister for war.

The issue of slavery was now becoming one of the key issues on which the camps divided. In 1845 it looked for a time as if Britain and the United States might go to war over Texas. O'Connell's sympathies were, as usual, against the slave-owners and he made this clear in a meeting of the Repeal Association. In a highly charged and controversial passage, he predicted that 'the American eagle, in its highest pride of flight', might be brought down, if it continued to support slavery. Many people shared Duffy's belief that this was a 'gratuitous interference in American affairs'.[50] 'Everybody is indignant at O'Connell meddling in the business,' a friend wrote to Davis, noting, 'Such talk must be supremely disgusting to the Americans, and to every man of honour and spirit.'[51] The Repeal Associations which had been founded in Baltimore, New Orleans, and other American cities dissolved themselves in disgust, and there was a permanent breach with Conciliation Hall. The Young Irelanders were resolutely unsympathetic to the plight of the American slaves. For example, Duffy insisted that the tenants in Mayo and Kerry were more badly treated than the slaves in Alabama and South Carolina, a ridiculous comparison because it denied that freedom itself counted for something.[52]

John Mitchel, himself to become a key defender of slavery, was beginning to play an important part in the movement. Friends with Duffy, he began writing for The Nation, and soon became one of its most important voices. Duffy initially found him a sullen young man who spoke slowly and delivered his opinions in what would have been considered an 'abrupt and dogmatic manner', except for the smile which accompanied them.[53] In the beginning Duffy was not impressed with Mitchel's journalism, but he thought that Mitchel gradually 'came to write with admirable vigour and skill'.[54] Mitchel had ambitions to be an orator but his pretensions were exposed at the '82 Club. Invited to deliver an oration on the memory of Thomas Davis, Mitchel's maiden speech was a complete disaster and he sat down having forgotten most of what he wanted to say. It was incidents like this which led O'Connell to later mock the 'juvenile orators' who presumed to challenge his authority at the Repeal Association.[55]

A controversial article by Mitchel in The Nation in November 1845 brought him to O'Connell's attention. In great detail, Mitchel had discussed how the railways in Ireland could be sabotaged easily, thus rendering them unserviceable for the movement of troops. O'Connell visited the office of The Nation, to remonstrate with Duffy for allowing this dangerous guide to guerrilla warfare to be published. He was furious that it left the Repeal Association open to prosecution and was determined to distance himself. At the next meeting in Conciliation Hall he declared that he was guarding the 'safety of the Association' and he spoke of his strong interest in maintaining the prosperity of the Irish railways. The crown solicitor immediately began a prosecution against The Nation for seditious libel, and it was rumoured that O'Connell had encouraged the government in taking it. Duffy was tried in June 1846 and was defended by Robert Holmes, who delivered a spectacular oration against the charges. The state prosecution collapsed and Duffy was released.

At some point before the trial, it is impossible to date it precisely, O'Connell sent for Duffy, and asked him to bring Mitchel with him.[56] Ever since the publication of the railway article he had viewed Mitchel as 'peculiarly hazardous to the safety of the Association'. O'Connell wanted to know if it was possible for them all to work together in peace. A new alliance with the Whigs was discussed and, according to Duffy, O'Connell threatened that unless this was supported he would end all connection between *The Nation* and the Association. Such a break would have bankrupted the paper and Duffy was forced to pledge his support.

O'Connell spoke increasingly rarely in the House of Commons, but returned to the chamber to make three major speeches on famine relief in 1846. However, it was clear to everyone that his powers were failing rapidly. On 3 April 1846 he spoke on the bill for the protection of life in Ireland. Because he had a lot of documents he wished to refer to in his speech, he decided to sit in the place normally reserved for the leader of the opposition, and he rested his papers on the red box. For two hours he spoke on the plight of Ireland, but it was soon painfully clear that his powers were gone. His voice only projected as far as the first few rows of the government benches, and no further. Disraeli cruelly compared it to a 'dumb show, a feeble old man muttering before the table', though he noted that 'respect for the great parliamentary personage kept us all orderly'.[57] It was impossible to hear the speech from the public gallery, but out of respect the MPs who heard the speech assisted the reporters with their accounts so that the speech was not lost.

On 30 April 1846 William Smith O'Brien was imprisoned in the Clock Tower of the House of Commons after being found guilty of contempt.[58] This was because of his repeated refusal to attend meetings of the railway committee. O'Brien became upset at O'Connell for not doing more to support his case, and for refusing to allow the Association to identify with his stand. In May O'Connell made various attempts to secure O'Brien's release, and he was freed at the end of the month, with Peel expressing his regret at the imprisonment.[59] By the summer Peel had been replaced as prime minister by Russell, and a Liberal government took power which was to prove appallingly ill-suited to deal with the problem of famine in Ireland.

The problems with the Young Irelanders could no longer be ignored. At a meeting of the Repeal Association on 15 June, Thomas Francis Meagher delivered an eloquent tribute to Davis, saying that '*we* looked upon him as our leader and our prophet'.[60] O'Connell was not present at the meeting, but Steele intervened to challenge

Meagher. Steele questioned what he meant by 'we', and whether he thought the people of Ireland had repudiated O'Connell for another leader. Meagher denied this, insisting that 'we' was a reference to the 'young gentlemen' who had supported Davis. O'Connell realised it was time to 'put down this mischievous knot' (in the words of one of his friends), and Steele rejoiced that he had at last decided to 'put these scamps in their proper position'.[61]

At a meeting of the Repeal Association on 13 July 1846 O'Connell laid a trap for the Young Irelanders. Two documents were presented. The first was a report on why Richard Lalor Sheil had not been opposed in the recent by-election in Dungarvan, Co. Waterford, after accepting an office of profit from the crown. The Young Irelanders challenged the report, believing that Sheil should have been opposed. The second document was a series of resolutions, later known as the peace resolutions, which O'Connell claimed reiterated the fundamental policy of the Association. These resolutions were an attack on the use of physical force, and a declaration that the Association's objectives would only be achieved through moral force. Meagher began by attacking the Dungarvan report and he argued that a victory there would have been 'an inspiriting example'.[62] O'Connell was imperious in his dismissal of Meagher. He mocked 'the young gentleman who came down with a ready-made speech', and claimed that 'two or three men from *The Nation* office [had] come here to create dissension'.[63] The report was carried without a division.

The peace resolutions were then discussed. The attack on them was led by John Mitchel. He refused to accept the position, defending the men of 1798 who had 'thought liberty worth some blood-letting'.[64] If this was calculated to provoke O'Connell it succeeded. O'Connell immediately interrupted and appealed to the members: 'What can this man's object be? He purports to be a man of peace, yet he preaches war.'[65] And, after a burning exchange with Mitchel, he declared that 'the man who pretended to profess the doctrines of peace, and still preached another, was betraying the Association and deceiving himself'.[66] Mitchel insisted that he approved of the resolutions, but O'Connell was not convinced. He revealed that the resolutions had been specifically framed to draw a line between Old Ireland and Young Ireland and he called on all members to agree to the resolutions fully and unconditionally, or be expelled. Denouncing one opponent, who wavered in his position, O'Connell demanded that he was 'bound to abhor physical force. The Repeal Association is entirely opposed to the use of such means, and any man who advocates it cannot be amongst us.'[67] The resolutions were passed amidst deafening cheers, with only Meagher voting against them.

O'Connell had hoped that this would lead to the secession of the Young Irelanders, but nothing happened in the short term. However, the cracks were all too visible. At two meetings of the Repeal Association on 27 July and 28 July the split finally came. It happened in O'Connell's absence, while he was away in London. The first meeting began with the reading of a letter from O'Connell declaring that there could be no compromise with anyone who would not accept the peace resolutions. William Smith O'Brien tried to intervene, and privately remonstrated with John O'Connell, but to no avail. For the first time, he aligned himself publicly with the Young Irelanders.[68] At the meeting the next day, a letter was read from Duffy justifying the position of The Nation. Mitchel then declared that the real cause of dissension in the hall was not physical force but the alliance with the Whigs and 'place-begging'.[69] Meagher joined the attack, speaking out against the necessity of the peace resolutions. Determined to quell the rebellion, John O'Connell demanded acceptance or expulsion. O'Brien intervened and tried to make a conciliatory speech, but after being interrupted by John O'Connell, he walked out of the hall. He was followed by Meagher, Mitchel, Duffy, and by a section of the meeting, as the split became a secession.

Despite some attempts at reconciliation, the wound was never healed and the Repeal movement never recovered. Popular opinion was divided, with few understanding the reasons for the split. As the leader of the movement, O'Connell was blamed for allowing it to happen. Doubts crystallised and would not go away, and his popularity began to fall. The decision to break from the Young Irelanders proved to be a costly final mistake. In the 1810s O'Connell had been the young man on the rise, and his calculated breaks with older, more intransigent elements succeeded as a result. But by the 1840s he was a man in decline, raging against his own fading powers as much as against the dangerous upstarts who threatened to contaminate his life-principles. Steele admitted in November 1846 that 'the people have ebbed away from him', and were alienated because of the split.[70] Whenever Steele tried to raise the subject O'Connell became excited and told him he must be mistaken, 'and he either takes up a book, or changes the subject'. Steele became depressed when he compared the O'Connell of 1843, at the zenith of his popularity, with the broken O'Connell of 1846. His spirits falling, and his health failing, O'Connell accepted that nothing more could be done to resuscitate the Repeal movement. He became increasingly gloomy whenever politics was discussed, and shrank away from any discussion of what had gone wrong. As the famine began to extract a terrible toll on the country, he mustered his fading energies for one final campaign to try and save his people.

Chapter 14 ∾

THE LAST DAYS OF 'THE FATHER OF THE COUNTRY', 1847

'If I had only the alternative of keeping the people alive or giving up the Repeal, I would give up the Repeal.'[1]
(DANIEL O'CONNELL TO THE REPEAL ASSOCIATION,
3 NOVEMBER 1845)

The terrible spectre of the famine haunted O'Connell's final days. In October 1846 he called for a national meeting of landowners in Ireland to confer with the government on measures of famine relief, but it was not taken up.[2] In December, he worked on a letter for the *Dublin Evening Post*, though ill-health seems to have prevented him from completing it. In it he begged the editor to use the newspaper's extensive circulation 'to arouse the fears and excite the attention of the resident landed proprietors of Ireland'.[3] He was disturbed that the landowners were 'by no means sufficiently alive to the horrible state of the country', and he feared that the country was 'only at the beginning of our calamities'.

The plea was dramatic and heart-felt: 'A NATION, it is starving.' O'Connell was aware that the problems of dysentery and typhus had been added to the 'all-prevalent famine' and he was left repeating the question 'What is to be done? What is to be done?' Predicting that no class would be safe from 'its dire effects', O'Connell sent detailed instructions to Kerry so that the poor would be protected there. He purchased ten tons of Indian meal in Britain and arranged for the

British navy to transport it to Cahirciveen.[4] Following this, he decided to buy ten tons of oatmeal, as all the time he looked for ways to alleviate the suffering of the people. The newspapers had calculated that thirty people were dying each day of hunger, but O'Connell feared that the figure was closer to three hundred and thirty. At the Repeal Association he proposed that the British government should raise a loan of forty million pounds, which would be applied to famine relief.[5] He noted sadly that only for the Union the Irish parliament could have raised the sum itself, and also that the country would have been better equipped to deal with it. But he derived no satisfaction from these observations.

Much of his time was spent at the Relief Committee Rooms on Dame Street. There he spent his time, 'closely muffled', studying figures and plans to relieve the starving.[6] One day John Mitchel entered and was placed in a chair near him. O'Connell said nothing, but gave 'a chilling, stately bow'. Mitchel was too afraid to engage him in conversation. He never saw him alive again. Though he blamed O'Connell for using 'his art and his eloquence to emasculate a bold and chivalrous nation', he recognised his greatness, and he could tell that O'Connell, who was full of 'tenderness and pity', was suffering intensely from seeing 'his well-beloved people perishing'.

This suffering was increasing all the time. In February 1847 O'Connell was diagnosed with 'intense bronchitis and generalised weakness', as well as anorexia, and he had difficulty in moving his arms.[7] There was no warmth in his hands, and he was unable to stop his right arm from trembling. The most obvious change was in his voice. It was now 'faint and feeble' and bore no resemblance to 'the stirring trumpet tones' of old.[8] One friend admitted that O'Connell could no longer be heard six yards off. But O'Connell refused to admit that the decline was as bad as it appeared. He insisted that he was deliberately economising his vocal powers and could make himself heard if he needed to be. Few believed him. It was the delusion of an old man convincing himself that 'the decay induced by years and sorrow was a voluntary economy of strength'.

Broken in mind and body, O'Connell found it difficult to walk, and his 'step was very slow'.[9] 'His mind was painfully agitated', as he reflected on 'the awful visitation of famine which had fallen on the country'. Having exhausted everything that could be done in Ireland, O'Connell realised that he must plead the case of his country before the British parliament. It was a humiliating prospect, begging for help in the chamber where he had abused and terrified his enemies for so long, but it needed to be done. On 28 January 1847 he left for London, to see what could be done for the starving country. Before he went, he asked Dr Daniel Murray, the archbishop of Dublin, for permission to bring his friend and confessor, the Rev. Dr John Miley, who had been his chaplain in Richmond, with him. Permission was granted and Miley joined O'Connell for his final months. O'Connell told Miley that he had little hope of changing anything: 'I know the vastness of this calamity. I have been proclaiming it for months, for a year, and they would not believe me. They believe it now, but they have no idea of its vastness . . . It is killing me.'[10] In London, O'Connell supported the scheme of the new lord lieutenant, the earl of Bessborough (formerly his old friend Lord Duncannon), to employ starving people in a railway-building scheme, but this was defeated. On 8 February he took his seat in the House of Commons for the very last time. The debate was on the state of Ireland and how to address the crisis. Rallying all his powers, O'Connell stood to make his final speech. But the task was beyond him. 'His voice was broken, hollow, and occasionally quite inaudible; his person was debilitated; the vigour of his eloquence was gone, and his appearance was that of one who was destined soon to descend into the grave.'[11] The wand of the magician was broken. He 'spoke very indistinctly', according to one reporter, and even *Hansard* began its report with the qualification 'Mr O'Connell was understood to say'. In an emotional and charged appeal, O'Connell begged the British parliament to do something for Ireland. As Oliver MacDonagh notes, 'He attempted no argument, attributed no blame, [but] threw his country upon the mercy of his foes.'[12] O'Connell admitted that 'Ireland is in your hands, in your power; if you do not save her she cannot save herself. I solemnly call on you to recollect that I predict, with the sincerest conviction, that one-fourth of her population will perish unless you come to her relief.'

His one request, which was ignored, was for 'a great national act of charity' to save the country. For years O'Connell had taunted and terrorised MPs from the very same spot. But now they listened to him in respectful silence, aware that this was the final performance of a falling giant.

Afterwards O'Connell spoke despairingly to Miley: 'I feel that I am gone. My physical power has departed from me. My voice is almost mute. I am oppressed with grief.'[13] For the sake of his health and for spiritual solace, O'Connell decided to set out on a trip to the continent. The plan was to go to France and from there embark on a pilgrimage to Rome to visit the tombs of the apostles and receive the blessing of Pope Pius IX. Knowing he would never return, O'Connell asked P.V. Fitzpatrick to look after his affairs, and instructed him to destroy his correspondence with Rose McDowell, even though 'it contains nothing disreputable'.[14] In a touching display of gratitude he thanked Fitzpatrick for keeping him going for so long by organising 'The O'Connell Tribute', and called him 'the best of *all* his friends' as he said farewell for the last time.[15] Miley noted that prayer had become O'Connell's only occupation, and admitted that 'He is perfectly prepared for death, and had rather not be diverted from it.'[16] On Monday 22 March O'Connell embarked on the *Prince Ernest* steamer from Folkestone to Boulogne, accompanied by his son Daniel, his servant, John Duggan, and Miley. At the hotel in Boulogne he cheered up when he recognised a familiar face, John Gully, the former MP for Pontefract, who was resting there.[17] A successful racehorse owner, Gully had won the Derby and the Oaks the previous year (with 'Pyrrhus the First' and 'Mendicant') and the two men reminisced about their days in parliament. From Boulogne O'Connell made his way to Paris, arriving on Friday 26 March. On Sunday 28 March he was visited by the Comte de Montalembert and a deputation from the committee for the defence of religious freedom. Montalembert had visited Derrynane in late 1830, and had received advice from O'Connell about how to 'emancipate the church from the temporal yoke' in France. At the time he had been disappointed with O'Connell, describing him in his diary as 'a demagogue', and dismissing his language as 'brusque, pompous, vulgar'. But with the passing of time he came to regret his youthful attacks, and he returned to his diary to write in the margin, 'Oh! What a fool!'[18] In Paris he hailed O'Connell as 'our master, our model, our glorious preceptor' and declared that 'we are all your children'.[19] O'Connell was too ill to respond, and he admitted that 'sickness and emotion close my mouth'. 'It is impossible for me to say what I feel,' he said, and he referred to the visit 'as one of the most significant events of my life'.

On Monday 29 March O'Connell and his party left on the five p.m. train for Orléans. Almost three hundred people gathered outside his hotel in Paris to see him off. From Orléans he went to Lyons, and on the journey was struck 'by an obstinate attack of dysentery'.[20] It snowed heavily at Lyons and the wintry weather did not help his condition. O'Connell was forced to spend eleven days at Lyons, resting on a sofa, and he was 'lamentably weak and sadly depressed in spirits'. A visitor tried to cheer him up by saying that recovery was possible, but O'Connell replied, 'Do not deceive yourself; I may not live three days.'[21] O'Connell's right arm trembled continually, and the left hand was so cold, even though he wore thick gloves, that it could only be warmed with difficulty. His face had grown thin and 'his look proclaimed an inexpressible sadness, the head hung upon the breast'. At night-time he was afflicted by 'griefs and terrors' and he insisted on Miley staying near him in case he awoke. A local doctor visited him at the hotel, and O'Connell told him, 'I am but the shadow of what I was, and I can scarcely recognise myself.'[22]

After recovering sufficiently to proceed, O'Connell embarked on a steamboat to Valence on 22 April. A French reporter noted the change to his health: 'Animation seems to have fled from the face, once so expressive, of the Liberator.'[23] As O'Connell made his way, slowly, to the steamboat, he was greeted by a large crowd which bowed in respect, but he was unable to pay them the slightest attention. As the reporter asked, 'How, said we to ourselves, is this the man who has filled the world with the thunder of his name, and made England tremble to her centre?' From Valence O'Connell made his way to Marseilles, before sailing on the Lombardo steamer to Genoa.

The party reached Genoa on Thursday 6 May, but it was unable to go any further. According to a doctor who examined him, on 7 May O'Connell 'suffered a violent headache, and his speech became quick and his movements spasmodically rapid'.[24] This condition worsened, and two days later he was in 'a slight state of delirium, with impeded speech, bounding pulse and marked injection of the face', which a doctor believed was the 'result of meningitis'. His speech became more laboured and he was unable to swallow. Feverish, he began to worry that he would be buried alive and he pleaded with his servant, Duggan, not to bury him until after he was dead.[25]

On 11 May an English doctor, who had been called in to examine him, diagnosed a 'new symptom of congestion of the brain'.[26] O'Connell imagined he was back at the Catholic Association, refighting the great issues of the day with Thomas Wyse. He asked Duggan if Wyse had brought forward his motion, and who had seconded it, and told him 'that Wyse was mad, and to call him should there be a division'.[27] The doctor wanted to treat him, but O'Connell showed 'great repugnance to swallow even the most simple medicine'. Dr Viviani, the oldest practitioner in Genoa, was also contacted for advice. His solution was to apply leeches, but although leeches were applied for three days they produced no improvement.

On the night of 13 May O'Connell went 'into a violent delirium'.[28] His voice barely audible, he took Duggan by the hands and bade him farewell, making him promise not to let anyone bury him until it was certain he was dead. O'Connell imagined that he was in London, addressing the House of Commons for one final time. It was said afterwards that he had hurled defiance at Peel, and shouted, 'I have got the Repeal! Hurrah! I have got it safely locked up in a box.'[29] But, unlike the Wyse comments, these do not appear in any contemporary account, although by this point O'Connell was so feverish and delusional they might very well have been said.

The next day, Friday 14 May, O'Connell was unable to speak or move for long periods. At two a.m. on the morning of Saturday 15 May he was so ill that Miley decided to administer the last rites. O'Connell was awake throughout, his hands clasped in prayer. He had a 'feverish thirst' but kept rejecting the drinks that were offered to him.[30] He would fall asleep and then awake suddenly, insisting that his doctors make sure he was dead before burying him.

In his final hours O'Connell spoke of nothing but 'his eternal interests and the bright hopes of eternity'.[31] He was constantly praying, reciting the litanies of the Virgin Mary and making 'continual efforts to articulate the Divine name of the Saviour'. Perhaps his final complete sentence was the conclusion of the prayer of St Bernard: 'to be merciful to me a sinner . . . and to lead me on toward Heaven along the way of the cross'.[32] O'Connell died at nine thirty-seven p.m. that evening. Miley noted, 'There was no struggle—no change visible upon the features, except that, as we gazed, it was plain that a dread mystery had cast its shadow over him.'[33] He wrote to O'Connell's son Morgan to tell him that 'the Liberator, your illustrious father—the father of his country—is dead! Dead!'[34] But then he corrected himself: 'No, I should say rather, *O'Connell is in Heaven*.' In the post-mortem examination it was discovered that there were lesions in several of O'Connell's organs, and that his brain was 'found engorged with blood throughout its entire extent and partially softened. Its membranes were inflamed and thickened.'[35] Another doctor also commented on the 'congested lungs, sound heart, and ossification of the aorta'.[36]

Along the journey, O'Connell had apparently expressed a wish that if he was unable to complete his pilgrimage his heart would be sent to Rome. This idea took its inspiration from the plan of Robert the Bruce to have his heart deposited at Jerusalem. This wish was followed and O'Connell's heart was sent to Rome, encased in a silver urn, while his body was embalmed in preparation for its return to Ireland. Concluding his magisterial study of O'Connell's life, Oliver MacDonagh noted that 'symbolically, this seems quite wrong. It [his heart] should surely have been laid in the Irish ground from which it had drawn, and to which it gave back so much.'[37] Fr Miley and O'Connell's son Daniel completed the pilgrimage and on 12 August had an audience with Pope Pius IX. The pope expressed his sadness on the death of O'Connell, and embraced Daniel as the son of 'the hero of Christianity'.[38]

At eleven thirty a.m. on Monday 2 August O'Connell's remains arrived in Dublin on board the *Duchess of Kent*. Many people had gathered to see the coffin, and some were overheard saying that they wanted to be able to tell their children and grandchildren that they saw 'the Liberator's coffin'.[39] The coffin was 'of regal magnificence', covered with rich crimson velvet from Genoa. The silver plate bore an inscription in Latin, the first line of which translated as 'Daniel O'Connell, Ireland's Liberator'.[40] The funeral mass took place on Wednesday 4 August at the Church of the Conception in Dublin. It was attended by mourners from Ireland and Britain, and from all around the world, with visitors from France, Germany, Italy, India, Columbia, and the United States, amongst other places. Afterwards, the funeral procession made its way around the city. The triumphal car which had brought O'Connell from Richmond Prison led the way, and massive crowds gathered to watch the procession along every street. St Stephen's Green was filled with mourners, but there was 'no noise, confusion, or disorder', just 'solemn and impressive' silence.[41] O'Connell was buried at Glasnevin Cemetery, which he had done so much to establish, and was some time later placed in a vault, fourteen feet long by eight feet broad, and seven high, with a round tower built on the spot. W.E. Gladstone described the 'soaring tower' as 'the pre-eminently national symbol of his country'.[42]

Writing from London, Charles Greville was unmoved by the death of O'Connell. He believed that at one time it would have 'excited the greatest interest and filled the world with political speculations', but now the news 'was heard almost with unconcern, so entirely had his importance vanished'.[43] In fact, he believed that O'Connell had for some time been 'morally and politically defunct', having 'quarrelled with half of his followers' and failed with his campaign for Repeal. That said, he noted that history would speak of O'Connell 'as one of the most remarkable men who ever existed', a man who, like Napoleon, had risen 'from the humblest situation to the height of empire'.[44] The *Spectator* compared O'Connell to Moses, Mohammed, and Napoleon, but complained that he had squandered his power after winning emancipation. 'His great deed was always in the future,' it claimed, 'to be performed.'[45] Thomas Steele took the death of O'Connell hardest. Life lost all meaning for him, and he attempted to commit suicide, throwing himself off Waterloo Bridge into the River Thames. However, he was rescued, and lingered on until 15 June 1848, when he finally passed away.[46] His body was taken back to Ireland and he is buried in Glasnevin Cemetery, at the foot of the monument to the man he had spent his life serving.

By the time of his death, O'Connell's international standing was immense. In France, for example, his reputation as one of the greatest figures of the age was never challenged. Honoré de Balzac, the novelist and playwright, once exclaimed that less than a handful of men had 'had an immense life'. One was Napoleon, and another was O'Connell, the man who 'incarnated in himself a people'.[47] When Jules Verne was writing his great novel *Twenty thousand leagues under the sea*, in 1869, he included a description of all the portraits that hung on Captain Nemo's wall. Alongside those of George Washington, 'the founder of the American Union', and Abraham Lincoln, 'who fell shot by a supporter of slavery', was one of Daniel O'Connell, 'the defender of Ireland'.[48] Perhaps not too surprisingly, when the novel was translated for publication in England in 1873 the reference to O'Connell was deleted, and many modern translations continue in this omission.

The Comte de Montalembert paid a heartfelt tribute to O'Connell after his death. He hailed him as the man who had 'reigned without ever having spilled one drop of blood and without encouraging one drop of blood or violent act'. And he credited him with having furthered the

Catholic cause more than any world leader. 'His fellow citizens christened him the Liberator,' he declared, insisting, 'He will be known by this title for all posterity.'[49] O'Connell exerted a lasting hold on the imagination of the French people. In May 1969, one month after retiring as president of the fifth republic, Charles de Gaulle made a surprise visit to Ireland. His grandmother, Joséphine-Marie de Gaulle, had written a biography of O'Connell and it was one of his favourite books growing up.[50] When he visited Kerry he made sure he went to Derrynane. There the symbol of French resistance and French honour during the second world war signed the visitors' book, and wrote 'In honour of the Liberator'.[51]

In Germany, too, O'Connell was long remembered. As a young man, Otto von Bismarck declared that his ambition was to have 'the career of a statesman in a free constitution, such as Peel, O'Connell, Mirabeau'.[52] When the great British historian A.J.P. Taylor wrote his study of Bismarck, he expressed surprise that O'Connell was on this list, concluding (with a sneer) that 'evidently principles did not matter to him'.[53] It seems that Bismarck changed his mind about O'Connell in his later years. T. Desmond Williams, the inspirational professor of modern history at University College Dublin, concluded his study of O'Connell's impact on Europe with a quote that was attributed to the older Bismarck: 'O'Connell was a man I think I would have shot.'[54]

In Ireland and Britain, O'Connell's legacy was equally complicated and contested. Cardinal John Henry Newman would later claim that his abhorrence for O'Connell delayed his move to the Roman Catholic Church. In *Apologia pro vita sua* he revealed that he had 'an unspeakable aversion to the policy and acts of Mr O'Connell' because he blamed O'Connell for advancing Catholicism by 'violence and intrigue'.[55] Others attributed their moves to the Roman Catholic religion directly to him: when O'Connell was preparing to leave Britain for the very last time he was visited by three men who assured him that it was his remarkable career which had persuaded them to become Catholics.

The greatest Irish writer in the English language, James Joyce, was a distant relation of O'Connell, and was immensely proud of the connection. O'Connell is referenced in a number of his works. In chapter seven of *Ulysses*, for example, he paid a glorious tribute to O'Connell's oratory: 'Gone with the wind. Hosts at Mullaghmast and Tara of the kings. Miles of ears of porches. The tribune's words, howled and scattered to the four winds. A people sheltered within his voice.'[56] John Henry Foley's monument to O'Connell in Dublin, which was completed by his student Thomas Brock and unveiled in 1882, also appears in a number of works. Paddy Dignam's funeral procession in *Ulysses* passes under 'the hugecloaked Liberator's form'.[57] Near the end of 'The dead', one of the greatest short stories in the English language, Gabriel Conroy 'nodded familiarly' to the statue, 'and waved his hand.—Good night, Dan, he said gaily.'[58]

Other Irish literary figures were more critical of O'Connell. W.B. Yeats called him 'the too compromised and compromising Daniel O'Connell' and dismissed him as 'The Great Comedian' of Irish politics.[59] He particularly disliked 'the bragging rhetoric and gregarious humour' of O'Connell's oratory. Similarly, Sean O'Faolain attacked O'Connell for not going ahead with Clontarf, and for his obnoxious treatment of Young Ireland. But he also praised O'Connell for being 'the greatest of all Irish realists', because he 'knew that if he could but once define, he would thereby create. He did define, he did create.'[60] The greatest tribute which O'Faolain paid him was that 'he thought a democracy and it rose. He defined himself, and the people became him.'

Éamon de Valera, as president of Ireland, officially reopened Derrynane Abbey in August 1967. In his speech he revealed that for many years he had felt that his own generation—the men and women who had fought in the 1916 Rising and the War of Independence—had not given O'Connell the credit he deserved. He admitted that this was because of 'the retreat from Clontarf', but he did not believe that this detracted from 'what a wonderful leader he was for the people'.[61] Situating O'Connell within the context of his time, de Valera spoke of 'the conditions of our people when he came to take over leadership. Our people had suffered from two centuries of spoliation and depression, and when he came it was after there had been two savage centuries of penal laws.' Therefore he argued that O'Connell's greatness lay in the way he had raised a people who were degraded and had given them confidence in themselves. He made his people realise that 'those who pretended they were superior were not superior in any way except that they had superior forces'. Similarly, Mary Robinson, the first female president of Ireland, has compared Daniel O'Connell to Nelson Mandela and Martin Luther King Jnr, and has credited him with establishing 'an effective model of non-violent agitation and political action' which has transformed the histories of some of the greatest countries in the world.[62] He was, simply, 'an individualist political personality of Colossian proportions'.

Perhaps the most striking tribute came from the four times prime minister of Britain, W.E. Gladstone, who acclaimed O'Connell as the 'prophet of a coming time' when his mission would be fulfilled. Gladstone insisted that when people talked about O'Connell they should say 'not only that he did much, but that he could not have done more'.[63] He believed that O'Connell was 'both over-censured and undervalued', a judgement which is surely as true in the twenty-first century as it was in the nineteenth. To claim that O'Connell polarised Ireland along sectarian lines, or betrayed the people by refusing to adopt a violent strategy, is to misread profoundly the reality of what Ireland was like in the nineteenth century, and what O'Connell was trying to achieve. In the 1810s and 1820s he raised a nation that was on its knees and won it its freedom. In the 1830s and 1840s he led a campaign for Irish rights first in the British parliament and then on the fields of Ireland, demonstrating to the world that the voice of a people could not be suppressed. From an early age O'Connell had cast himself as the hero in the story of the Irish nation, and his entire career reveals the advantages and disadvantages of such an unashamedly self-centered approach. O'Connell forged a new Irish nation in the fires of his own idealism, intolerance, and determination. For a people that was broken, humiliated, and defeated, he became its chieftain, its leader, its Liberator.

ABBREVIATIONS

DAUNT, *Personal recollections*
William J. O'Neill Daunt, *Personal recollections of the late Daniel O'Connell.* 2 vols, London, 1848.

DIB
James McGuire and James Quinn (eds), The Royal Irish Academy's *Dictionary of Irish Biography.* 9 vols, Cambridge, 2009.

DUFFY, *Young Ireland*
Charles Gavan Duffy, *Young Ireland: a fragment of Irish history.* London, 1880.

FITZPATRICK, *Correspondence*
W.J. Fitzpatrick (ed.), *Correspondence of Daniel O'Connell, the Liberator.* 2 vols, New York, 1888.

GRANT, *Random recollections*
[Grant, James], *Random recollections of the House of Commons.* Philadelphia, 1836.

GREVILLE, *Memoirs*
Henry Reeve (ed.), *The Greville memoirs: a journal of the reigns of King George IV, King William IV and Queen Victoria. By the late Charles C.F. Greville.* 8 vols, London, 1897–99.

MACDONAGH, *Life*
Michael MacDonagh, *The life of Daniel O'Connell.* London, 1903.

O'CONNELL CORR.
M.R. O'Connell (ed.), *The correspondence of Daniel O'Connell.* 8 vols, Shannon and Dublin, 1972–80.

O'CONNELL, *Recollections*
John O'Connell, *Recollections and experiences during a parliamentary career from 1833 to 1848.* 2 vols, London, 1849.

OXFORD DNB
H.C.G. Matthew and Brian Harrison (eds), *Oxford Dictionary of National Biography.* 60 vols, Oxford, 2004.

SHAW, *State Trials*
[Anon.], *Shaw's authenticated report of the Irish state trials.* Dublin, 1844.

REFERENCES

Introduction (pp vii–x)
1. W.E.H. Lecky, *Leaders of public opinion in Ireland* (2 vols, London, 1903), ii, 313.
2. Ibid., ii, 195.
3. Ibid., ii, 196.

Prologue (pp 1–4)
1. W.E. Gladstone, 'Daniel O'Connell', in *The Nineteenth Century*, vol. xxv (1889), 149.
2. William Fagan, *The life and times of Daniel O'Connell* (2 vols, Cork, 1847–8), i, 116.
3. Lord Mahon (ed.), *Memoirs of the Right Honourable Sir Robert Peel* (2 vols, London, 1857), i, 116.
4. Fagan, *Life*, i, 646.
5. Ibid., i, 650.
6. The report of the *Morning Herald* (quoted in ibid., i, 649).
7. Ibid., i, 649.
8. Ibid., i, 653.
9. Greville, *Memoirs*, i, 208.
10. *Parliamentary debates*, xxi, col. 1402.
11. Ibid., col. 1409.
12. Ibid., col. 1414.
13. Fagan, *Life*, i, 654.
14. Memorandum of Rickard O'Connell (Fitzpatrick (ed.), *Correspondence*, i, 184).
15. Ibid., i, 185.

Chapter 1 'The Man Who Discovered Ireland' (pp 7–13)
1. [Frederick Marryat], *Diary of a Blasé* (Philadelphia, 1836), p. 9.
2. John Richie to Daniel O'Connell, 23 January 1841 (O'Connell (ed.), *O'Connell Corr*, vii, 10).
3. Ibid., ii, 10.
4. Daunt, *Personal recollections*, ii, 138.
5. Ibid.
6. Ibid., i, 143.
7. Ibid., i, 69.
8. Ibid., i, 70.
9. Ibid., ii, 61; *O'Connell Corr.*, vii, 115.

10. *The Christian Recorder*, 25 September 1873.
11. Daunt, *Personal recollections*, i, 43.
12. Ibid., i, 130.
13. Ibid., i, 129.
14. Wilmot Harrison (ed.), *"Thomas Moore" Anecdotes* (London, 1899), p. 281.
15. Daunt, *Personal recollections*, i, 129.
16. Ibid., i, 14.
17. Ibid., ii, 9–10.
18. Duffy, *Young Ireland*, 350.
19. O'Connell, *Recollections*, ii, 84.
20. Ibid., ii, 85.
21. C.M. O'Connell, *Excursions in Ireland during 1844 and 1850* (London, 1852), p. 224.
22. O'Connell, *Recollections*, ii, 86.
23. Greville, *Memoirs*, i, 228.
24. O'Connell, *Recollections*, ii, 88.
25. O'Connell, *Recollections*, i, 229.
26. Ibid., i, 230.
27. Ibid., i, 228.
28. Ibid., i, 234.
29. MacDonagh, *Life*, p. 367.
30. O'Connell, *Recollections*, i, 235.
31. MacDonagh, *Life*, p. 369.
32. [Mask], *St. Stephen's; Or, Pencillings of Politicians* (London, 1839), p. 163.
33. Ibid., p. 142.
34. Lady Dorchester (ed.), *Recollections of a long life by Lord Broughton (John Cam Hobhouse)* (6 vols, London, 1841–52), v, 17.

Chapter 2 'King of the Beggars', 1830 (pp 14–26)

1. Quoted by Lord Alvanley (*Hansard*, 3rd series, xxvii, col. 1000).
2. Grant, *Random recollections*, p. 5.
3. Ibid., p. 10.
4. Ibid., p. 33.
5. O'Connell, *Recollections*, i, 7.
6. *Parliamentary debates*, xxii, col. 56.
7. [Mask], *St. Stephen's*, p. 160.
8. Grant, *Random recollections*, p. 200.
9. Dorchester (ed.), *Recollections of a long life*, iv, 8.
10. O'Connell, *Recollections*, i, 85.
11. *Parliamentary debates*, xxii, col. 93.
12. *Parliamentary debates*, xxii, col. 94.
13. *Parliamentary debates*, xxii, cols. 212; 269; 799.

14. *Parliamentary debates*, xxii, col. 215.

15. Daniel O'Connell to Isaac Lyon Goldsmid, 11 September 1829 (*O'Connell Corr.*, iv, 95–6).

16. Mary Robinson, 'Daniel O'Connell: a tribute' in *History Ireland* (Winter 1997).

17. *Parliamentary debates*, xxii, cols. 718–19.

18. *Parliamentary debates*, xxii, col. 721.

19. *Parliamentary debates*, xxii, cols. 1332–3.

20. [Mask], *St. Stephen's*, p. 160.

21. Daniel O'Connell to Jeremy Bentham, 22 February 1831 (*O'Connell Corr.*, viii, 229).

22. Mary O'Connell to Daniel O'Connell, 1 March 1830 (*O'Connell Corr.*, iv, 131).

23. *O'Connell Corr.*, iv, 161.

24. Daniel O'Connell to Archbishop Murray, March 1830 (*O'Connell Corr.*, iv, 127).

25. Daniel O'Connell to Bishop Doyle, 19 March 1830 (*O'Connell Corr.*, iv, 141).

26. Richard Scott to Daniel O'Connell, 30 June 1830 (*O'Connell Corr.*, iv, 180).

27. *O'Connell Corr.*, iv, 184.

28. Richard Scott to Daniel O'Connell, 6 July 1830 (*O'Connell Corr.*, iv, 185).

29. Daniel O'Connell to John Primrose, 7 July 1830 (*O'Connell Corr.*, iv, 186).

30. Daniel O'Connell to P.V. Fitzpatrick, 24 June 1830 (*O'Connell Corr.*, iv, 175); Daniel O'Connell to P.V. Fitzpatrick, 31 August 1830 (*O'Connell Corr.*, iv, 200).

31. £24,524.16.9 was raised between 9 January 1831 and 14 April 1831 (*O'Connell Corr.*, iv, 299).

32. MacDonagh, *Life*, p. 217.

33. Greville, *Memoirs*, vi, 86.

34. *O'Connell Corr.*, iv, 209.

35. Ibid., 214.

36. Ibid., 215.

37. Ibid., 220; *Annual Register* (1831), p. 176.

38. Daniel O'Connell to Sir Henry Hardinge, 24 October 1830 (*O'Connell Corr.*, iv, 220).

39. Greville, *Memoirs*, ii, 328.

40. *Hansard*, 3rd series, xxiv, col. 549.

41. *O'Connell Corr.*, viii, 234.

42. Daniel O'Connell to the editor of the *Northampton Mercury*, 11 February 1832 (*O'Connell Corr.*, viii, 233).

43. Daniel O'Connell to Richard Newton Bennett, 31 December 1830 (*O'Connell Corr.*, iv, 247).

44. Daniel O'Connell to Bennett, 31 December 1830 (*O'Connell Corr.*, iv, 247).

45. Mary O'Connell to Daniel O'Connell, 1 December 1830 (*O'Connell Corr.*, iv, 240).

46. Daniel O'Connell to R.N. Bennett, 7 December 1830 (*O'Connell Corr.*, iv, 244).

47. Daniel O'Connell to R.N. Bennett, 21 January 1831 (*O'Connell Corr.*, iv, 262).

48. Marquess of Anglesey (ed.), *One-leg: the life and letters of Henry William Paget, first marquess of Anglesey* (London, 1961), p. 244.

49. Greville, *Memoirs* (1875 edition), ii, 96.

Chapter 3 The Arrest of O'Connell, 1831 (pp 27-33)

1. Quoted in Duffy, *Young Ireland*, p. 653.

2. Greville, *Memoirs* (1875 edition), ii, 98.

3. MacDonagh, *Life*, p. 218.

4. D.R. Pigot to Lord Chief Justice John Whiteside, 1 October 1871 (Private Collection, held by Michael Cuming). I would like to thank Professor David Dickson for providing me with a transcript of this correspondence.

5. *Annual Register* (1832), p. 301.

6. Greville, *Memoirs* (1875 edition), ii, 106.

7. MacDonagh, *Life*, p. 375.

8. *Annual Register* (1832), p. 306.

9. MacDonagh, *Life*, p. 220.

10. Greville, *Memoirs* (1875 edition), ii, 107.

11. O'Connell, *Recollections*, i, 66; W.J. Fitzpatrick (ed.), *The life, times, and correspondence of the Right Rev. Dr. Doyle* (2 vols, Dublin, 1861), ii, 260.

12. O'Connell, *Recollections*, i, 167.

13. W.B. MacCabe, (ed.), *The last days of O'Connell* (Dublin, 1847), p. 58.

14. Ibid., p. 49.

15. Ibid., p. 56.

16. Ibid., p. 57.

17. *Annual Register* (1832), p. 312.

18. MacDonagh, *Life*, p. 222.

19. Greville, *Memoirs* (1875 edition), ii, 114.

20. D.R. Pigot to Lord Chief Justice, John Whiteside, 1 October 1871 (Private Collection, held by Michael Cuming).

21. *O'Connell Corr.*, iv, 258.

22. Greville, *Memoirs* (1875 edition), ii, 139.

23. Anglesey (ed.), *One-leg*, pp 248-50.

24. Daniel O'Connell to Edward Littleton (A. Aspinall (ed.), *Three early nineteenth century diaries* (London, 1952), pp 351-2.

25. Daniel O'Connell to his constituents, 8 October 1833 (Mary Francis Cusack (ed.), *The speeches and public letters of the Liberator* (2 vols, Dublin, 1875), ii, 417).

26. Fitzpatrick (ed.), *The life, times, and correspondence of the Right Rev. Dr. Doyle*, ii, 344.

Chapter 4 'The Great Political Leviathan', 1831–1834 (pp 34–62)

1. *New York Tribune*, 12 May 1853. It was one of Frederick Douglass's favourite quotes from O'Connell and he claimed that he first read the words 'with a shudder'.

2. Daniel O'Connell to John Redmond, 21 July 1830 (*O'Connell Corr.*, viii, 236).

3. *O'Connell Corr.*, iv, 320.

4. Ibid., iv, 272–3.

5. Daniel O'Connell to Mary O'Connell, 2 March 1831 (*O'Connell Corr.*, iv, 284).

6. Daniel O'Connell to Richard Barrett, 19 May 1831 (*O'Connell Corr.*, iv, 322).

7. See *O'Connell Corr.*, iv, 315–6, and see Daniel O'Connell to Edward Stanley, 8 May 1831 (*O'Connell Corr.*, iv, 317).

8. Daniel O'Connell to Richard Barrett, 19 May 1831 (*O'Connell Corr.*, iv, 322–3).

9. *O'Connell Corr.*, iv, 324–5.

10. Daniel O'Connell to Richard Barrett, 19 May 1831 (*O'Connell Corr.*, iv, 324).

11. Daniel O'Connell to Richard Barrett, 19 May 1831 (*O'Connell Corr.*, iv, 322).

12. *O'Connell Corr.*, iv, 313.

13. *O'Connell Corr.*, iv, 329.

14. *O'Connell Corr.*, iv, 343.

15. Daniel O'Connell to P.V. Fitzpatrick, 19 July 1832 (*O'Connell Corr.*, iv, 427).

16. A.B. King to Daniel O'Connell, 4 August 1832 (*O'Connell Corr.*, iv, 434).

17. Daniel O'Connell to P.V. Fitzpatrick, 19 July 1832 (*O'Connell Corr.*, iv, 427).

18. Daniel O'Connell to Richard Barrett, 5 October 1831 (*O'Connell Corr.*, iv, 355).

19. Henry Hunt to Daniel O'Connell, 25 November 1831 (*O'Connell Corr.*, iv, 363).

20. Daniel O'Connell to Jeremy Bentham, 6 October 1828 (*O'Connell Corr.*, viii, 204).

21. Daniel O'Connell to Henry Hunt, 30 November 1831 (*O'Connell Corr.*, iv, 369).

22. Daniel O'Connell to Leslie Grove Jones, 14 January 1832 (*O'Connell Corr.*, iv, 399).

23. Daniel O'Connell to P.V. Fitzpatrick, 16 August 1839 (*O'Connell Corr.*, vi, 272).

24. Daniel O'Connell to P.V. Fitzpatrick, 14 September 1833 (*O'Connell Corr.*, v, 70).

25. *O'Connell Corr.*, iv, 402.

26. Greville, *Memoirs*, ii, 316.

27. Daniel O'Connell to John Primrose, 3 May 1832 (*O'Connell Corr.*, iv, 416).

28. Daniel O'Connell to John Primrose, [1 March 1834] (*O'Connell Corr.*, v, 108).

29. Daniel O'Connell to John Primrose, 3 March 1834 (*O'Connell Corr.*, v, 109).

30. Daniel O'Connell to Edward Lytton Bulwer, [c. June 1832] (*O'Connell Corr.*, iv, 420); Andrew Brown, 'Edward Lytton Bulwer' in *Oxford DNB*.

31. *Blackwood's Magazine*, vol. 87 (1860), p. 284.

32. Ibid., p. 285.

33. Le Marchant's diary (Aspinall (ed.), *Three early nineteenth century diaries*, p. 278).

34. Kathryn M. Burton, 'Gédeon D'Orsay' in *Oxford* DNB.

35. *O'Connell Corr.*, iv, 448.

36. *O'Connell Corr.*, iv, 441.

37. *Hansard*, 3rd series, xv, col. 148.

38. February 1833, Le Marchant's diary (Aspinall (ed.), *Three early nineteenth century diaries*, p. 295).

39. Dorchester (ed.), *Recollections of a long life*, iv, 281.

40. Daniel O'Connell to Richard Barrett, [c. 11 July 1834] (*O'Connell Corr.*, v, 152).

41. Le Marchant (Aspinall (ed.), *Three early nineteenth century diaries*, p. 295).

42. *O'Connell Corr.*, v, 9.

43. Daniel O'Connell to P.V. Fitzpatrick, 6 March 1833 (*O'Connell Corr.*, v, 14).

44. 5 March 1833 (*Hansard*, 3rd series, xvi, col. 232).

45. *Hansard*, 3rd series, xvi, col. 260.

46. *Hansard*, 3rd series, xvi, col. 239.

47. MacDonagh, *Life*, p. 228.

48. *Random recollections*, i, 95.

49. MacDonagh, *Life*, p. 229.

50. Daniel O'Connell to P.V. Fitzpatrick, 8 March 1833 (*O'Connell Corr.*, v, 15).

51. Daniel O'Connell to P.V. Fitzpatrick, 27 May 1833 (*O'Connell Corr.*, v, 33).

52. Daniel O'Connell to Richard Barrett, 7 June 1833 (*O'Connell Corr.*, v, 39).

53. Daniel O'Connell to P.V. Fitzpatrick, 13 June 1833 (*O'Connell Corr.*, v, 43).

54. Aspinall (ed.), *Three early nineteenth century diaries*, p. 314.

55. Daunt, *Personal recollections*, i, 7.

56. Feargus O'Connor, *A series of letters from Feargus O'Connor to Daniel O'Connell* (London, 1836), p. 41.

57. Ibid., p. 53.

58. Ibid., p. 13.

59. Ibid., p. 25.

60. Ibid., p. 27.

61. *O'Connell Corr.*, v, 48.

62. Daniel O'Connell to P.V. Fitzpatrick, 26 June 1833 (*O'Connell Corr.*, v, 50).

63. *O'Connell Corr.*, v, 44.

64. *O'Connell Corr.*, vi, 143.

65. *O'Connell Corr.*, v, 89.

66. O'Connell, *Recollections*, i, 220.

67. Daniel O'Connell to P.V. Fitzpatrick, 5 July 1833 (*O'Connell Corr.*, v, 52).

68. Daniel O'Connell to Richard Barrett, 8 July 1830 (*O'Connell Corr.*, iv, 187).

69. *O'Connell Corr.*, iv, 188.

70. *O'Connell Corr.*, v, 56.

71. O'Connell, *Recollections*, i, 223.

72. Grant, *Random recollections*, p. 29.

73. Daniel O'Connell to P.V. Fitzpatrick, 5 August 1833 (*O'Connell Corr.*, v, 57).

74. Daniel O'Connell to P.V. Fitzpatrick, 13 September 1833 (*O'Connell Corr.*, v, 68).

75. P.M. Geoghegan, 'Edward Littleton' in *DIB*.

76. Daniel O'Connell to Edward Littleton, 9 October 1833 (*O'Connell Corr.*, v, 77–80); *O'Connell Corr.*, v, 91.

77. Edward Littleton to Daniel O'Connell, 25 October 1833 (*O'Connell Corr.*, v, 83).

78. *O'Connell Corr.*, v, 95.

79. Ibid., v, 99.

80. Grant, *Random recollections*, p. 164.

81. 5 March 1833 (Aspinall (ed.), *Three early nineteenth century diaries*, p. 312).

82. Dorchester (ed.), *Recollections of a long life*, iv, 336.

83. O'Connell, *Recollections*, i, 81.

84. Daniel O'Connell to Michael Staunton, 9 April 1834 (*O'Connell Corr.*, v, 120).

85. Daniel O'Connell to P.V. Fitzpatrick, c. 12 April 1834 (*O'Connell Corr.*, v, 123).

86. Daniel O'Connell to a friend [c. 1 April 1834] (*O'Connell Corr.*, v, 118).

87. O'Connell, *Recollections*, i, 85.

88. MacDonagh, *Life*, pp 234–5.

89. *Hansard*, 3rd series, xxii, col. 1093.

90. Ibid., col. 1092.

91. Grant, *Random recollections*, p. 168.

92. *Hansard*, 3rd series, xxii, col. 1157.

93. Daniel O'Connell to Edward Dwyer, 24 April 1834 (*O'Connell Corr.*, v, 126); O'Connell, *Recollections*, i, 84.

94. Daniel O'Connell to Edward Dwyer, 24 April 1834 (*O'Connell Corr.*, v, 126).

95. Grant, *Random recollections*, p. 38.

96. Daniel O'Connell to P.V. Fitzpatrick, 25 April 1834 (*O'Connell Corr.*, v, 127).

97. O'Connell, *Recollections*, i, 88.

98. Ibid., i, 95.

99. *O'Connell Corr.*, v, 146.

100. Greville, *Memoirs*, iii, 105.

101. Daniel O'Connell to Richard Barrett, [c. 11 July 1834] (*O'Connell Corr.*, v, 151).

102. *Hansard*, 3rd series, xxiv, col. 1099.

103. Edward Littleton to Lord Wellesley, 4 July 1834 (Henry Reeve (ed.), *Memoir and correspondence relating to political occurrences in June and July 1834 by the Right Hon. Edward John Littleton, first Lord Hatherton* (London, 1872), p. 52).

104. *Hansard*, 3rd series, xxiv, col. 1111.

105. Dorchester (ed.), *Recollections of a long life*, iv, 353.

106. Daniel O'Connell to P.V. Fitzpatrick, 8 July 1834 (*O'Connell Corr.*, v, 149).

107. Reeve (ed.), *Memoir and correspondence relating to political occurrences in June and July 1834 by the Right Hon. Edward John Littleton*, p. 20.
108. MacDonagh, *Life*, p. 239.
109. Greville, *Memoirs*, iii, 111.
110. Greville, *Memoirs*, iii, 120.
111. *Hansard*, 3rd series, xxiii, col. 894.
112. Gladstone, 'Daniel O'Connell', p. 151.
113. Daniel O'Connell to P.V. Fitzpatrick, 8 July 1834 (*O'Connell Corr.*, v, 149–50).
114. Daniel O'Connell to P.V. Fitzpatrick, 16 August 1839 (*O'Connell Corr.*, vi, 272).
115. Daniel O'Connell to Thomas Mooney, 13 June 1834 (*O'Connell Corr.*, v, 144).
116. *O'Connell Corr.*, v, 193.
117. Daniel O'Connell to P.V. Fitzpatrick, 17 October 1834 (*O'Connell Corr.*, v, 194).
118. Daniel O'Connell to Richard Barrett, c. 21 October 1834 (*O'Connell Corr.*, v, 194–5).
119. *O'Connell Corr.*, v, 191.
120. Daniel O'Connell to P.V. Fitzpatrick, 17 November 1834 (*O'Connell Corr.*, v, 201).
121. Daniel O'Connell to Mary O'Connell, 21 November 1834 (*O'Connell Corr.*, v, 204).
122. Daniel O'Connell to Bindon Scott, 15 August 1834 (*O'Connell Corr.*, v, 60).
123. *O'Connell Corr.*, v, 85.
124. Daniel O'Connell to Mary O'Connell, 1 December 1834 (*O'Connell Corr.*, v, 213).
125. Daniel O'Connell to Mary O'Connell, 17 December 1834 (*O'Connell Corr.*, v, 232).
126. Daniel O'Connell to Mary O'Connell, 13 December 1834 (*O'Connell Corr.*, v, 229).
127. Daniel O'Connell to Mary O'Connell, 18 December 1834 (*O'Connell Corr.*, v, 234).
128. Daniel O'Connell to Mary O'Connell, 17 December 1834 (*O'Connell Corr.*, v, 232).
129. *O'Connell Corr.*, v, 243; *Freeman's Journal*, 26 December 1834.
130. Daniel O'Connell to Mary O'Connell, 25 December 1844 (*O'Connell Corr.*, v, 242).

Chapter 5 Public Anger, Private Agony, 1835–1836 (pp 63–82)

1. Daniel O'Connell to Mary O'Connell, 12 January 1835 (*O'Connell Corr.*, v, 255).
2. *O'Connell Corr.*, v, 256.
3. Ibid., v, 257.
4. Daniel O'Connell to P.V. Fitzpatrick, 25 March 1835 (*O'Connell Corr.*, v, 285).

5. Daniel O'Connell to Mary O'Connell, 14 January 1835 (*O'Connell Corr.*, v, 258).

6. Daniel O'Connell to his brother John O'Connell, 15 January 1835 (*O'Connell Corr.*, v, 260).

7. *The Times*, 19 September 1835.

8. Daniel O'Connell to P.V. Fitzpatrick, 9 March 1835 (*O'Connell Corr.*, v, 279).

9. Daniel O'Connell to Lawrence Finn, 14 March 1835 (*O'Connell Corr.*, v, 283).

10. Fitzpatrick, *Correspondence*, i, 532.

11. Daniel O'Connell to Unknown, 16 March 1835 (*O'Connell Corr.*, iv, 283).

12. Daniel O'Connell to P.V. Fitzpatrick, 4 September 1835 (*O'Connell Corr.*, v, 330).

13. Daniel O'Connell to P.V. Fitzpatrick, 25 March 1835 (*O'Connell Corr.*, v, 285).

14. Daniel O'Connell to P.V. Fitzpatrick, 4 September 1835 (*O'Connell Corr.*, v, 330).

15. Daniel O'Connell to P.V. Fitzpatrick, 14 April 1835 (*O'Connell Corr.*, v, 289–90).

16. Daniel O'Connell to P.V. Fitzpatrick, 23 March 1835 (*O'Connell Corr.*, v, 284).

17. *O'Connell Corr.*, v, 357.

18. Daniel O'Connell to Joseph Denis Mullen, 24 May 1836 (*O'Connell Corr.*, v, 375).

19. Daniel O'Connell to P.V. Fitzpatrick, 11 September 1835 (*O'Connell Corr.*, v, 332).

20. O'Connell, *Recollections*, i, 135.

21. *O'Connell Corr.*, v, 270.

22. O'Connell, *Recollections*, i, 124.

23. Ibid., i, 129.

24. Daniel O'Connell to P.V. Fitzpatrick, 19 February 1835 (*O'Connell Corr.*, v, 271).

25. Daniel O'Connell to P.V. Fitzpatrick, 19 February 1835 (*O'Connell Corr.*, v, 271); Daniel O'Connell to P.V. Fitzpatrick, 20 February 1835 (*O'Connell Corr.*, v, 272).

26. *Hansard*, 3rd series, xxvi, col. 394.

27. Daniel O'Connell to P.V. Fitzpatrick, 27 February 1835 (*O'Connell Corr.*, v, 276).

28. *O'Connell Corr.*, v, 276.

29. Daniel O'Connell to P.V. Fitzpatrick, 3 June 1838 (*O'Connell Corr.*, vi, 165).

30. Gladstone, 'Daniel O'Connell', p. 162.

31. Daniel O'Connell to P.V. Fitzpatrick, 27 February (*O'Connell Corr.*, v, 275).

32. Daniel O'Connell to Richard Barrett, [21 February 1835] (*O'Connell Corr.*, v, 274).

33. *Hansard*, 3rd series, xxvi, col. 397.

34. Daniel O'Connell to P.V. Fitzpatrick, 10 April 1835 (*O'Connell Corr.*, v, 288).

35. Daniel O'Connell to P.V. Fitzpatrick, 14 April 1835 (*O'Connell Corr.*, v, 289).

36. Daniel O'Connell to P.V. Fitzpatrick, 14 April 1835 (*O'Connell Corr.*, v, 289).

37. MacDonagh, *Life*, p. 246.

38. Greville, *Memoirs*, iii, 261.

39. *Hansard*, 3rd series, xxvii, cols. 1008–9.

40. Lord Alvanley to Daniel O'Connell, [21 April 1835] (*O'Connell Corr.*, v, 295).

41. Daniel O'Connell to George Dawson Damer, 1 May 1835 (*O'Connell Corr.*, v, 299).

42. *O'Connell Corr.*, v, 301.

43. MacDonagh, *Life*, p. 249.

44. Earl of Malmesbury, *Memoirs of an ex-minister* (2 vols, London, 1884), i, 65.

45. MacDonagh, *Life*, p. 250.

46. Ibid., *Life*, p. 253.

47. Daniel O'Connell to P.V. Fitzpatrick, 11 September 1835 (*O'Connell Corr.*, v, 331).

48. [Anon.], *Ireland and O'Connell* (Edinburgh, 1835), p. 4.

49. Ibid., p. 16.

50. Ibid., pp 15–16.

51. *Hansard*, vol. 33, col. 91.

52. Daniel O'Connell to Charles Pearson, 2 December 1834 (*Hansard*, 3rd series, xxxiii, col. 28).

53. *Hansard*, 3rd series, xxxi, col. 469.

54. Daniel O'Connell to Charles Pearson, 2 December 1834 (*O'Connell Corr.*, v, 215); *Hansard*, 3rd series, xxxiii, col. 28).

55. Daniel O'Connell to Alexander Raphael, 29 May 1835 (*O'Connell Corr.*, v, 307).

56. Daniel O'Connell to Alexander Raphael, 1 June 1835 (*O'Connell Corr.*, v, 308).

57. Daniel O'Connell to Alexander Raphael, 8 June 1835 (*O'Connell Corr.*, v, 310).

58. Daniel O'Connell to Alexander Raphael, 27 July 1835 (*O'Connell Corr.*, v, 322).

59. Alexander Raphael to Daniel O'Connell, 28 July 1835 (*O'Connell Corr.*, v, 323).

60. Alexander Raphael to Daniel O'Connell, 5 August 1835 (*O'Connell Corr.*, v, 325).

61. [Anon.], *Considerations on the case of Raphael and O'Connell* (Dublin, 1836).

62. Ibid., p. 16.

63. Duffy, *Young Ireland*, p. 6.

64. *The Times*, 25 November 1836.

65. [James Grant], *The British Senate, Or, A second series of random recollections of the Lords and Commons* (2 vols, Philadelphia, 1838), i, 201.

66. *Hansard*, 3rd series, xxxi, col. 276.

67. Ibid., col. 286.

68. Ibid., col. 468.

69. *O'Connell Corr.*, vi, 69.

70. See P.M. Geoghegan, *King Dan: the rise of Daniel O'Connell* (Dublin, 2008).

71. [Benjamin Disraeli], *The letters of Runnymede* (London, 1836), p. 70.

72. Ibid., p. 75.

73. Ibid., p. 145.

74. Ibid., pp 145–6.

75. W.S. Gibson, *A memoir of Lord Lyndhurst* (London, 1869), p. 29.

76. Jonathan Parry, 'Benjamin Disraeli', in *Oxford* DNB. He was lord chancellor on three separate occasions but by this time had only held the office twice.

77. Theodore Martin, *A life of Lord Lyndhurst from letters and papers in possession of his family* (London, 1884), pp 348–9.

78. 9 May 1836 (*Hansard*, 3rd series, xxxiii, cols. 734–5).

79. MacDonagh, *Life*, p. 258.

80. Daniel O'Connell to P.V. Fitzpatrick, 26 October 1836 (*O'Connell Corr.*, v, 400).

81. Patrick Maume, 'Maurice Daniel O'Connell' in DIB.

82. Daniel O'Connell to Richard Barrett, 4 September 1836 (*O'Connell Corr.*, v, 393).

83. Daniel O'Connell to P.V. Fitzpatrick, 9 September 1836 (*O'Connell Corr.*, v, 396).

84. Daniel O'Connell to Richard Barrett, 4 September 1836 (*O'Connell Corr.*, v, 393).

85. *O'Connell Corr.*, v, 406.

Chapter 6 O'Connell in Parliament, 1835–1840 (pp 83–94)

1.   [Mask], *St. Stephen's*, p. 133.

2.   O'Connell, *Recollections*, i, 85.

3.   Ibid., i, 84.

4.   [Mask], *St. Stephen's*, p. 138.

5.   Ibid.

6.   Grant, *Random recollections*, p. 169.

7.   Ibid., p. 164.

8.   Ibid., p. 165.

9.   [Mask], *St. Stephen's*, p. 137.

10. Ibid., p. 135.

11. Grant, *Random recollections*, p. 166.

12. Ibid.

13. MacDonagh, *Life*, p. 273; the account also appears in Michael MacDonagh, *The reporter's gallery* (London, 1913). This is normally said to have taken place during O'Connell's great speech on coercion, but that was before Dickens was employed by the paper. See Jim Cooke, *Charles Dickens and Ireland: an anthology* (Dublin, 1999), p. 26.

14. Grant, *Random recollections*, p. 166.

15. Ibid.

16. *Hansard*, 3rd series, xxviii, cols. 979–97.
17. Grant, *Random recollections*, p. 72.
18. Ibid., p. 91.
19. *Hansard*, 3rd series, xliv, col. 837, a slightly different version of the lines can be found in Dorchester (ed.), *Recollections of a long life*, v, 160.
20. Grant, *Random recollections*, p. 168.
21. [Mask], *St. Stephen's*, p. 136.
22. MacDonagh, *Life*, p. 287.
23. Ibid., p. 40.
24. Ibid., pp 283–4.
25. Grant, *The British Senate*, i, 16.
26. *Hansard*, 3rd series, xxxiv, col. 528.
27. Grant, *The British Senate*, i, 9.
28. Ibid., i, 12.
29. Ibid., i, 14.
30. Ibid., i, 175.
31. Ibid., i, 183.
32. Ibid., i, 188.
33. Ibid., i, 193.
34. G.O. Trevelyan (ed.), *The life and letters of Lord Macaulay* (2 vols, London, 1876), ii, 76.
35. *Hansard*, 3rd series, liv, col. 1093.
36. Trevelyan (ed.), *The life and letters of Lord Macaulay*, ii, 76.
37. Ibid., ii, 77.

Chapter 7 Despair and Decline, 1837–1839 (pp 95–112)

1. Daunt, *Personal recollections*, i, 257.
2. Daniel O'Connell to P.V. Fitzpatrick, 4 September 1837 (*O'Connell Corr.*, vi, 84).
3. Michael Slater, 'Charles Dickens' in *Oxford DNB*.
4. Ibid.
5. Daniel O'Connell to Richard Barrett, 23 March 1843 (*O'Connell Corr.*, vii, 192).
6. A.V. Kirwan to Daniel O'Connell, 10 December 1837 (*O'Connell Corr.*, vi, 103).
7. Daniel O'Connell to A.V. Kirwan, 8 December 1837 (*O'Connell Corr.*, v, 102).
8. Daniel O'Connell to A.V. Kirwan, 11 December 1837 (*O'Connell Corr.*, vi, 105).
9. A.V. Kirwan to Daniel O'Connell, [c. 12 December 1837] (*O'Connell Corr.*, vi, 106).
10. *O'Connell Corr.*, vi, 34.
11. Ibid., vi, 14.
12. Duffy, *Young Ireland*, p. 139.
13. *O'Connell Corr.*, vi, 32.

14. Daniel O'Connell to Richard Barrett, 21 April 1837 (*O'Connell Corr.*, vi, 32).

15. Daniel O'Connell to Richard Sullivan, 7 July 1837 (*O'Connell Corr.*, vi, 56).

16. Daniel O'Connell to Pierce Mahony, 22 July 1837 (*O'Connell Corr.*, vi, 73).

17. Daniel O'Connell to P.V. Fitzpatrick, 26 March 1838 (*O'Connell Corr.*, vi, 149).

18. Grant, *The British Senate*, i, 113.

19. Ibid., i, 115.

20. Ibid., i, 159.

21. *Hansard*, 3rd series, xxxix, col. 795.

22. Ibid., col. 792.

23. Grant, *The British Senate*, i, 210.

24. *Hansard*, 3rd series, xxxix, col. 807.

25. *O'Connell Corr.*, vi, 108.

26. Daniel O'Connell to R.B. Foster, 19 December 1837 (*O'Connell Corr.*, v, 108).

27. O'Connell, *Recollections*, i, 176.

28. See F.A. D'Arcy, 'The artisans of Dublin and Daniel O'Connell, 1830–47: an unquiet liaison', in *Irish Historical Studies*, vol. 17, no. 66 (Sept., 1970), pp 221–43.

29. MacDonagh, *Life*, p. 267.

30. D'Arcy, 'The artisans of Dublin and Daniel O'Connell', p. 221.

31. Ibid., p. 237.

32. MacDonagh, *Life*, p. 268.

33. Daniel O'Connell to P.V. Fitzpatrick, 10 February 1838 (*O'Connell Corr.*, vi, 133).

34. Christine Kinealy (ed.), *Lives of Victorian political figures II. Volume I. Daniel O'Connell* (London, 2007), 157.

35. Daniel O'Connell to P.V. Fitzpatrick, 15 February 1838 (*O'Connell Corr.*, vi, 134).

36. A.C. Benson and Viscount Esher (eds), *The letters of Queen Victoria* (3 vols, New York, 1907), i, 186.

37. Daunt, *Recollections*, ii, 262.

38. K.D. Reynolds, 'Sir Augustus Frederick D'Este' in *Oxford DNB*.

39. *O'Connell Corr.*, vi, 1.

40. *O'Connell Corr.*, vi, 198.

41. Daniel O'Connell to P.V. Fitzpatrick, 3 June 1838 (*O'Connell Corr.*, vi, 165).

42. Daniel O'Connell to P.V. Fitzpatrick, 18 June 1838 (*O'Connell Corr.*, vi, 171).

43. Christine Kinealy (ed.), *Lives of Victorian political figures II. Volume I. Daniel O'Connell*, 158.

44. Ibid.

45. Daunt, *Recollections*, i, 37.

46. Daniel O'Connell to P.V. Fitzpatrick, 15 June 1838 (*O'Connell Corr.*, vi, 170).

47. Daniel O'Connell to D.R. Pigot, 30 September 1838 (*O'Connell Corr.*, vi, 186).

48. *O'Connell Corr.*, vi, 175.

49. MacDonagh, *Life*, p. 262.
50. Duffy, *Young Ireland*, p. 6.
51. Daniel O'Connell to P.V. Fitzpatrick, 28 October 1838 (*O'Connell Corr.*, vi, 196).
52. *O'Connell Corr.*, vi, 203.
53. O'Connell, *Recollections*, i, 178.
54. Ibid.
55. *O'Connell Corr.*, vi, 211.
56. Ibid., vi, 213–14.
57. Gladstone, 'Daniel O'Connell', p. 157.
58. *O'Connell Corr.*, vi, 236.
59. Daniel O'Connell to Richard More O'Ferrall, 7 May 1839 (*O'Connell Corr.*, vi, 238).
60. Daniel O'Connell to P.V. Fitzpatrick, 10 May 1839 (*O'Connell Corr.*, vi, 242).
61. Daniel O'Connell to Richard More O'Ferrall, 29 November 1839 (*O'Connell Corr.*, vi, 287).
62. *O'Connell Corr.*, vi, 335.
63. Daniel O'Connell to P.V. Fitzpatrick, 14 June 1840 (*O'Connell Corr.*, vi, 335).
64. Daniel O'Connell to P.V. Fitzpatrick, 11 May 1839 (*O'Connell Corr.*, vi, 243).
65. Daniel O'Connell to Dr Thomas O'Brien Costello, 16 May 1839 (*O'Connell Corr.*, vi, 247).
66. Oliver MacDonagh, *The emancipist* (London, 1989), p. 126.
67. Duffy, *Young Ireland*, p. 460.
68. MacDonagh, *Life*, p. 270.
69. Daniel O'Connell to Kate O'Connell, 1 May 1839 (*O'Connell Corr.*, vi, 236).
70. Daniel O'Connell to P.V. Fitzpatrick, 18 September 1837 (*O'Connell Corr.*, vi, 85).
71. The line is 'No craving void left aching in the breast' (Alexander Pope, *Eloisa to Abelard*).
72. Daniel O'Connell to Betsey Ffrench, 28 June 1839 (*O'Connell Corr.*, vi, 253).
73. Daniel O'Connell to Betsey Ffrench, 8 July 1839 (*O'Connell Corr.*, vi, 259).
74. Daniel O'Connell to P.V. Fitzpatrick, 8 August 1839 (*O'Connell Corr.*, vi, 267).
75. Daniel O'Connell to P.V. Fitzpatrick, 24 August 1839 (*O'Connell Corr.*, vi, 278).
76. Daniel O'Connell to P.V. Fitzpatrick, 7 August 1839 (*O'Connell Corr.*, v, 266).
77. Ibid.
78. Daniel O'Connell to P.V. Fitzpatrick, 8 August 1839 (*O'Connell Corr.*, vi, 268).
79. Ibid.

Chapter 8 The Resurrection of O'Connell (pp 115–32)
1. Quoted by Lord Alvanley, *Hansard*, vol. 27, c. 1000.
2. Daniel O'Connell to P.V. Fitzpatrick, 30 May 1840 (*O'Connell Corr.*, vi, 333).
3. Duffy, *Young Ireland*, p. 34.

4. William J. O'Neill Daunt, *Ireland and her agitators* (Dublin, 1845), p. 215. The initial name was the 'National Association for full and prompt Justice or Repeal', but it was renamed the 'Loyal National Repeal Association' in July 1840.

5. MacDonagh, *The emancipist*, p. 201.

6. Fitzpatrick, *Correspondence*, ii, 293.

7. Duffy, *Young Ireland*, p. 35.

8. Ibid., p. 36.

9. Ibid., p. 37.

10. MacDonagh, *Life*, p. 289.

11. Jacob Venedey, *Ireland and the Irish during the Repeal years*, trans. William B. McCabe (Dublin, 1844), p. 137; James Grant, *Impressions of Ireland and the Irish* (2 vols, London, 1844), i, 70.

12. See P.M. Geoghegan, *King Dan: the rise of Daniel O'Connell.*

13. Daunt, *Agitators*, p. 330.

14. Grant, *Impressions*, i, 70.

15. MacDonagh, *Life*, p. 291.

16. O'Connell, *Recollections*, i, 74.

17. Duffy, *Young Ireland*, p. 190; Duffy, *Four years of Irish history*, p. 399.

18. Venedey, *Ireland and the Irish*, p. 137.

19. Duffy, *Young Ireland*, p. 176.

20. Charles Gavan Duffy, *Four years of Irish history* (London, 1883), p. 399.

21. Duffy, *Young Ireland*, p. 173.

22. Grant, *Impressions*, i, 87.

23. Duffy, *Young Ireland*, p. 179.

24. Daniel O'Connell to William Smith O'Brien, 9 November 1844 (*O'Connell Corr.*, vii, 295).

25. Duffy, *Young Ireland*, p. 180.

26. Ibid., p. 22.

27. Ibid., p. 254.

28. Ibid., p. 41.

29. *O'Connell Corr.*, vii, 9.

30. [Henry Cooke] *The Repealer repulsed!* (Belfast, 1841), p. 19.

31. Ibid., p. 38.

32. *The Times*, 25 January 1841.

33. Daunt, *Personal recollections*, ii, 19.

34. Ibid., ii, 22.

35. O'Connell, *Recollections*, ii, 121.

36. Daunt, *Personal recollections*, ii, 30.

37. Ibid., ii, 32.

38. Daniel O'Connell to Charles Bianconi, December 1844 (*O'Connell Corr.*, vii, 297).

39. Daunt, *Personal recollections*, ii, 45.

40. MacDonagh, *Life*, pp 204–5.

41. Ibid., p. 293.

42. MacDonagh, *The emancipist*, p. 207.

43. Daunt, *Personal recollections*, ii, 83.

44. Ibid., ii, 84.

45. *O'Connell Corr.*, vii, 175.

46. Daunt, *Personal recollections*, ii, 88.

47. Ibid., ii, 97.

48. Ibid., ii, 98.

49. Issue n. 34 (Duffy, *Young Ireland*, p. 170).

50. Duffy, *Young Ireland*, p. 288.

51. [Anon.], *Shaw's authenticated report of the Irish state trials* (Dublin, 1844), p. 277.

52. Daunt, *Personal recollections*, ii, 11.

53. Ibid., ii, 139–40.

54. Ibid., ii, 12.

55. Duffy, *Young Ireland*, p. 191.

56. O'Connell, *Recollections*, ii, 223.

57. Daunt, *Personal recollections*, ii, 140.

58. Ibid., ii, 141.

59. Duffy, *Young Ireland*, p. 193.

60. Daunt, *Agitators*, p. 268; for a full report of the three-day debate see John Levy (ed.), *A full and revised report of the three days' discussion in the corporation of Dublin of the Repeal of the Union* (Dublin, 1843).

61. Duffy, *Young Ireland*, p. 194; *O'Connell Corr.*, vii, 189.

62. Levy (ed.), *A full and revised report of the three days' discussion*, p. 37.

63. Ibid., pp 41–2.

64. Ibid., p. 44.

65. Daunt, *Agitators*, p. 271.

66. Levy (ed.), *A full and revised report of the three days' discussion*, p. 193 (emphasis as in original).

67. MacDonagh, *Life*, p. 301.

68. Duffy, *Young Ireland*, p. 208.

69. Ibid., p. 214.

70. Ibid., p. 209.

71. Levy (ed.), *A full and revised report of the three days' discussion*, p. 203.

72. Ibid., p. 207.

73. Jacob Venedey, *Ireland and the Irish*, pp 110–11.

74. MacDonagh, *Life*, p. 307.

75. Daunt, *Personal recollections*, ii, 141.

76. Duffy, *Young Ireland*, p. 217.

77. Ibid., p. 222.

Chapter 9 'The Moses of Ireland' and the Year of Repeal, 1843 (pp 133–65)

1. Gladstone, 'Daniel O'Connell', pp 149–50.
2. Shaw, *State trials*, p. 48.
3. O'Connell, *Recollections*, ii, 243.
4. Grant, *Impressions*, i, 74.
5. Shaw, *State trials*, p. 44.
6. Ibid., p. 449.
7. Grant, *Impressions*, i, 77.
8. Shaw, *State trials*, p. 29.
9. Ibid., p. 19.
10. Ibid., p. 20.
11. Venedey, *Ireland and the Irish*, p. 29.
12. Duffy, *Young Ireland*, p. 217.
13. Ibid., p. 219.
14. Ibid., p. 244.
15. Ibid., p. 245.
16. Ibid., p. 246.
17. Paul Bew, *Ireland: the politics of enmity 1789-2006* (Oxford, 2007), p. 160.
18. Shaw, *State trials*, p. 29.
19. *The Nation*, 20 May 1843.
20. Ibid.
21. Shaw, *State trials*, p. 31.
22. Ibid., p. 30.
23. Donald A. Kerr, *Peel, priests and politics* (Oxford, 1982), p. 86.
24. O'Connell discussed this in his speech at Lismore (Shaw, *State trials*, p. 68).
25. Lenihan's account was read by Michael MacDonagh (MacDonagh, *Life*, p. 314).
26. Shaw, *State trials*, p. 32.
27. Ibid., p. 265.
28. MacDonagh, *The emancipist*, p. 230; MacDonagh, *Life*, p. 315.
29. Ibid.
30. Shaw, *State trials*, p. 643.
31. MacDonagh, *Life*, p. 317.
32. *The Nation*, 17 June 1843.
33. O'Connell, *Recollections*, ii, 306; Venedey, *Ireland and the Irish*, p. 27.
34. Venedey, *Ireland and the Irish*, p. 28.
35. Ibid., p. 30.
36. Ibid., p. 39.
37. Ibid., p. 31.
38. Ibid., p. 142.
39. Ibid., p. 43.
40. Ibid., p. 44.

41. Ibid., p. 48.

42. Shaw, *State trials*, p. 34.

43. Venedey, *Ireland and the Irish*, p. 116; see also Shaw, *State trials*, p. 39.

44. Venedey, *Ireland and the Irish*, p. 122.

45. Ibid., p. 127.

46. *New York Herald*, 12 October 1838.

47. *Notes and Queries*, 9th series, vol. lx (1902), 170.

48. [Anon.], *Memoirs of James Gordon Bennett and his times* (New York, 1855), pp 331–42.

49. Venedey, *Ireland and the Irish*, p. 126.

50. Ibid., p. 142.

51. Ibid., p. 145.

52. Shaw, *State trials*, p. 36.

53. Ibid., p. 388.

54. Ibid., p. 40.

55. Ibid., p. 43.

56. Ibid., p. 46.

57. Venedey, *Ireland and the Irish*, p. 191.

58. Ibid., p. 193.

59. Shaw, *State trials*, pp 47, 643.

60. O'Connell, *Recollections*, ii, 292.

61. Ibid., ii, 294.

62. Shaw, *State trials*, p. 48.

63. Ibid., p. 51.

64. Venedey, *Ireland and the Irish*, p. 151.

65. Ibid., p. 152.

66. Ibid., p. 153.

67. Shaw, *State trials*, p. 51.

68. O'Connell, *Recollections*, ii, 274.

69. Ibid., ii, 278.

70. Shaw, *State trials*, p. 56.

71. Ibid., p. 61.

72. O'Connell admitted this at Mullaghmast on 1 October (Shaw, *State trials*, p. 75).

73. Shaw, *State trials*, p. 64.

74. Ibid., p. 65.

75. Ibid., pp 67–8.

76. Ibid., p. 68.

77. Duffy, *Young Ireland*, p. 344.

78. Shaw, *State trials*, p. 73.

79. Ibid., pp 74, 92; Duffy, *Young Ireland*, p. 351.

80. William Howitt and Mary Howitt (eds), *Howitt's journal of literature and popular progress, vol. 1* (London, 1847), 333.

81. Duffy, *Young Ireland*, p. 351.
82. John Mitchel, *The crusade of the period, and the last conquest of Ireland (perhaps)* (New York, 1878), p. 126.
83. Shaw, *State trials*, p. 75.
84. Ibid., p. 93.
85. Ibid., p. 83.
86. Ibid., p. 84.
87. Ibid., p. 85.
88. Duffy, *Young Ireland*, p. 381.
89. Daunt, *Agitators*, p. 285.
90. Duffy, *Young Ireland*, p. 370.
91. MacDonagh, *Life*, p. 331.
92. Duffy, *Young Ireland*, p. 371.
93. Shaw, *State trials*, p. 319.
94. Duffy, *Young Ireland*, p. 374.
95. Ibid., p. 378.
96. MacDonagh, *Life*, p. 332.
97. Ibid., p. 380.
98. Ibid., p. 404.
99. W.H.A. Williams (ed.), *Daniel O'Connell, the British press, and the Irish famine: killing remarks* (Ashgate, 2003), p. 63.
100. Raikes' diary, quoted in Duffy, *Young Ireland*, pp 381–2.

Chapter 10 The Trial of Daniel O'Connell, 1844 (pp 166–82)

1. Lady Trevelyan (ed.), *Works of Lord Macaulay* (8 vols, London, 1866), viii, 261.
2. Spoken at his trial (Shaw, *State trials*, p. 471).
3. Duffy, *Young Ireland*, p. 398.
4. Daniel O'Connell to Pierce O'Mahony, 17 December 1843 (*O'Connell Corr.*, vii, 231).
5. *O'Connell Corr.*, vii, 233.
6. Daniel O'Connell to P.V. Fitzpatrick, 3 January 1844 (*O'Connell Corr.*, vii, 234).
7. Duffy, *Young Ireland*, p. 391.
8. Ibid., p. 392.
9. MacDonagh, *Life*, pp 328, 333.
10. Duffy, *Young Ireland*, p. 393.
11. Duffy, *Four years of Irish history*, p. 150.
12. John Mitchel said it was more like thirty-three yards (Mitchel, *Last conquest*, p. 138).
13. Shaw, *State trials*, introduction.
14. From the *Quarterly Review* (1844), quoted in Duffy, *Young Ireland*, p. 400.
15. See Annual Register (1845), pp 71–4.

16. Shaw, *State trials*, introduction.
17. Duffy, *Young Ireland*, p. 411.
18. Ibid., p. 440; see also Sarah Wise, *The Italian boy: murder and grave robbery in 1830s London* (London, 2004).
19. Duffy, *Young Ireland*, p. 412.
20. *The Nation* quoted in Duffy, *Young Ireland*, p. 422.
21. MacDonagh, *Life*, p. 337.
22. See for example, Shaw, *State trials*, p. 112.
23. Ibid., p. 203.
24. Ibid., p. 355.
25. Ibid., p. 355.
26. Ibid. p. 356.
27. Ibid., p. 358.
28. Ibid., p. 402.
29. Duffy, *Young Ireland*, p. 432.
30. Ibid., p. 531.
31. Shaw, *State trials*, p. 466.
32. Ibid., p. 480.
33. Ibid., p. 470.
34. Ibid., p. 473.
35. Ibid., p. 474.
36. Ibid., pp 475–6.
37. Ibid., p. 479.
38. Ibid., p. 481.
39. Ibid., p. 482.
40. Ibid., p. 485.
41. Ibid., p. 507.
42. Ibid., p. 516.
43. Ibid., p. 667.
44. Ibid., p. 669.
45. Ibid., p. 670.
46. Ibid., p. 672.
47. A.C. Benson and Lord Esher (eds), *The letters of Queen Victoria* (3 vols, New York, 1907), ii, 681.
48. Duffy, *Young Ireland*, p. 443.
49. *O'Connell Corr.*, vii, 243.
50. *Hansard*, lxxii, col. 684.
51. MacDonagh, *Life*, p. 340.
52. Daniel O'Connell to William Smith O'Brien, 2 April 1844 (*O'Connell Corr.*, vii, 252).
53. Duffy, *Young Ireland*, p. 474.
54. Ibid., p. 471.

55. Ibid., p. 473.
56. Account of a lawyer present (*The Irish Times*, 7 December 1874, reprinted 7 December 2009).

Chapter 11 The Prisoner, 1844 (pp 183–96)
1. Grant, *Impressions*, i, 66–7.
2. Duffy, *Young Ireland*, p. 491.
3. Daunt, *Agitators*, p. 299.
4. Duffy, *Young Ireland*, p. 497.
5. Daunt, *Agitators*, p. 299.
6. Daniel O'Connell to his daughter, 1 August 1844 (*O'Connell Corr.*, vii, 261).
7. Duffy, *Young Ireland*, p. 496.
8. Grant, *Impressions*, i, 94.
9. Duffy, *Young Ireland*, p. 493.
10. Grant, *Impressions*, i, 74.
11. Duffy, *Young Ireland*, p. 492.
12. Ibid., p. 508.
13. Grant, *Impressions*, i, 64–5.
14. Daunt, *Agitators*, p. 298.
15. Duffy, *Young Ireland*, p. 494.
16. Daunt, *Agitators*, p. 298.
17. Duffy, *Young Ireland*, p. 494.
18. Ibid., p. 495.
19. Ibid., p. 497.
20. Grant, *Impressions*, i, 69.
21. Ibid., i, 80.
22. Ibid., i, 97.
23. Ibid., i, 78.
24. C.M. O'Connell, *Excursions in Ireland during 1844 and 1850* (London, 1852), p. 23.
25. Daunt, *Agitators*, p. 300.
26. Daniel O'Connell to Margaret O'Mara, 1 May 1844 (*O'Connell Corr.*, vii, 255).
27. Daniel O'Connell to Margaret O'Mara, 21 June 1844 (*O'Connell Corr.*, vii, 258).
28. Duffy, *Young Ireland*, pp 530–31.
29. Williams (ed.), *Killing remarks*, p. 86.
30. Daunt, *Agitators*, p. 308.
31. Duffy, *Young Ireland*, p. 517.
32. I would like to thank Mr Justice Adrian Hardiman for his assistance on this point.
33. Report from the *Morning Chronicle*, quoted in MacCabe (ed.), *Last days*, 59.

34. Daunt, *Agitators*, p. 309.
35. Ibid.; Duffy, *Young Ireland*, p. 520.
36. MacCabe (ed.), *Last days*, p. 61; Duffy, *Young Ireland*, p. 521.
37. Duffy, *Young Ireland*, p. 521.
38. Daunt, *Agitators*, p. 310.
39. MacCabe (ed.), *Last days*, p. 64.
40. Ibid., p. 71.
41. Ibid., p. 72.
42. MacDonagh, *Life*, pp 351–2.
43. Duffy, *Young Ireland*, p. 522.
44. Daunt, *Agitators*, p. 312.
45. Mitchel, *Last conquest*, p. 151.
46. Daunt, *Agitators*, p. 314.
47. Ibid., p. 316.
48. Duffy, *Young Ireland*, p. 523.

Chapter 12 Daniel O'Connell and the Campaign against Slavery (pp 197–210)

1. Quoted in Christine Kinealy, 'The Liberator: Daniel O'Connell and anti-slavery' in *History Today*, vol. 57, issue 12 (December 2007), 51–7.
2. Daniel O'Connell, *Daniel O'Connell upon American slavery, with other Irish testimonies* (New York, 1860), p. 40.
3. Frederick Douglass, *Life and times of Frederick Douglass* (London, 1996), p. 180.
4. Speech of 29 September 1845 (O'Connell, *Daniel O'Connell upon American slavery*, p. 33).
5. O'Connell, *Daniel O'Connell upon American slavery*, p. 31.
6. Douglass, *Life and times of Frederick Douglass*, pp 181–2.
7. See Bruce Nelson, '"Come out of such a land, you Irishmen": Daniel O'Connell, American slavery, and the making of the "Irish race"' in *Éire-Ireland*, 42:1 and 2 (Spring/Summer 2007), p. 64; Kenneth Charlton, 'The state of Ireland in the 1820s: James Cropper's plan' in *Irish Historical Studies*, 17 (March 1971), 320–29.
8. O'Connell, *Daniel O'Connell upon American slavery*, p. 8.
9. Mary Francis Cusack (ed.), *The speeches and public letters of the Liberator* (2 vols, Dublin, 1875), ii, 425.
10. O'Connell revealed this negotiation in a speech in September 1844 (O'Connell, *Daniel O'Connell upon American slavery*, p. 32).
11. Ibid., p. 5.
12. Ibid., p. 9.
13. Ibid., p. 25.
14. Ibid., p. 13.
15. [Anon.], *Ireland and O'Connell*, p. 12.

16. O'Connell, *Daniel O'Connell upon American slavery*, p. 14.
17. *O'Connell Corr.*, vi, 257, 283.
18. Daniel O'Connell to Joseph Sturge, 7 July 1838 (quoted in Howard Temperley, 'The O'Connell-Stevenson contretemps' in *The Journal of Negro History* (vol. xlvii, October 1962, no. 4), 219).
19. Daniel O'Connell to Andrew Stevenson, 10 August 1838.
20. Temperley, 'The O'Connell-Stevenson contretemps', p. 225.
21. Ibid., p. 226.
22. Ibid., p. 227.
23. *Richmond Enquirer*, 21 September and 16 October 1838.
24. Temperley, 'The O'Connell-Stevenson contretemps', p. 229.
25. Ibid., p. 230.
26. O'Connell, *Daniel O'Connell upon American slavery*, p. 18.
27. Ibid., p. 20.
28. Lucretia Mott to Daniel O'Connell, 17 June 1840 (*O'Connell Corr.*, vi, 337).
29. Daniel O'Connell to Lucretia Mott, 20 June 1840 (*O'Connell Corr.*, vi, 338).
30. John Bowring to Daniel O'Connell, 22 October 1840 (*O'Connell Corr.*, vi, 374).
31. William Lloyd Garrison quoted in Nelson, '"Come out of such a land, you Irishmen": Daniel O'Connell [and] American slavery', p. 58.
32. O'Connell, *Daniel O'Connell upon American slavery*, p. 23.
33. William Lloyd Garrison to Theobald Mathew, 5 October 1849 (W.M. Merrill and Louis Ruchames (eds), *The letters of William Lloyd Garrison*, vol. iii (Cambridge, Mass., 1973), 671).
34. William Lloyd Garrison, 22 March 1842 (Merrill and Ruchames (eds), *The letters of William Lloyd Garrison*, p. 63).
35. *O'Connell Corr.*, vi, 383.
36. See *O'Connell Corr.*, vii, 145–6.
37. O'Connell, *Daniel O'Connell upon American slavery*, pp 38–40.
38. Ibid., p. 40.
39. Gerrit Smith to Daniel O'Connell, 28 July 1843 (*O'Connell Corr.*, vii, 215).
40. James Haughton to Daniel O'Connell, 1 October 1842 (*O'Connell Corr.*, vii, 176–7).
41. William Lloyd Garrison to Richard Allen, 2 July 1842 (Merrill and Ruchames (eds), *The letters of William Lloyd Garrison*, p. 93); Nelson, '"Come out of such a land, you Irishmen": Daniel O'Connell [and] American slavery', p. 69.
42. *O'Connell Corr.*, vii, 200.
43. O'Connell, *Daniel O'Connell upon American slavery*, p. 28.
44. Ibid., p. 29.
45. Ibid., p. 30.
46. Ibid., p. 31.
47. Venedey, *Ireland and the Irish*, p. 124.

48. *O'Connell Corr.*, vii, 218.

49. William Lloyd Garrison to Daniel O'Connell, 8 December 1843 (Merrill and Ruchames (eds), *The letters of William Lloyd Garrison*, pp 229–32).

50. William Lloyd Garrison to Richard D. Webb, 1 July 1847 (Merrill and Ruchames (eds), *The letters of William Lloyd Garrison*, p. 489).

51. Daunt, *Personal recollections*, i, 282.

52. Ibid., i, 283.

53. Ibid., i, 285.

54. Ibid., i, 287.

55. Ibid., i, 287–8.

56. *Pilot*, 4 October 1843 (quoted in Lawrence J. McCaffrey, *Daniel O'Connell and the Repeal year* (Lexington, 1966), pp 74–5).

57. Daniel O'Connell to Richard Barrett, 23 March 1843 (*O'Connell Corr.*, vii, 192).

58. Charles Dickens, *The life and adventures of Martin Chuzzlewit, his relatives, friends and enemies* (Leipzig, 1844), p. 389.

59. Patricia Ingham (ed.), *The life and adventures of Martin Chuzzlewit* (London, 2004), p. 812.

60. Dickens, *Martin Chuzzlewit*, p. 391.

61. Duffy, *Young Ireland*, p. 738.

62. Ibid., p. 739.

63. Charles Lenox Remond to Charles B. Ray, 30 June 1840 (C. Peter Ripley (ed.), *The black abolitionist papers: volume 1, the British Isles, 1830–1865* (Chapel Hill, 1985), 73).

64. Daunt, *Personal recollections*, i, 13–14.

Chapter 13 Young Ireland and the Fall of O'Connell, 1844–1846 (pp 212–27)

1. Daniel O'Connell to Charles Gavan Duffy, some time before the founding of the *Nation* (Duffy, *Four years of Irish history*), p. 58.

2. Assessment of Dr B. J. O'Neil (MacDonagh, *The emancipist*, p. 338).

3. Fitzpatrick, *Correspondence*, ii, 331.

4. Daunt, *Personal recollections*, ii, 244.

5. Howitt and Howitt (eds), *Howitt's journal of literature and popular progress, vol. 1*, p. 332.

6. Ibid., p. 330.

7. Ibid., p. 333.

8. Duffy, *Young Ireland*, p. 584.

9. Gladstone, 'Daniel O'Connell', p. 164; M.F. Cusack, *The Liberator, his life and times, political, social and religious* (London, 1872), ii, 702.

10. *O'Connell Corr.*, vii, 280.

11. Duffy, *Young Ireland*, p. 599.

12. Ibid., p. 602.

13. See Duffy, *Young Ireland*, pp 625–8.

14. Quoted by Raikes (in Duffy, *Young Ireland*, p. 628).

15. Duffy, *Young Ireland*, pp 654–5.

16. Richard Davis, *The Young Ireland Movement* (Dublin, 1987), p. 171.

17. Daniel O'Connell to Thomas Davis, 30 October 1844 (Duffy, *Young Ireland*, p. 629).

18. Duffy, *Young Ireland*, p. 639.

19. Ibid., p. 688.

20. Duffy, *Four years of Irish history*, p. 115.

21. Duffy, *Young Ireland*, p. 737.

22. Ibid., p. 657.

23. Duffy, *Four years of Irish history*, pp 61–2.

24. Duffy, *Young Ireland*, p. 657.

25. Kerr, *Peel, priests and politics*, p. 312.

26. Duffy, *Young Ireland*, p. 695.

27. Ibid., p. 698.

28. Ibid., p. 701.

29. Ibid., p. 702.

30. Ibid., p. 704.

31. MacDonagh, *The emancipist*, p. 269.

32. Ibid., p. 270.

33. Duffy, *Young Ireland*, p. 707.

34. Ibid., p. 708.

35. Thomas MacNevin to William Smith O'Brien (quoted in Duffy, *Young Ireland*, p. 712).

36. Duffy, *Young Ireland*, p. 722.

37. Ibid., p. 728.

38. Daniel O'Connell to T.M. Ray, 17 September 1845 (*O'Connell Corr.*, vii, 342).

39. MacDonagh, *Life*, p. 376.

40. See the description in *O'Connell Corr.*, vii, 344.

41. *The Times*, 25 December 1845.

42. Fitzpatrick, *Correspondence*, ii, 365–6.

43. *O'Connell Corr.*, vii, 353.

44. Daniel O'Connell to William Smith O'Brien, 20 December 1845 (*O'Connell Corr.*, vii, 352).

45. MacDonagh, *Life*, p. 387.

46. MacDonagh, *The emancipist*, p. 277.

47. William Smith O'Brien to Daniel O'Connell, 18 December 1845 (*O'Connell Corr.*, vii, 350).

48. *O'Connell Corr.*, vii, 351.

49. Daniel O'Connell to William Smith O'Brien, 20 December 1845 (*O'Connell Corr.*, vii, 351).

50. Duffy, *Young Ireland*, p. 738.

51. Ibid., p. 746.
52. Duffy, *Four years of Irish history*, p. 34.
53. Duffy, *Young Ireland*, p. 731.
54. Duffy, *Four years of Irish history*, p. 11.
55. Ibid., pp 203–10.
56. Ibid., p. 144.
57. Benjamin Disraeli, *Lord George Bentinck, a political biography* (London, 1905) p. 103.
58. *O'Connell Corr.*, viii, 15.
59. *O'Connell Corr.*, viii, 39.
60. Martin Crean to Daniel O'Connell, 15 June 1846 (*O'Connell Corr.*, viii, 46).
61. Thomas Steele to Daniel O'Connell, 16 June 1846 (*O'Connell Corr.*, viii, 48).
62. Duffy, *Four years of Irish history*, p. 185.
63. Ibid., p. 189.
64. Ibid., p. 191.
65. Ibid., p. 192.
66. Ibid., p. 193.
67. Ibid., p. 194.
68. Ibid., p. 228.
69. Ibid., p. 232.
70. Daunt, *Personal recollections*, ii, 253.

Chapter 14 The Last Days of 'The Father of the Country', 1847 (pp 228–38)

1. MacDonagh, *The emancipist*, p. 277.
2. *O'Connell Corr.*, viii, 122.
3. Daniel O'Connell to F.W. Conway, 10 December 1846 (*O'Connell Corr.*, viii, 152–3).
4. Daniel O'Connell to Maurice O'Connell, 13 January 1847 (*O'Connell Corr.*, viii, 159), and MacDonagh, *The emancipist*, p. 311.
5. Daunt, *Personal recollections*, p. 263; Williams (ed.), *Killing remarks*, p. 224.
6. Mitchel, *Last conquest*, p. 233.
7. Report of Dr O'Neil (MacDonagh, *The emancipist*, p. 338).
8. Daunt, *Personal recollections*, ii, 256.
9. Ibid., ii, 263.
10. Funeral oration of Fr Miley (MacCabe (ed.), *Last days*, p. 236).
11. Daunt, *Personal recollections*, ii, 264.
12. MacDonagh, *The emancipist*, p. 313.
13. MacCabe (ed.), *Last days*, p. 236.
14. Daniel O'Connell to P.V. Fitzpatrick, 1 March 1847 (*O'Connell Corr.*, viii, 164).
15. Fitzpatrick, *Correspondence*, ii, 411.
16. Miley to Fitzpatrick (Fitzpatrick, *Correspondence*, ii, 408).
17. MacCabe (ed.), *Last days*, p. 79.

18. Pierre Joannon, 'O'Connell, Montalembert, and the birth of Christian Democracy in France', in M.R. O'Connell (ed.), *Daniel O'Connell: political pioneer* (Dublin, 1991), p. 105.

19. MacCabe (ed.), *Last days*, p. 81.

20. Ibid., p. 83.

21. Daunt, *Personal recollections*, ii, 269.

22. Fitzpatrick, *Correspondence*, ii, 412–13.

23. MacCabe (ed.), *Last days*, p. 84.

24. MacDonagh, *The emancipist*, p. 338.

25. Duggan's diary (in Cusack, *Life and times*, p. 760).

26. MacCabe (ed.), *Last days*, p. 88.

27. Cusack, *Life and times*, p. 760.

28. MacDonagh, *The emancipist*, p. 338.

29. MacDonagh, *Life*, p. 409.

30. MacCabe (ed.), *Last days*, p. 93.

31. Fr John Miley to Morgan O'Connell, 15 May 1847 (MacCabe (ed.), *Last days*, p. 87).

32. MacCabe (ed.), *Last days*, p. 98.

33. Fr John Miley to Morgan O'Connell, 16 May 1847 (MacCabe (ed.), *Last days*, p. 90).

34. Fr John Miley to Morgan O'Connell, 16 May 1847 (MacCabe (ed.), *Last days*, p. 89).

35. MacCabe (ed.), *Last days*, p. 95.

36. MacDonagh, *The emancipist*, p. 338.

37. Ibid., p. 318.

38. MacCabe (ed.), *Last days*, p. 105.

39. Ibid., p. 201.

40. Ibid., p. 204.

41. Ibid., p. 247.

42. Gladstone, 'Daniel O'Connell', p. 150.

43. Greville, *Memoirs*, vi, 84.

44. Ibid., vi, 88.

45. Bew, *Ireland*, p. 215.

46. Fitzpatrick, *Correspondence*, ii, 292.

47. Frederick Lawton, *Balzac* (Montana, 2004), p. 112.

48. Jules Verne, *Twenty thousand leagues under the sea* (trans. William Butcher) (Oxford, 1998), p. 248.

49. Quoted (and translated) in Geraldine Grogan, *The noblest agitator* (Dublin, 1991), p. 14.

50. Joséphine-Marie de Gaulle, *Le Libérateur de l'Irlande, ou Vie de Daniel O'Connell* (2nd edition, Lille, 1851).

51. *The Irish Times*, 9 December 2009.

52. A.J.P. Taylor, *Bismarck: the man and the statesman* (London, 1955), p. 19.
53. Ibid.
54. T. Desmond Williams, 'O'Connell's impact on Europe' in K.B. Nowlan and M.R. O'Connell (eds), *Daniel O'Connell: portrait of a radical* (Belfast, 1984), p. 106.
55. MacDonagh, *Life*, p. 403.
56. James Joyce, *Ulysses* (Paris, 1922), p. 121.
57. Ibid., p. 77.
58. James Joyce, 'The dead', in *Dubliners* (first published 1914, London, 1993), p. 216.
59. A.N.N. Jeffares, *A new commentary on the poems of W.B. Yeats* (Stanford, 1994), p. 339; R.F. Foster, *W.B. Yeats: a life* (2 vols, London, 1997–2005), ii, 444.
60. Sean O'Faolain, *King of the beggars: a life of Daniel O'Connell* (Dublin, 1986), p. 330.
61. *The Irish Times*, 21 August 1967.
62. Mary Robinson, 'Daniel O'Connell: a tribute' in *History Ireland* (Winter 1997).
63. Gladstone, 'Daniel O'Connell', p. 168.

BIBLIOGRAPHY

PRIMARY SOURCES

Manuscript Sources

National Library of Ireland

MSS 1503–1504   Reminiscences of Daniel O'Connell by his daughter, Ellen Fitzsimon, 1843 and 1876.

MSS 13,621-13,651   O'Connell correspondence.

MS 15,476   Papers of W.J. Fitzpatrick relating to his work on O'Connell.

University College Dublin Archives

P12   Extensive collection of O'Connell correspondence.

Private Collection

John Whiteside letters held by Michael Cuming in London.

Printed Sources

I PARLIAMENTARY AND LEGAL RECORDS
Hansard
Parliamentary Debates

II PAMPHLETS

[Anon.] *Ireland and O'Connell*. Edinburgh, 1835.

[Anon.] *Considerations on the case of Raphael and O'Connell*. Dublin, 1836.

[Anon.] *Shaw's authenticated report of the Irish state trials*. Dublin, 1844.

[Cooke, Henry]. *The Repealer repulsed!* Belfast, 1841.

Leahy, David (ed.). *The judgement of Lord Denman*. London, 1844.

Levy, John (ed.) *A full and revised report of the three days' discussion in the corporation of Dublin of the Repeal of the Union*. Dublin, 1843.

O'Connell, Daniel. *Daniel O'Connell upon American slavery, with other Irish testimonies*. New York, 1860.

O'Connor, Feargus. *A series of letters from Feargus O'Connor to Daniel O'Connell*. London, 1836.

III NEWSPAPERS AND MAGAZINES

Annual Register
Bentley's Magazine
Blackwood's Magazine
The Christian Recorder
Courier
Dublin Evening Post
Dublin Magazine
The Eclectic Magazine
Freeman's Journal
Freemasons' Quarterly Review
Household Words
The Irish Times
Morning Chronicle
Morning Register
The Nation
New Monthly Magazine
New York Herald
New York Tribune
Notes and Queries
Pilot
Richmond Enquirer
The Times

IV DIARIES, MEMOIRS, SPEECHES AND CORRESPONDENCE

Anglesey, Lord (ed.). *One-leg: the life and letters of Henry William Paget, first marquess of Anglesey.* London, 1961.

[Anon.]. *Memoirs of James Gordon Bennett and his times.* New York, 1855.

Aspinall, A. (ed.). *Three early nineteenth century diaries.* London, 1952.

Benson, A.C. and Esher, Lord (eds). *The letters of Queen Victoria.* 3 vols. New York, 1907.

Colchester, Lord (ed.). *The diary and correspondence of Charles Abbot, Lord Colchester.* 3 vols. London, 1861.

Courtenay, Ellen. *A narrative by Miss Ellen Courtenay, of most extraordinary cruelty, perfidy and depravity, perpetrated against her by Daniel O'Connell, Esq., MP for Kerry.* London, 1832.

Cumming, James Slator. *A six years' diary.* London, 1847.

Cusack, Mary Francis (ed.). *The speeches and public letters of the Liberator.* 2 vols. Dublin, 1875.

Daunt, William J. O'Neill. *Personal recollections of the late Daniel O'Connell.* 2 vols. London, 1848.

[Disraeli, Benjamin]. *The letters of Runnymede.* London, 1836.

Dixon, Hepworth (ed.). *Lady Morgan's memoirs: autobiography, diaries and correspondence.* 2 vols. London, 1863.

Dorchester, Lady (ed.). *Recollections of a long life by Lord Broughton* (John Cam Hobhouse). 6 vols. London, 1841–52.

Fitzpatrick, W.J. (ed.). *The life, times, and correspondence of the Right Rev. Dr. Doyle.* 2 vols. Dublin, 1861.

— *Correspondence of Daniel O'Connell, the Liberator.* 2 vols. New York, 1888.

Froude, James Anthony (ed.). *Letters and memorials of Jane Welsh Carlyle, prepared for publication by Thomas Carlyle.* New York, 1883.

[Grant, James]. *Random recollections of the House of Commons.* Philadelphia, 1836.

— *The British Senate, Or, A second series of random recollections of the Lords and Commons.* 2 vols. Philadelphia, 1838.

Haydon, F.W. (ed.). *Benjamin Robert Haydon: correspondence and table-talk.* 2 vols. Boston, 1877.

Kapp, Friedrich (ed.). *Letters of Alexander von Humboldt to Varnhagen von Ense.* New York, 2007.

Mahon, Lord (ed.). *Memoirs of the Right Honourable Sir Robert Peel.* 2 vols. London, 1857.

Malmesbury, Lord. *Memoirs of an ex-minister.* 2 vols. London, 1884.

[Mask]. *St. Stephen's; Or, Pencillings of Politicians.* London, 1839.

Maxwell, Herbert. *The Creevey papers: a selection from the correspondence and diaries of the late Thomas Creevey, MP.* 2 vols. London, 1904.

Merrill, W.M. and Ruchames, Louis (eds). *The letters of William Lloyd Garrison. Volume III. No union with slave-holders.* Cambridge, Mass., 1973.

Mitchel, John. *The crusade of the period, and the last conquest of Ireland (perhaps).* New York, 1878.

O'Connell, John. *Recollections and experiences during a parliamentary career from 1833 to 1848.* 2 vols. London, 1849.

O'Connell, John (ed.). *The life and speeches of Daniel O'Connell MP.* 2 vols. Dublin, 1846.

O'Connell, M. R. (ed.). *The correspondence of Daniel O'Connell.* 8 vols, Shannon and Dublin, 1972–80.

Reeve, Henry (ed.). *The Greville memoirs: a journal of the reigns of King George IV, King William IV and Queen Victoria. By the late Charles C.F. Greville.* 3 vols. London, 1875.

— *The Greville memoirs: a journal of the reigns of King George IV, King William IV and Queen Victoria. By the late Charles C.F. Greville.* 8 vols. London, 1897–99.

— *Memoir and correspondence relating to political occurrences in June and July 1834 by the Right Hon. Edward John Littleton, first Lord Hatherton.* London, 1872.

Ripley, C.P. (ed.). *The black abolitionist papers. Volume I. The British isles, 1830–1865.* Chapel Hill, 1985.

Taylor, Tom (ed.). *The autobiography and journals of Benjamin Robert Haydon.* 3 vols. London, 1853.

Trevelyan, G.O. (ed.). *The life and letters of Lord Macaulay.* 2 vols. London, 1876.

Tuckerman, Bayard. *The diary of Philip Hone, 1828–1851.* 2 vols. New York, 1889.

V CONTEMPORARY AND NEAR-CONTEMPORARY WORKS

[Anon.]. *Anecdotes of O'Connell, John Philpot Curran, Grattan, Father O'Leary, and Swift.* Dublin, n.d.

[Anon.]. *A diary of royal movements of Queen Victoria.* London, 1883.

Brightwell, Cecilia. *Memorials of the life of Amelia Opie.* Norwich, 1854.

Brougham, Henry. *The life and times of Henry Lord Brougham.* 3 vols. London, 1871.

Cusack, M.F. *The Liberator, his life and times, political, social and religious.* London, 1872.

Daunt, William J. O'Neill. *Ireland and her agitators.* Dublin, 1845.

de Gaulle, Joséphine-Marie. *Le Libérateur de l'Irlande, ou Vie de Daniel O'Connell.* 2nd edition, Lille, 1851.

Dickens, Charles. *The life and adventures of Martin Chuzzlewit, his relatives, friends and enemies.* Leipzig, 1844.

Disraeli, Benjamin. *Lord George Bentinck, a political biography.* London, 1905.

Douglass, Frederick. *Life and times of Frederick Douglass.* London, 1996.

Duffy, Charles Gavan. *Young Ireland: a fragment of Irish history.* London, 1880.

— *Four years of Irish history, 1845–1849.* London, 1883.

— *Thomas Davis: the memoirs of an Irish patriot, 1840–1846.* London, 1890.

— *Young Ireland: a fragment of Irish history.* 2 vols. Final Revision. London, 1896.

Dunlop, Robert. *Daniel O'Connell and the revival of national life in Ireland.* London, 1908.

Fagan, William. *The life and times of Daniel O'Connell.* 2 vols. Cork, 1847–8.

Fitzpatrick, W.J. *Secret service under Pitt.* Dublin, 1892.

Gibson, W.S. *A memoir of Lord Lyndhurst.* London, 1869.

Gilchrist, J.P. *A brief history of the origin and history of ordeals . . . Also, a chronological register of the principal duels.* London, 1821.

Gladstone, W.E. 'Daniel O'Connell'. In *The Nineteenth Century,* vol. xxv (1889).

Grant, James. *Impressions of Ireland and the Irish.* 2 vols. London, 1844.

Gullion, Slieve. 'Leinster and Munster in the summer of 1844'. In *Irish Monthly,* xl (Oct. 1912).

Harrison, Wilmot (ed.). *"Thomas Moore" Anecdotes.* London, 1899.

Howitt, William and Howitt, Mary (eds). *Howitt's journal of literature and popular progress.* Vol. 1. London, 1847.

Huish, Robert. *The memoirs private and political of Daniel O'Connell.* London, 1836.

Ingham, Patricia (ed). *The life and adventures of Martin Chuzzlewit.* London, 1999.

Kinealy, Christine (ed.). *Lives of Victorian political figures II. Volume 1. Daniel O'Connell.* London, 2007.

Lecky, W.E.H. *Leaders of public opinion in Ireland.* 2 vols. London, 1903.

Luby, T.C. *The life and times of Daniel O'Connell.* Glasgow, n.d.

MacCabe, W.B. (ed.). *The last days of O'Connell.* Dublin, 1847.

Madden, D.O. *Ireland and its rulers since 1829.* 2 vols. London, 1843–4.

— *Revelations of Ireland in the past generation.* Dublin, 1877.

[Marryat, Frederick]. *Diary of a Blasé.* Philadelphia, 1836.

Martin, Theodore. *A life of Lord Lyndhurst from letters and papers in possession of his family.* London, 1884.

Maume, Patrick (ed.). *Reminiscences of Daniel O'Connell.* Dublin, 2005.

Millingen, J.G. *The history of duelling.* 2 vols. London, 1841.

Mitchel, John. *The crusade of the period, and Last conquest of Ireland (perhaps).* New York, 1878.

Montalembert, Charles. *De l'avenir politique de l'Angleterre.* Paris, 1856.

O'Connell, C.M. *Excursions in Ireland during 1844 and 1850.* London, 1852.

O'Keeffe, C.M. *Life and times of Daniel O'Connell.* Dublin, 1864.

Phillips, Charles. *Curran and his contemporaries.* Various editions, London, 1850 and New York, 1862.

Plowden, Francis. *The history of Ireland from its Union with Great Britain in January 1801 to October 1810.* 3 vols. Dublin, 1811.

Pollock, Frederick (ed.). *Macready's reminiscences and selections from his diaries and letters.* New York, 1875.

Roche, James. *Critical and miscellaneous essays. By an octogenarian.* 2 vols. Cork, 1850–51.

Sabine, Lorenzo. *Notes on Duels and Duelling.* Boston, 1855.

Sheahan, Thomas. *'Articles' of Irish manufacture, or, Portions of Cork history.* Cork, 1833.

Shee, Martin Archer. *The life of Sir Martin Archer Shee.* 2 vols. London, 1860.

Taylor, W.C. (ed.). *Ireland, social, political and religious: Gustave de Beaumont.* Introduction by Tom Garvin and Andreas Hess. Cambridge, Mass., 2006.

[Taylor, W.C.]. *Reminiscences of Daniel O'Connell. By a Munster farmer.* London, 1847.

Trevelyan, Lady (ed.). *Works of Lord Macaulay.* 8 vols. London, 1866.

Venedey, Jacob. *Ireland and the Irish during the Repeal years,* trans. William B. McCabe. Dublin, 1844.

Verne, Jules. *Twenty thousand leagues under the sea* (trans. William Butcher). Oxford, 1998.

SECONDARY SOURCES

Adelman, Paul. *Peel and the Conservative party, 1830–50.* London, 1989.

Ahern, Dennis J. 'O'Connell tribute 1843'. In *Mallow Field Club Journal,* 25 (2007).

Aldous, Richard. *The lion and the unicorn: Gladstone vs Disraeli.* London, 2006.

Bew, Paul. *Ireland: the politics of enmity 1789–2006*. Oxford, 2007.

Bew, Paul and Maume, Patrick. 'The great advocate'. In *Dublin Review of Books*, 8 (Winter 2008–09). www.drb.ie.

Bishop, Erin I. 'Was O'Connell faithful? Ellen Courtenay revisited'. In *Éire-Ireland*, 31: 3–4 (1996).

— *The world of Mary O'Connell* [1778–1836]. Dublin, 1999.

Blake, Robert. *Disraeli*. London, 1987.

Bric, Maurice J. 'Daniel O'Connell and the debate on anti-slavery, 1820–50'. In Dunne, Tom and Geary, Lawrence M. (eds), *History and the public sphere: essays in honour of John A. Murphy*. Cork, 2005.

Cecil, David. *The young Melbourne and Lord M*. London, 2001.

Charlton, Kenneth. 'The state of Ireland in the 1820s: James Cropper's plan'. In *Irish Historical Studies*, xvii (1971).

Colantonio, Laurent. 'French interpretations of Daniel O'Connell from the last years of the restoration to the second republic'. In Maher, Eamon and Neville, Grace (eds), *France-Ireland: anatomy of a relationship*. Frankfurt, 2004.

Comerford, R.V. and Delaney, Enda (eds). *National questions: reflections on Daniel O'Connell and contemporary Ireland*. Dublin, 2000.

Cooke, Jim. *Charles Dickens and Ireland: an anthology*. Dublin, 1999.

Crimmins, J.E. 'Jeremy Bentham and Daniel O'Connell: their correspondence and radical alliance, 1828–1831'. In *Historical Journal*, 40 (1997).

Cronin, Maura. '"Of one mind?": O'Connellite crowds in the 1830s and 1840s'. In Jupp, Peter and Magennis, Eoin (eds), *Crowds in Ireland, c. 1720–1920*. Basingstoke, 2000.

D'Arcy, F.A. 'The artisans of Dublin and Daniel O'Connell, 1830–47: an unquiet liaison'. In *Irish Historical Studies*, vol. 17, no. 66 (Sept., 1970).

Davis, Richard. *The Young Ireland Movement*. Dublin, 1987.

Earls, Tony. 'The opportunity of being useful: Daniel O'Connell's influence on John Hubert Plunkett'. In Geary, L.M. and McCarthy, A.J. (eds), *Ireland, Australia and New Zealand: history, politics and culture*. Dublin, 2008.

Fitzsimons, Bob. 'The Tralee election of 1832'. In *Journal of the Kerry Archaeological and Historical Society*, ser. 2, 2 (2003).

Foster, R.F. *W.B. Yeats: a life*. 2 vols. London, 1997–2005.

Geoghegan, P.M. *The Irish Act of Union*. Dublin, 1999.

— *King Dan: the rise of Daniel O'Connell, 1775–1829*. Dublin, 2008.

Grogan, Geraldine. *The noblest agitator: Daniel O'Connell and the German Catholic movement, 1830–1850*. Dublin, 1991.

— 'O'Connell and German Catholicism during the Kulturkampf'. In *Studies: an Irish Quarterly Review*, 91:362 (2002).

— 'Nineteenth-century European co-operation: Ireland, France and Germany'. In Maher, Eamon and Neville, Grace (eds), *France-Ireland: anatomy of a relationship*. Frankfurt, 2004.

Gwynn, Denis. *O'Connell and Ellen Courtenay*. Oxford, 1930.

Hill, Jacqueline. *From patriots to unionists: Dublin civic politics and Irish Protestant patriotism, 1660–1840*. Oxford, 1997.

Hilton, Boyd. 'The ripening of Robert Peel'. In Bentley, Michael (ed.), *Public and private doctrine: essays in British history presented to Maurice Cowling*. Cambridge, 1993.

Hoppen, K. Theodore. *Elections, politics, and society in Ireland, 1832–85*. Oxford, 1984.

— 'Riding a tiger: Daniel O'Connell, reform, and popular politics in Ireland, 1800–1847'. In Blanning, T.C.W. and Wende, Peter (eds), *Reform in Great Britain and Germany, 1750–1850*. Oxford, 1999.

Hurd, Douglas. *Sir Robert Peel: a biography*. London, 2007.

Hyman, Louis. *The Jews of Ireland: from earliest times to the year 1910*. Shannon, 1972.

Jeffares, A.N.N. *A new commentary on the poems of W.B. Yeats*. Stanford, 1994.

Jenkins, Lee M. 'The black O'Connell: Frederick Douglass and Ireland'. In *Nineteenth Century Studies*, 13 (1999).

Joyce, James. *Ulysses*. Paris, 1922.

— *Dubliners*. London, 1993 (first published in 1914).

Kelly, James. '*That damned thing called honour:' duelling in Ireland*. Cork, 1996.

Kerr, Donald A. *Peel, priests and politics*. Oxford, 1982.

— 'The Catholic church in the age of O'Connell'. In Bradshaw, Brendan and Keogh, Dáire (eds), *Christianity in Ireland: revisiting the story*. Dublin, 2002.

Kinealy, Christine. 'The Liberator: Daniel O'Connell and anti-slavery'. In *History Today* (December 2007).

Lawton, Frederick. *Balzac*. Montana, 2004.

Lehane, Shane. 'O'Connell—the Liberator: his death, funeral, and local reaction'. In *The Kerry Magazine*, 9 (1998).

MacCartney, Donal (ed.). *The world of Daniel O'Connell*. Dublin, 1980.

MacDonagh, Michael. *The life of Daniel O'Connell*. London, 1903.

MacDonagh, Oliver. *The hereditary bondsman: Daniel O'Connell, 1775–1829*. London, 1988.

— *The emancipist: Daniel O'Connell, 1830–1847*. London, 1989.

Macintyre, A.D. *The Liberator: Daniel O'Connell and the Irish party, 1830–47*. London, 1965.

Maume, Patrick. 'Repelling the Repealer: William McComb's caricatures of Daniel O'Connell'. In *History Ireland*, 13:2 (2005).

McCaffrey, Lawrence. *Daniel O'Connell and the Repeal year*. Lexington, 1966.

McElroy, Martin. 'The local Protestant landed elite and the impact of O'Connellism, 1826–35'. In *Irish history: A research yearbook*, 1. Dublin, 2002.

Moley, Raymond. *Daniel O'Connell: nationalism without violence*. New York, 1974.

Murphy, Angela F. 'Daniel O'Connell and the "American Eagle" in 1845: slavery, diplomacy, nativism, and the collapse of America's first nationalist movement'. In *Journal of American Ethnic History*, 26:2 (2007).

Murphy, Paula. 'John Henry Foley's O'Connell monument'. In *Irish Arts Review Yearbook*, 11 (1995).

Nelson, Bruce. '"Come out of such a land, you Irishmen": Daniel O'Connell, American slavery, and the making of the "Irish race"'. In *Éire-Ireland*, 42:1 and 2. Spring/Summer 2007.

Neville, Grace. '"I hate France with a mortal hatred": Daniel O'Connell and France'. In Maher, Eamon and Neville, Grace (eds), *France-Ireland: anatomy of a relationship*. Frankfurt, 2004.

Nowlan, Kevin and O'Connell, M.R. (eds). *Daniel O'Connell: portrait of a radical*. Belfast, 1984.

O'Connell, M.R. 'Daniel O'Connell: income, expenditure and despair'. In *Irish Historical Studies*, xvii (1970).

O'Connell, M.R. (ed.). *Daniel O'Connell: political pioneer*. Dublin, 1991.

O'Dowd, Mary. 'O'Connell and the lady patriots: women and O'Connellite politics, 1824–1845'. In Blackstock, Allan and Magennis, Eoin (eds), *Politics and political culture in Britain and Ireland, 1750–1850: essays in tribute to Peter Jupp*. Belfast, 2007.

O'Faolain, Sean. *King of the beggars: a life of Daniel O'Connell*. Dublin, 1986, first published in 1938.

Ó Fearghail, Fearghus. 'Daniel O'Connell's Roman bequest'. In Keogh, Dáire and McDonnell, Albert, *The Irish College, Rome, and its world*. Dublin, 2008.

O'Ferrall, Fergus. *Catholic emancipation: Daniel O'Connell and the birth of Irish democracy, 1820–30*. Dublin, 1985.

— 'Daniel O'Connell, "the Liberator", 1775–1847: changing images'. In *Ireland: A journal of history and society* (1994).

Owens, Gary. 'Visualizing the Liberator: self-fashioning, dramaturgy, and the construction of Daniel O'Connell'. In *Éire-Ireland*, 33:3/4-34:1 (1998).

Pickering, Paul A. '"Irish first": Daniel O'Connell, the native manufacture campaign, and economic nationalism, 1840–44'. In *Albion*, 32:4 (2000).

Quinn, James. *John Mitchel*. Dublin, 2008.

Riach, Douglas. 'Daniel O'Connell and American anti-slavery'. In *Irish Historical Studies*, vol. 20 (1977).

Robinson, Mary. 'Daniel O'Connell: a tribute'. In *History Ireland* (Winter 1997).

Shannon, Richard. *Gladstone*. 2 vols. London, 1999–2000.

Taylor, A.J.P. *Bismarck: the man and the statesman*. London, 1955.

Temperley, Howard. 'The O'Connell-Stevenson contretemps'. In *The Journal of Negro History*. vol. xlvii, no. 4. October 1962.

Tierney, Michael (ed.). *Daniel O'Connell: nine centenary essays*. Dublin, 1949.

Trench, C.C. *The Great Dan: a biography of Daniel O'Connell*. London, 1984.

Uí Ógáin, Ríonach. *Immortal Dan: Daniel O'Connell in Irish folk tradition*. Dublin, n.d.

Vaughan, W.E. (ed.). *A new history of Ireland: Ireland under the Union*. Volume v. Oxford, 1989.

Williams, W.H.A. (ed.). *Daniel O'Connell, the British press, and the Irish famine: killing remarks* (Ashgate, 2003).

Wise, Sarah. *The Italian boy: murder and grave robbery in 1830s London*. London, 2004.

BIOGRAPHICAL DICTIONARIES

Matthew, H.C.G. and Harrison, Brian (eds). *Oxford Dictionary of National Biography*. 60 vols. Oxford, 2004. Website: www.oxforddnb.com.

McGuire, James and Quinn, James (eds). *The Royal Irish Academy's Dictionary of Irish Biography*. 9 vols. Cambridge, 2009. Website: dib.cambridge.org.

INDEX

Reviews of Patrick Geoghegan's *King Dan*:

'Geoghegan's well-thought-out, refreshing iconoclasm disturbs some stagnant pieties and enhances his already considerable reputation as a historian . . . A fine piece of historical detective work . . . the sparkling narrative . . . further enhancing his reputation as one of the leaders of the new generation of Irish historians.'
PROFESSOR PAUL BEW AND DR PATRICK MAUME, *DUBLIN REVIEW OF BOOKS*, 2008

'A very readable and fresh look at one of the great figures in modern Irish history, and a fascinating insight into aspects of Irish life in the early 19th century. O'Connell's colourful early life—high spending, constant debt, duelling, womanising and involvement with the United Irishmen—is worthy of a historical novel.'
PROFESSOR MARY E. DALY, *THE IRISH TIMES*

'This volume has about it a freshness and readability and carries its scholarship lightly.'
PROFESSOR DONAL MCCARTNEY, PROFESSOR EMERITUS OF MODERN IRISH HISTORY AT UCD, *MAIL ON SUNDAY*

'History lecturer and broadcaster, Dr Patrick Geoghegan succeeds in explaining some of the biographical puzzles about O'Connell.'
MARTIN MANSERGH, *THE IRISH INDEPENDENT*

'In his biography, Geoghegan ultimately casts O'Connell as a protean figure who helped create the modern Ireland. It was the towering achievement of his life . . . Geoghegan's book helps rescue his subject from fading into irrelevance in the mists of history.'
THE SUNDAY TIMES